Contents

HISTORY-SOCIAL SCIENCE FOR CALIFORNIA

OUR NATION

WILLIAM E. WHITE, Ph.D.
PROGRAM AUTHOR

SAVVAS LEARNING COMPANY

Savvas Learning Company LLC, 15 East Midland Avenue, Paramus, NJ 07652

ISBN-13: 978-0-328-16673-2
ISBN-10: 0-328-16673-1
45 22

A Book About the United States

Do you know where the "people's house" is located? That's what one President called the White House, the President's home in Washington, D.C. Over time, the White House has grown and changed to reflect the many Presidents and families who have lived there. Similarly, the growth and changes in our nation reflect the diverse people who have made the United States their home.

This book—*your* book—is about the United States. Like the United States, your book is unique in many ways.

The White House

Flags of the United States and the state of California

First, you can write in it. As you read, you will complete time lines and mark locations on maps. You will also answer questions by circling, underlining, or writing information in your book.

Second, every unit in your book begins with a Study Journal. In your Study Journal, you will write what you already know about our nation, as well as what you learn about our nation.

Finally, your book has many photographs and drawings of the people, locations, and events that have made our nation what it is today. These pictures will bring the history of the United States to life for you.

What You Will Learn

Your book begins by describing the cultures of American Indians, the earliest people to live in what is now the United States. For centuries they have developed unique ways of life in regions across North America. When Europeans came to North America, they too found a land that was filled with a variety of people, natural features, and riches. As Europeans began to settle here, they exchanged goods and ideas with American Indians. Over time, settlers learned to use their area's resources, develop a variety of beliefs, and form their own systems of rules and laws. But life was not always easy or peaceful. Some settlers fought with American Indians or bought and sold people from Africa. Some disagreed with other settlers about what to believe and how to live.

You will learn how English settlers in North America came to have strong ideas about freedom and how people should be ruled. During the American Revolution, many people risked their lives to form a new nation in which their ideas of freedom could became a reality—the United States of America. You will also discover how documents from our nation's early days, such as the Declaration of Independence and the Constitution, continue to play an important role in defining and protecting the rights of our nation's citizens.

In the 1400s, the Americas were a "New World" to Europeans, but American Indians had already lived here for thousands of years.

In 1776, Americans declared their independence from British rule.

Settlers began moving into the Far West, including California, in the 1800s.

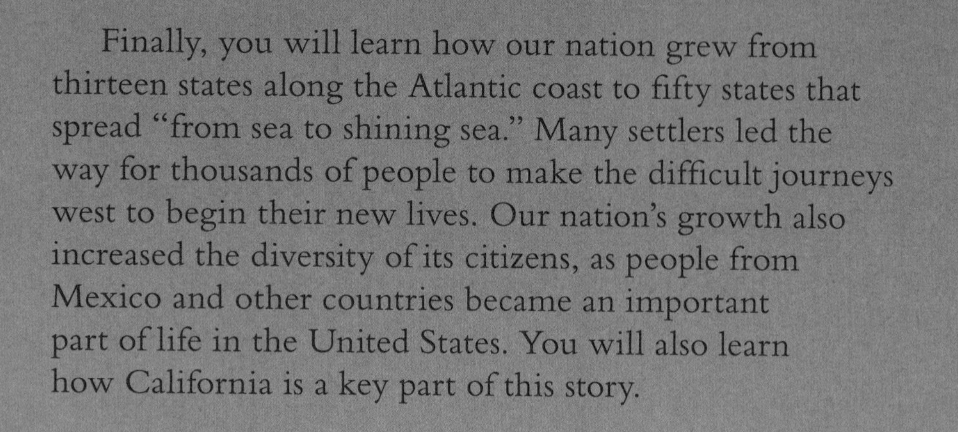

Finally, you will learn how our nation grew from thirteen states along the Atlantic coast to fifty states that spread "from sea to shining sea." Many settlers led the way for thousands of people to make the difficult journeys west to begin their new lives. Our nation's growth also increased the diversity of its citizens, as people from Mexico and other countries became an important part of life in the United States. You will also learn how California is a key part of this story.

The Next Step

As you read the history of the United States, you will discover what the land and people were like here before the creation of the United States. You will witness our nation's courageous beginnings and how it continues to grow and change. Most importantly, you will find out why you are an important part of the ongoing story of the United States. Turn the page to begin your journey into the story of *Our Nation.*

These students are visiting our nation's capital city, Washington, D.C.

Name:

Unit 1

Study Journal

In this unit you will learn how American Indians lived before the arrival of European explorers. You will be able to describe the ways of life of people of the Desert Southwest, the Pacific Northwest, the Eastern Woodlands, and the Great Plains. Complete the activities on these pages as you read the unit.

What I know about . . .

American Indians:

American Indian Cultural Regions

Complete the chart to show how American Indian groups adapted to their region's geography and climate.

Cultural Region	Major Resources	Food	Shelter	Technology
Desert Southwest				
Pacific Northwest				
Eastern Woodlands				
Great Plains				

Complete these sections as you read the unit.

Write a paragraph about American Indian ways of life using three of the following vocabulary words:

- adapt
- agriculture
- economy
- specialize
- surplus
- technology

What cultural region do you find most interesting? Write four sentences describing a day in the life of an American Indian living in that region.

1.

2.

3.

4.

Choose two cultural regions that might have been trading partners. Draw pictures of the items they might trade. Then write a caption explaining why these might be trade items.

I have learned . . .

Name:

H-SS 5.1.1 Describe how geography and climate influenced the way various nations lived and adjusted to the natural environment, including locations of villages, the distinct structures that they built, and how they obtained food, clothing, tools, and utensils.

Lesson 1

How did geography and climate affect how early people lived?

SET THE SCENE If you moved to a new place, would you need to buy a winter coat? Would you do the same daily activities and chores? Often when people move, they have to change how they live to fit their new surroundings. How did American Indians learn to live in different parts of North America?

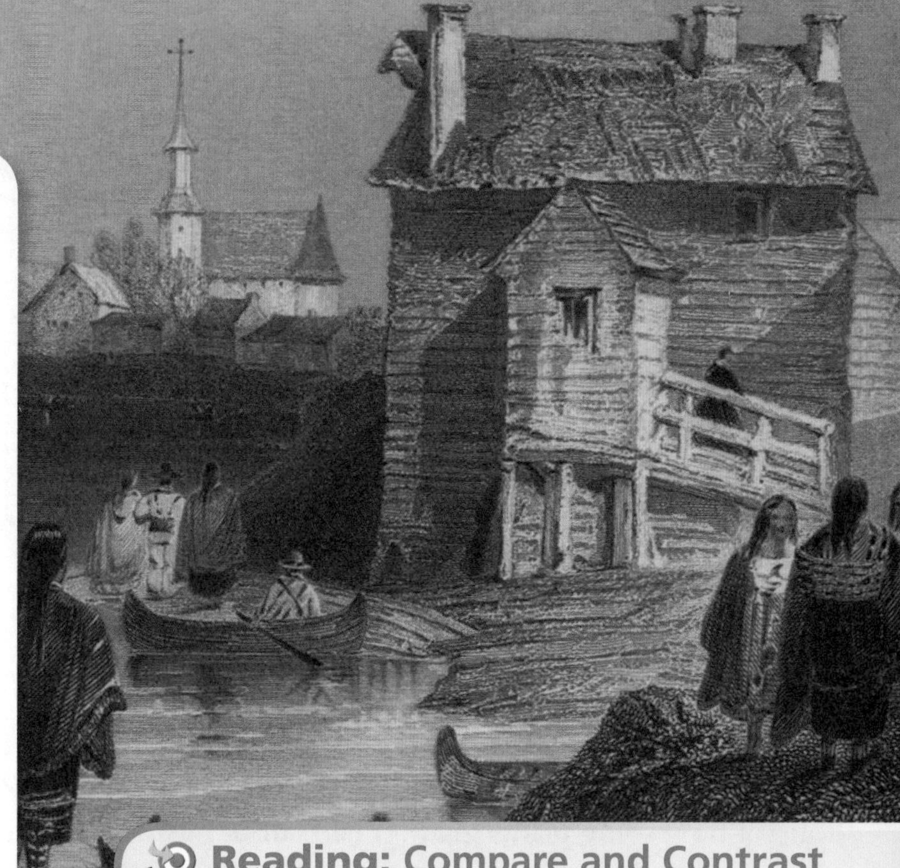

Preview the Lesson

Vocabulary

nomad *(n.)* a person with no permanent home who travels from place to place

migration *(n.)* movement from one place to another

agriculture *(n.)* the skill of raising plants and animals for human use

adapt *(v.)* to change the way one lives to fit different conditions

technology *(n.)* the use of scientific knowledge to solve problems

archaeology *(n.)* the study of objects to learn about life in the past

artifact *(n.)* an object made by people

Vocabulary Activity The word part *-ology* means "the study or use" of something. Knowing this can help you predict and remember word meanings. Circle two words above with the word part *-ology*.

Reading: Compare and Contrast

Reading Skill

When you compare and contrast, you look to see how ideas are alike and different. As you read about each of the American Indian cultural regions on pages 6–9, underline the sentence in the first paragraph on each page that tells about the amount of resources in each region.

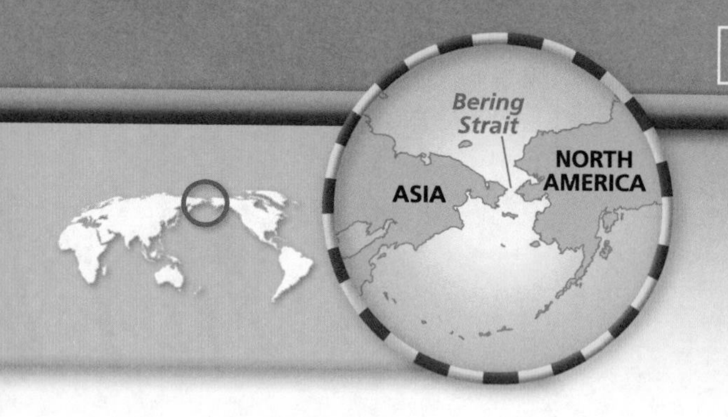

Nomads may have migrated to North America from Asia.

The First North Americans

There are many ideas about how and when people first arrived in North America. One theory says that people first came to North America from Asia between 40,000 and 10,000 years ago. This was during the last Ice Age, or a period when cold temperatures froze much of Earth's water into huge sheets of ice called glaciers. Many scientists believe that so much of Earth's water was contained in glaciers that there was less water in the oceans than there is now. As a result, areas that today are underwater may have been above water. One place where this may have happened is the Bering Strait, between Asia and North America.

Many scientists believe that **nomads,** or people with no permanent home who travel from place to place, traveled across the Bering Strait on a land bridge. Why? Animals were the nomads' main food source. As animals crossed the land bridge, nomads followed and hunted them. This **migration,** or movement from one place to another, may have made these nomads the first North Americans. Today, the relatives of these early people are called American Indians.

Ways of Life Change

About 7,000 years ago, some American Indian groups changed how they got their food. Besides gathering wild plants and hunting, they learned to control how some plants grow. The skill of raising plants and animals for human use is called **agriculture.** With agriculture, people no longer had to move from place to place to follow their food sources. Now they could live in one place and plant their own food, or crops, year after year. Often they chose to live near rivers or streams in order to water their crops and provide drinking water.

1. Compare and Contrast **Underline a sentence that compares the amount of water in the oceans during the Ice Age and today.**

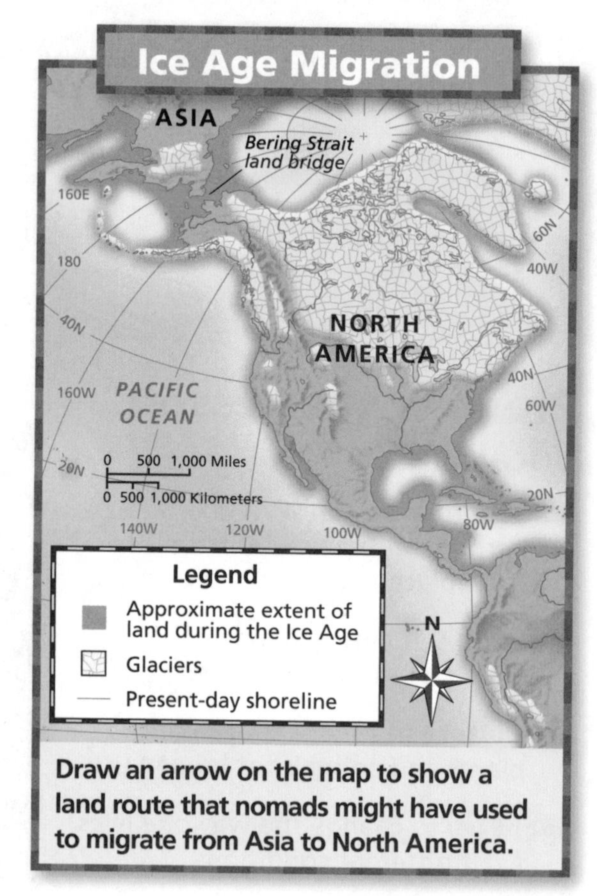

Draw an arrow on the map to show a land route that nomads might have used to migrate from Asia to North America.

2. Underline a sentence in the text that explains the effect that agriculture had on where some American Indians chose to live.

Cause and Effect

About 7,000 Years Ago

Some early American Indian groups develop agriculture.

Cultural Regions Develop

Over time, American Indian groups migrated to places across North America. Each area they moved to had its own natural environment. An environment is an area's physical conditions, such as geography, climate, and natural resources. Geography is an area's landforms and bodies of water. Climate is an area's usual weather. Natural resources are useful materials, such as soil, plants, and animals. To meet their needs, groups had to **adapt,** or change how they lived to fit these different conditions. For example, groups in cold climates needed heavier clothing than groups in warm climates.

In areas with similar environments, American Indian groups adapted to meet their needs in ways that were alike. Historians call these areas cultural regions. The map below shows four American Indian cultural regions: the Desert Southwest, the Pacific Northwest, the Eastern Woodlands, and the Great Plains.

3. What factors influenced how American Indians adapted to environments in North America?

Cause and Effect

______

______

______

______

American Indian Cultural Regions

PACIFIC NORTHWEST
PACIFIC OCEAN
NORTH AMERICA
GREAT PLAINS
EASTERN WOODLANDS
DESERT SOUTHWEST
ATLANTIC OCEAN
Gulf of Mexico
N

Legend

______

______

______

______

Present-day national border
Present-day state border

0 500 1,000 Miles
0 500 1,000 Kilometers

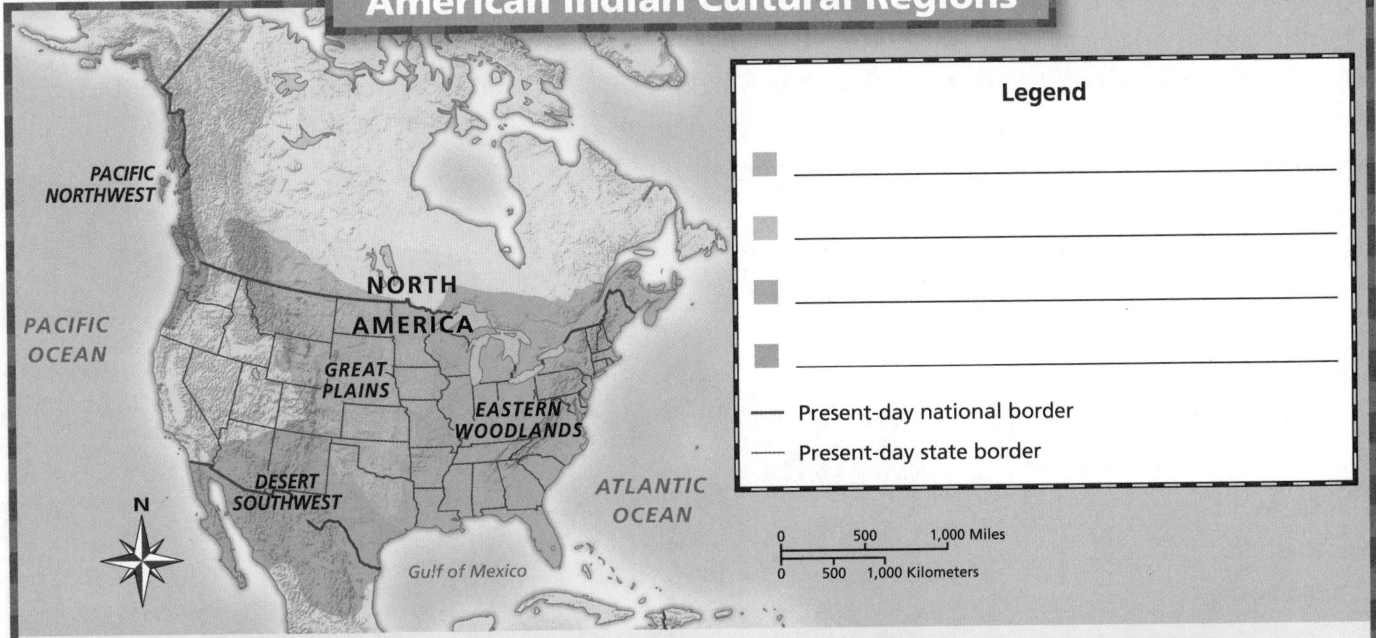

Use information from the map to label the four American Indian cultural regions in the legend.

Desert Southwest Cultural Region

Life in the Desert Southwest could be difficult. The region's hot, dry climate often made plants, animals, and water hard to find. American Indian groups developed many technologies to help them adapt to these harsh conditions. **Technology** is the use of scientific knowledge to solve problems.

One problem was getting food. Agriculture could give people a stable food source, but much of the region was too dry for farming. An early group we now call the Anasazi (ah nuh SAH zee) used technology to solve this problem. The Anasazi dug ditches to bring water from streams to fields of crops, such as corn, beans and cotton. This technology is called irrigation.

People of the Desert Southwest used technology to store their crops too. Groups such as the Navajo (NAH vah ho) used pottery jars and woven baskets to store crops for long periods of time. They often decorated their pottery with symbols and other designs.

The use of adobe was another important technology in the Desert Southwest. Adobe is clay that is baked in the sun to make strong bricks. Some groups used adobe bricks to construct villages of large, apartment-style buildings with many rooms. The Anasazi are sometimes called "cliff dwellers" because they built their homes into the sides of cliffs. A later group called the Hopi built their homes on top of flat areas called mesas. Adobe was also used to build dome-shaped ovens called *hornos.* These ovens were used to make cornbread and other foods.

4. Circle technologies that helped American Indians adapt to life in the Desert Southwest.
Main Idea and Details

This *horno (above)* is made of adobe. Buildings made of adobe *(below)* can still be seen throughout the Desert Southwest region.

Pacific Northwest Cultural Region

Unlike American Indians of the Desert Southwest, groups in the Pacific Northwest had little need for agriculture. They lived in a narrow area of coastal land between present-day California and Alaska. People such as the Haida and the Kwakiutl (kwah kee OO tuhl) found plenty of food and other natural resources in this region's ocean, rivers, and forests.

Sea animals were an important resource to people of the Pacific Northwest. Fish, especially salmon, provided food for many of the region's people. Some groups also hunted whales for meat and other uses. Oil made from whale fat could be used for cooking.

The region's forests provided many useful resources. Groups hunted deer and gathered nuts and berries for food in the forests. People also used wood from tall trees to make many things. A dugout canoe carved from a single log could be as long as 75 feet and hold up to 50 people. Large cedar-wood plank houses sheltered up to ten families. Finely carved wooden bowls and utensils, such as spoons, filled the plank houses. People even wove tree bark into clothing.

Many groups also developed ways to control who used their area's resources. In a village, different families claimed their own resources. Chiefs and their relatives controlled the best hunting and fishing grounds. Other families claimed resources too, but the chief decided how and when they could use them.

5. How did the resources of the Pacific Northwest affect the lives of the people who lived there?
Main Idea and Details

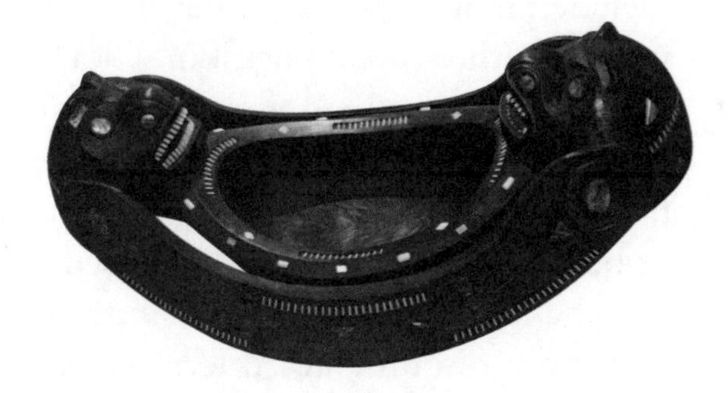

The Tlingit (TLING kit) used this finely carved wooden dish *(above)* during special feasts. The Hupa built wooden plank houses *(below).*

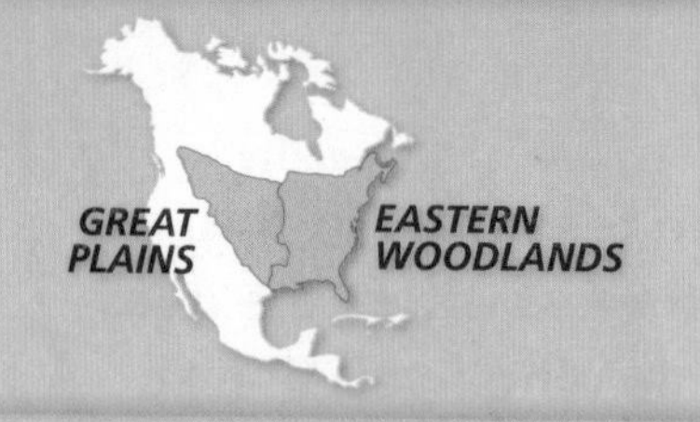

Eastern Woodlands Cultural Region

Like the Pacific Northwest, the Eastern Woodlands provided many resources. However, the area east of the Mississippi River has a wide range of climates and geographic features. For example, there are large bodies of water as well as farmland, forests, and mountains. The climate can be hot in the summer and cold in the winter. People adapted to meet their needs in these different conditions.

The forests of the Eastern Woodlands provided many useful plants and animals. Important animals included rabbits, bears, and deer. Deer provided meat as well as leather called buckskin. Clothing made from buckskin lasted a long time and kept people warm during the cold winters. People made other objects from forest trees. Strong, flexible birch bark was woven or bent into baskets. It was also used to make canoes.

The many bodies of water in the region were important resources to American Indians of the Eastern Woodlands. People used their canoes to travel and fish in the region's lakes and rivers. Rich soil on land near the water was often used to grow crops. Groups who lived near the Atlantic Ocean fished and collected seashells to make beads for decorating their clothes.

Different groups of the Eastern Woodlands had different types of shelter. The Ojibwa lived in dome-shaped structures called wigwams. These homes were made of bent wooden poles covered with bark or animal skins. The Mohawk had very different homes. They lived in wooden longhouses up to 200 feet long.

6. Compare and Contrast **Compare and contrast the housing of the Ojibwa and the Mohawk.**

The Ojibwa lived in bark wigwams such as this one *(above)*. The Mohawks' wooden longhouses *(below)* housed many related families.

Horses, which were first brought to the Americas by Europeans, changed the way of life of many American Indian groups of the Great Plains.

Great Plains Cultural Region

To find resources, some American Indians of the Great Plains traveled farther and more often than groups in other cultural regions. The Great Plains is a large, flat grassland west of the Mississippi River. The climate can be dry, but land near rivers provides rich farmland. Large herds of buffalo once lived throughout this region. To adapt to this environment, some groups farmed, some hunted, and some did both.

For many Great Plains groups, spring was the season for planting crops. During planting season, groups such as the Pawnee lived in villages. Their homes were soil-covered, dome-shaped structures called earth lodges. They planted crops such as beans, squash, and sunflowers.

In the summer, the Mandan and other groups left their homes for a buffalo hunt. Buffalo provided large amounts of meat but could be used to make many other things too. Buffalo bones were made into tools, such as knives and scrapers. Tendons, which connect muscles to bones, became strings for bows. Buffalo skins were used to make clothes and shelters. During hunting season, the group lived in cone-shaped portable tents made out of wooden poles and buffalo skins. These tents were called tepees. The poles and skins could also be made into a sledlike cart called a travois (truh VOY).

In the fall, hunting groups returned to their village to harvest, or gather, crops. Some groups then set out for another buffalo hunt before the winter.

7. Circle the kinds of housing that Great Plains people used and underline the seasons when they lived there. *Main Idea and Details*

Summary

American Indians adapted to many different environments across North America. How did American Indians of each cultural region make their shelter?

Skill

Site Maps

Learn More How do we know about early American Indians and their cultures? Archaeology (ahr key AHL uh jee) is one way. **Archaeology** is the study of objects to learn about life in the past. An **artifact** is an object made by people. Artifacts help us learn about how people live. Sites are places where artifacts are found. The objects found at a site can tell us about the ways of life of people in the past. For example, artifacts such as spearheads have to do with hunting. Farming groups left artifacts such as hoes and other farming tools, as well as containers for storing crops. The illustration below shows what the site map of an American Indian village from long ago might look like. Use it to answer the questions below.

Try It

1. Label a source of water. *Identify*
2. Circle the place that used to be the American Indians' home. *Identify*
3. In the legend, circle an artifact that tells you the people here grew crops. *Analyze*
4. In which cultural region do you think this village could have been located? Why? *Analyze*

____

____

____

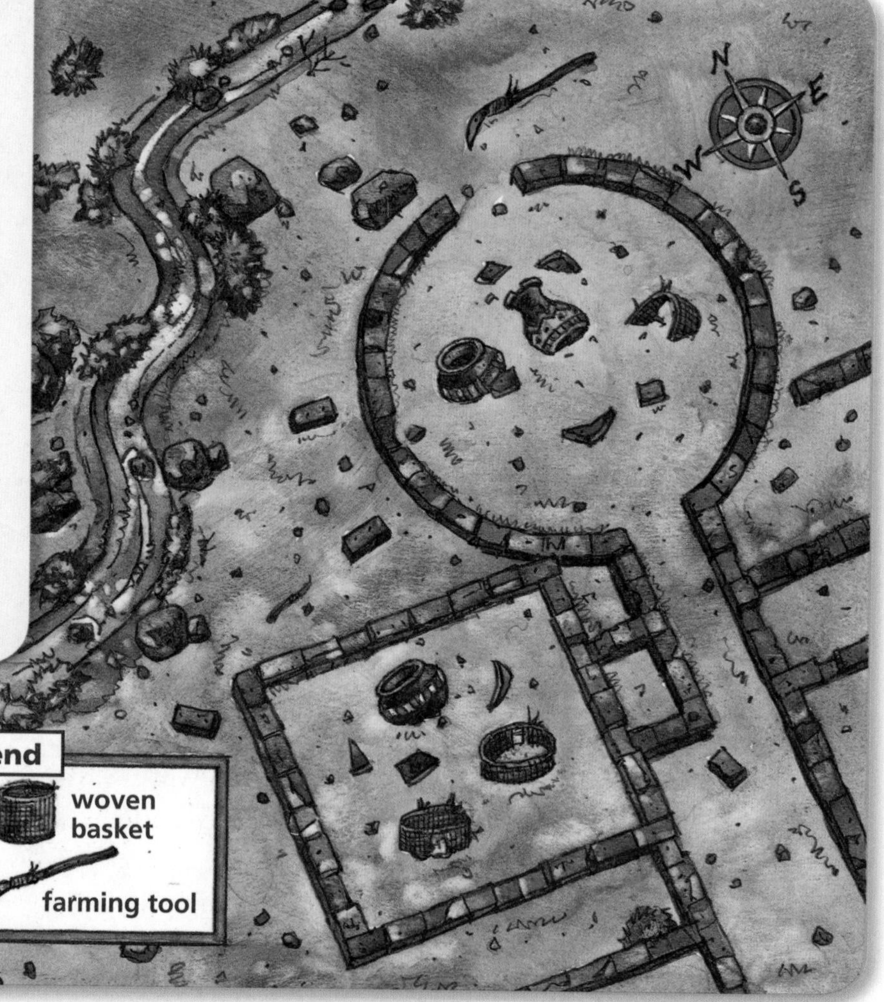

Name:

H-SS 5.1.2 Describe their varied customs and folklore traditions.

Lesson 2

What common ways of life developed among American Indian cultures?

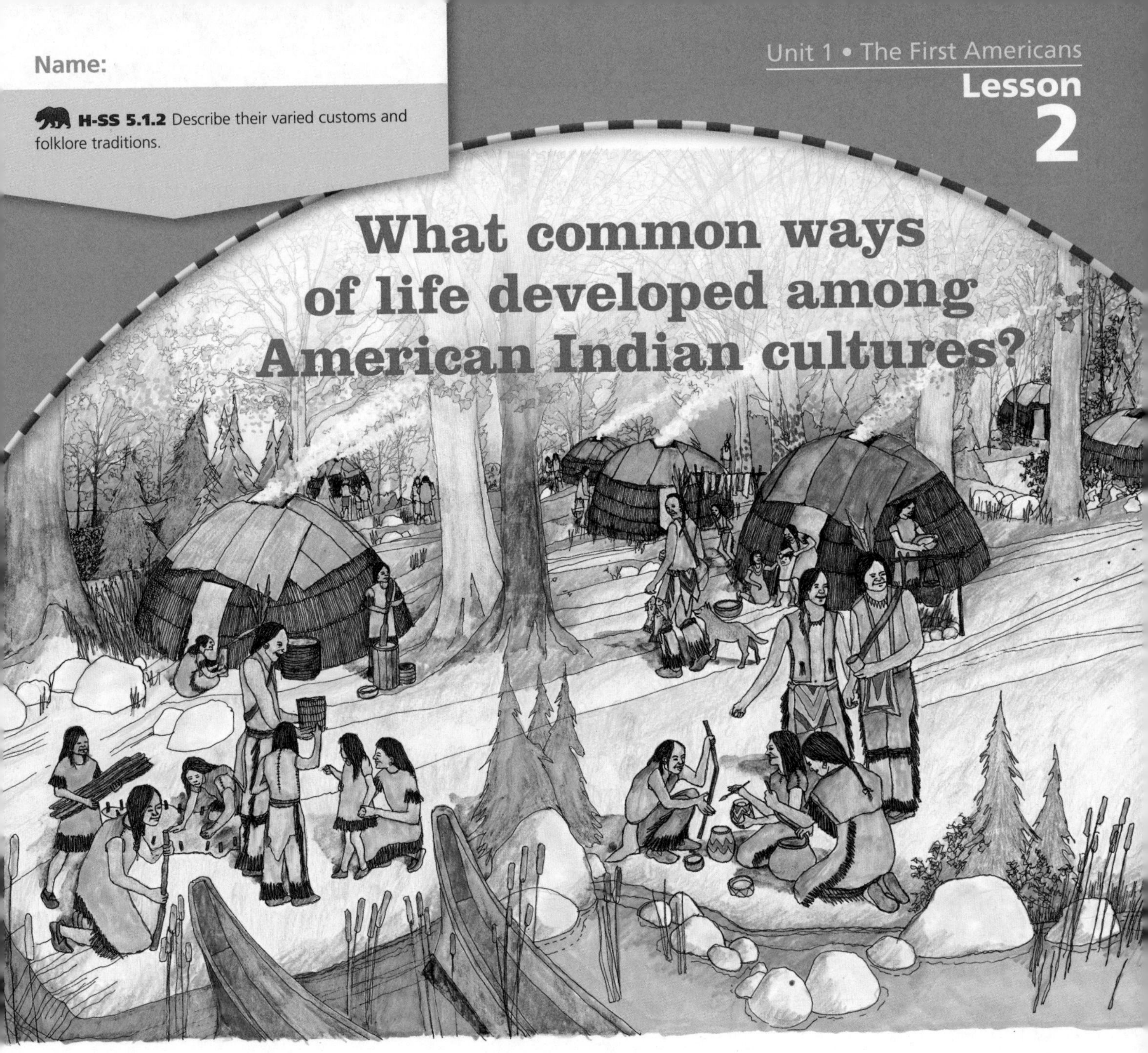

Preview the Lesson

Vocabulary

custom *(n.)* an accepted way of doing something

tradition *(n.)* a set of customs that people create over time

folklore *(n.)* a group's stories and customs

ceremony *(n.)* a set of activities done for a special purpose

religion *(n.)* a system of faith or worship

Vocabulary Activity A *compound word* is made up of two or more smaller words. Circle the word above that is made up of two words with the meanings "people" and "stories."

SET THE SCENE If someone asked you to describe your culture, what would you say? You might talk about holidays you celebrate, music and stories you enjoy, or activities you do with friends and family. How do American Indians express their culture?

Reading: Main Idea and Details

A *main idea* states what a paragraph is mostly about. Writers often include a topic sentence that clearly states a paragraph's main idea. As you read, underline the topic sentence in each paragraph on page 12.

Cultural Practices Develop

As American Indian groups adapted to different regions, they developed unique customs. A **custom** is an accepted way of doing something, such as greeting people or making food. Many of these customs then became part of a group's tradition. A **tradition** is a set of customs that people create over time.

In each cultural region, people developed traditional roles that helped their group meet its needs. In many Eastern Woodlands villages, men collected resources by hunting and fishing. Women used other resources to make clothing and food containers. However, these roles varied by region. In some regions, women provided resources by farming. In the Desert Southwest, some men wove cotton cloth. Children learned by helping with chores in most groups. Grandparents, aunts and uncles, and parents all helped teach children the group's traditions.

Passing on traditions is still important to American Indian groups today. Most American Indian groups did not have a written language. Therefore, people developed oral, or spoken, traditions to help pass the group's folklore from generation to generation. **Folklore** is a group's stories and customs. Most American Indian stories were spoken, chanted, or sung. Many of these stories continue to be passed along today.

1. Why are stories important to many American Indian groups?
Main Idea and Details

This Havasupai storyteller of the Desert Southwest is helping pass on his people's tradition to new generations.

Celebrations and Ceremonies

Celebrations and ceremonies have always been, and continue to be, an important part of American Indian life. A **ceremony** is a set of activities done for a special purpose. Many of these activities are related to a group's resources or religion. **Religion** is a system of faith or worship. In many American Indian groups, these activities include music and dancing.

American Indian celebrations and ceremonies have served a variety of purposes. Some honored nature. In the Eastern Woodlands, the Iroquois held harvest celebrations when crops were gathered. Other ceremonies had social purposes. In the Pacific Northwest, Wakashan chiefs held large feasts called potlatches. At a potlatch, the chief gave away goods to other members of the village to show how well he controlled the group's resources.

Many ceremonies had religious importance too. The Cheyenne of the Great Plains held large dances that lasted many days to meet their group's spiritual needs. In the Desert Southwest, the Hopi spoke about the group's gods in the kachina ceremony.

2. Circle three main purposes for American Indian celebrations and ceremonies. *Main Idea and Details*

These kachina dolls represent important figures in Hopi culture.

Summary

Over time, American Indian cultures have developed traditions that play an important role in their ways of life. How are these traditions handed down today?

Primary Source

Artifacts: Winter Counts

Learn More

American Indian arts also help pass on traditions. For example, the Yanktonai of the Great Plains kept track of their history by creating winter counts. Winter counts are artifacts that tell us about the life of the Yanktonai. Winter counts were made by drawing pictures of important events on an animal hide. They were called winter counts because the Yanktonai called each year a "winter."

Each Yanktonai group had people who kept the winter count. Once each year, leaders of the group picked an important event from the past year, such as a buffalo hunt or a battle. The keepers of the winter count drew a picture on the hide to show the event. They knew the meaning of all the pictures. By telling the story of each picture, they passed the group's history on to others. Study this winter count and then answer the questions below.

1. **Circle the tepee symbols on the winter count above.** *Identify*
2. **Draw your own winter count symbol for an important event in your life.** *Apply*

My Winter Count

Name:

Lesson 3

H-SS 5.1.3 Explain their varied economies and systems of government.

How did American Indian groups work together?

SET THE SCENE Do you ever trade part of your lunch with a friend? Trading and other ways of working together can help people build strong relationships and meet each other's needs. How do you think American Indians worked together to meet their needs?

Preview the Lesson

Vocabulary

surplus *(n.)* more than is needed

specialize *(v.)* to focus on one kind of product or activity

economy *(n.)* a system for organizing resources, such as money and goods

interact *(v.)* to talk to and work with others

barter *(v.)* to trade goods for other goods without the use of money

government *(n.)* a system of laws and the people who carry them out

Vocabulary Activity Looking for word parts can help you figure out word meanings. Circle the prefix *inter-* above in *interact*. Use a dictionary to look up the meaning of *inter-*. Write its meaning below.

Reading: Compare and Contrast

Reading Skill

Comparing and contrasting information will help you look for similarities and differences between two or more things. As you read, underline details in both paragraphs on page 16 that show that different cultural regions produced different goods.

People Trade Goods and Ideas

As you have learned, people in American Indian groups had different roles. However, they also worked together to meet their needs. Within a group, people worked together to learn better ways to hunt and farm. Over time, groups learned how to produce a food **surplus,** or more than was needed. Once their food needs were met, people had time to do other things, such as carve wood or weave cloth. Some groups began to **specialize,** or focus on one kind of product or activity. Some groups of the Desert Southwest specialized in weaving cotton cloth. In the Eastern Woodlands, some groups specialized in making birch-bark goods. When a group could produce many items, it developed an economy. An **economy** is a system for organizing resources, such as money and goods.

Groups not only worked together to meet their needs, they also interacted with other groups. To **interact** means to talk to and work with others. As groups interacted, they introduced each other to new goods and ideas. When a group could not produce certain goods, they might trade their surplus food and specialized goods with other groups in order to meet their needs. Often the groups bartered with each other for the goods they wanted. To **barter** is to exchange goods for other goods without the use of money. Groups sometimes traveled a long way to trade. For example, groups of the Great Plains traded their buffalo products for agricultural products from groups of the Desert Southwest.

1. Compare and Contrast **Write the goods traded between the cultural regions in the chart below.**

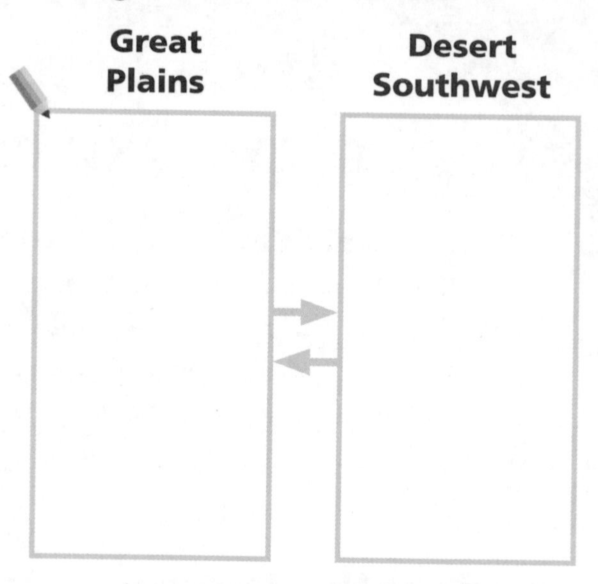

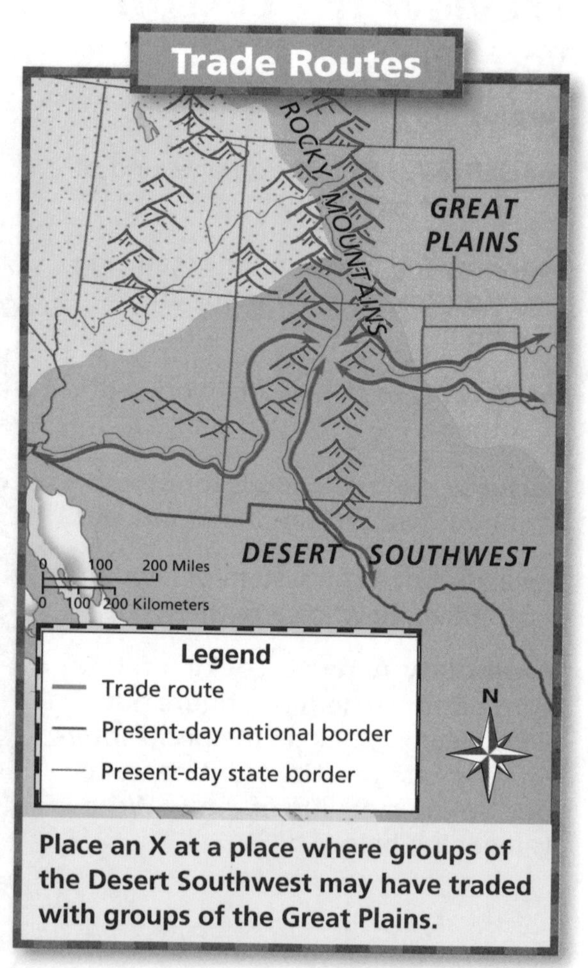

Place an X at a place where groups of the Desert Southwest may have traded with groups of the Great Plains.

Systems of Order

Interacting helped American Indians meet their needs, but it could lead to problems. Some groups fought over resources. Sometimes these groups formed governments to create order. A **government** is a system of laws and the people who carry them out.

One government was the Iroquois Confederacy in the Eastern Woodlands. An American Indian leader named Deganawidah (day gahn uh WEE duh) helped form this government. He wanted to unite five Iroquois groups under one set of laws. He asked a chief named Hiawatha (hi uh WAH thuh) to explain the idea to the groups, and they soon agreed. A group of chiefs from all five groups formed a council that later became the Iroquois Confederacy. They met whenever they had questions about land use, trade, or war. The council discussed an issue until every chief agreed on a decision.

Groups in other regions had governments too. Like the Iroquois, some groups had a large, powerful government. In the Great Plains, the Cheyenne had a council of chiefs that ruled over all Cheyenne groups. Other groups, such as the Papago of the Desert Southwest, had small village councils that handled local issues.

2. Summarize how the Iroquois Confederacy developed. Include the most important events.
Sequence

Hiawatha *(right)* used his speaking skills to convince American Indian leaders to form the Iroquois Confederacy. Created over 500 years ago, this government still exists today.

Summary

American Indian groups interacted with each other in many ways. How did American Indians work together to meet their needs and solve problems?

Biography

Ben Nighthorse Campbell, b. 1933

Learn More Ben Nighthorse Campbell was the first American Indian U.S. Senator to head the Indian Affairs Committee. Born in Auburn, California, Campbell is a member of the Northern Cheyenne. His mother was Portuguese and his father was a Northern Cheyenne. Today, Campbell lives in Colorado and is a member of the Council of 44 Chiefs.

Campbell has done much to bring attention to issues facing American Indians today. In 1989 he helped write a law that created the National Museum of the American Indian, which opened in 2004 in Washington, D.C. He was elected to the United States Senate in 1992 and 1998. In 1997 he became the first American Indian to head the Senate's Indian Affairs Committee. Campbell also celebrates American Indian traditions by making Cheyenne jewelry, a skill he learned from his father.

Answer the questions below.

1. **In college, Campbell studied physical education and fine arts. Circle something he has done that relates to fine arts.** *Identify*

2. **Why do you think it is helpful to have Campbell lead the Senate's Indian Affairs Committee?** *Analyze*

____

____

____

____

____

____

Name:

Unit 2

Study Journal

In this unit you will learn how, why, and where Europeans explored the Americas. Complete the activities on these pages as you read the unit.

What I know about . . .

European explorers:

European Explorers

Classify information about European explorers in the chart below.

Explorer	Year	Sponsor Country	Area Explored
Columbus			
Da Gama			
Vespucci			
Pizarro			
Hudson			
La Salle			

Complete these sections as you read the unit.

Fill in these boxes to show how European explorers' goals changed when they came to the Americas and realized that these lands were not a part of Asia.

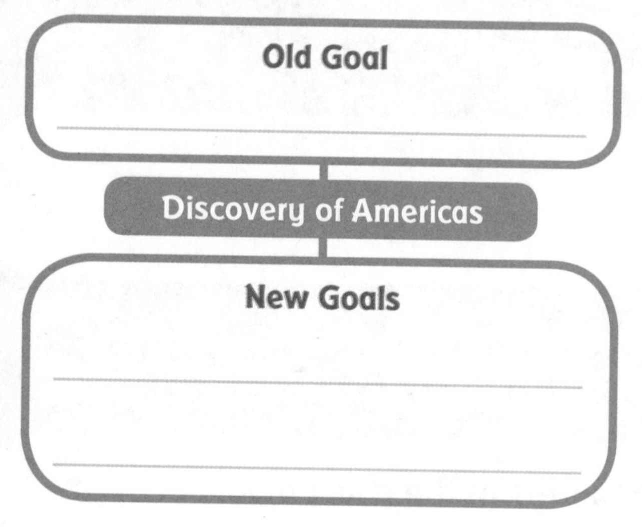

Write a topic sentence for a paragraph explaining how European explorers found their way on the seas. Use three of the following vocabulary terms:

- **astrolabe**
- **latitude**
- **magnetic compass**
- **cartographer**
- **longitude**
- **navigation**

For each explorer listed at the right, write in his accomplishment for the correct year on the time line below:

- **Vasco Núñez de Balboa**
- **Hernando de Soto**
- **Jacques Cartier**

I have learned . . .

Name:

H-SS 5.2.1 Describe the entrepreneurial characteristics of early explorers (e.g., Christopher Columbus, Francisco Vásquez de Coronado) and the technological developments that made sea exploration by latitude and longitude possible (e.g., compass, sextant, astrolabe, seaworthy ships, chronometers, gunpowder).

Lesson 1

Why did Europeans sail to new places?

SET THE SCENE Would you set sail in dangerous seas without a clear idea of where you were going? In the 1400s, many European sailors did just that as they searched for new sea routes to Asia. What do you think caused them to take such risky journeys?

Preview the Lesson

Vocabulary

navigation *(n.)* a science used by sailors to find their place and plan their route

magnetic compass *(n.)* a tool that shows which direction is north

astrolabe *(n.)* a tool that helped sailors use the sun and stars to find their location

expedition *(n.)* a long and carefully organized trip

entrepreneur *(n.)* a person who starts a new business

latitude *(n.)* a distance north or south of the equator, usually measured in degrees

longitude *(n.)* a distance east or west of the prime meridian, usually measured in degrees

Vocabulary Activity The suffix *-ion* means "the act of." Circle the words above that have the suffix *-ion.*

People

Marco Polo
Christopher Columbus
Queen Isabella
King Ferdinand
Francisco Vásquez de Coronado
Bartolomeu Dias
Vasco da Gama

Reading: Cause and Effect

Reading Skill

A *cause* is what makes something happen. An *effect* is what happens as a result of the cause. Signal words such as *because* and *since* can help you find causes and effects. As you read page 22, underline the sentences that include words that signal cause and effect.

1300 | 1350

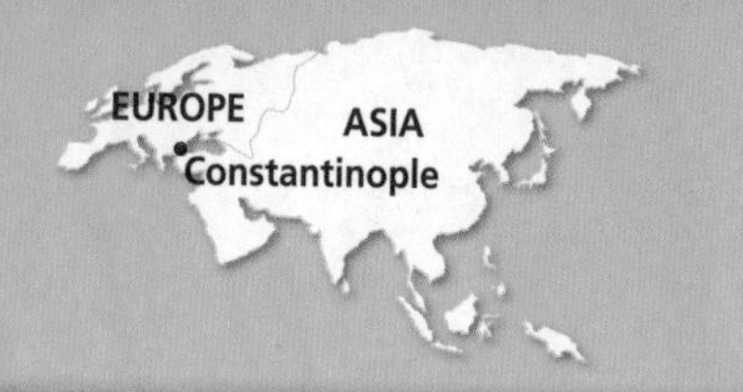

1295 Marco Polo returns to Europe from Asia.

Europe Expands Trade with Asia

In 1295 most Europeans knew little about Asia, or "the East." But that year a merchant named Marco Polo returned to Europe after many years in Asia and wrote a book about its unique cultures. Because of Polo's book, European interest in Asia began to grow. Over time, trade for Asian goods, such as spices and silk, increased and became an important part of Europe's economy.

Trade between Asia and Europe was difficult and costly, though. Many goods moved along land routes called the Silk Road. Traders on the Silk Road faced bad weather, illness, and thieves. Because of these risks, the farther goods traveled, the more costly they became.

Trade became even harder in 1453. That year the Ottoman Turks captured Constantinople and blocked trade through the city. But Europeans still wanted Asian goods. Prices increased as the supply of goods dropped. Since Europeans wanted to continue their trade with Asia, they began looking for new routes to the East.

1. Cause and Effect **What factors caused Europeans to seek new trade routes to Asia?**

The Silk Road

EUROPE
ASIA
Venice
Constantinople
Antioch
Mediterranean Sea
Tyre
Baghdad
Merv
Kashi
Anxi
Xian
Luoyang
HIMALAYAS
AFRICA
ARABIA
INDIA
INDIAN OCEAN
N
0 750 1,500 Miles
0 750 1,500 Kilometers

Legend
- Silk Road
- Sea route
- Ottoman Empire, 1453
- Present-day China

Circle the city of Constantinople, which was located on the Silk Road between Europe and Asia.

1500

1492 Christopher Columbus sets out to reach Asia by sailing west.

Ideas About Sea Travel Change

Until the 1400s, sea travel by Europeans was limited. Why? Most of the maps used by European sailors were poor and their ships were unsteady. These problems made it too risky to sail long distances.

By the 1400s, trade with Asia had brought new technologies in navigation to Europe. **Navigation** is a science used by sailors to find their place and plan their route. The **magnetic compass,** a tool that shows which direction is north, came to Europe from China. The **astrolabe** was a tool that helped sailors use the sun and stars to find their location. It came to Europe from Arabia. Europeans also began to build ships called caravels, which had better sails. Because of these new technologies, Europeans felt it was now possible to search for new sea routes to Asia.

Exploration Brings Hopes of Riches

Many sailors became eager to lead expeditions to find new trade routes. An **expedition** is a long and carefully organized trip. For example, Christopher Columbus believed he could reach Asia by sailing west, something no European had ever done before. However, much like **entrepreneurs** (ahn truh preh NOORS), or people who start new businesses, sailors needed people to sponsor, or pay for, these trips. Kings and queens often agreed to sponsor an expedition when they felt it would bring them wealth and power. In 1492 Queen Isabella and King Ferdinand of Spain agreed to sponsor Columbus's expedition because they wanted to control new routes to the riches of Asia. Successful expeditions could also bring wealth to the explorers. A later Spanish explorer, Francisco Vásquez de Coronado, explored southwestern North America because he heard rumors that the region contained cities made of gold.

2. Cause and Effect **How did trade affect European navigation?**

Technologies such as the magnetic compass *(left)* and gunpowder came to Europe from China.

3. Cause and Effect **Underline why kings and queens were willing to sponsor expeditions.**

Summary

Many factors and events affected trade with Asia in the 1400s. What effects did the desire to continue trade with Asia have on Europe?

Skill

Lines of Latitude and Longitude

Learn More Navigators use lines of latitude and longitude to plan their routes. These lines create a global grid that can plot any location on Earth. A line of **latitude** marks a distance north or south of the equator. Sailors began using astrolabes to measure latitude in the 1400s. A line of **longitude** marks a distance east or west of the prime meridian. Sailors could not measure longitude accurately until the 1700s.

Latitude and longitude are both measured in degrees. To locate a place, you use both measurements. For each question below, find and circle the location on the map. Then draw lines along the lines of longitude and latitude that meet closest to that place. The first question has been done for you.

Try It

1. **In the 1400s, Prince Henry the Navigator sent expeditions south from Lagos, Portugal. Near which lines of latitude and longitude is Lagos located?** *Identify*

____

2. **In 1488 Bartolomeu Dias of Portugal reached the Cape of Good Hope in Africa. What are the nearest lines of latitude and longitude for the Cape?** *Identify*

____

3. **Vasco da Gama of Portugal sailed around the Cape in 1497. He was the first European to reach India by sea. Near which line of latitude is Calicut, India?** *Identify*

____

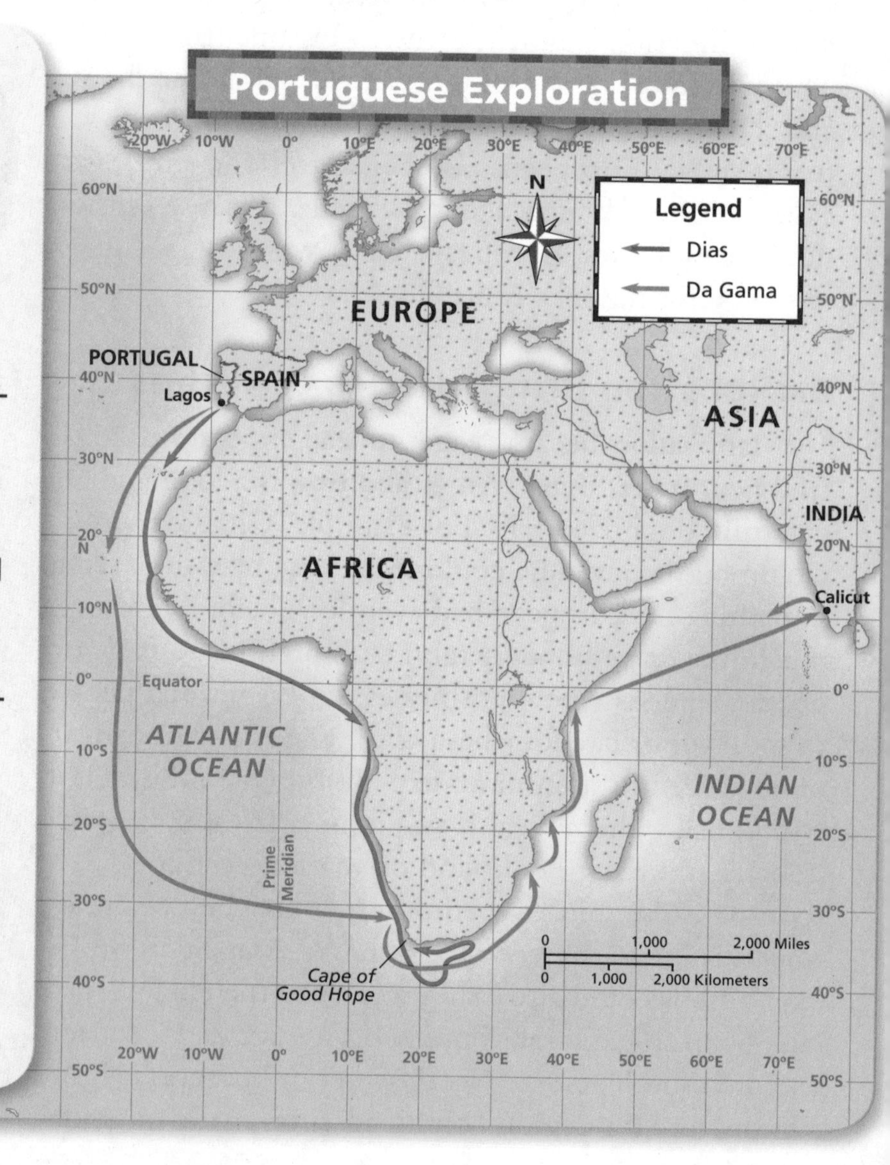

Name:

H-SS 5.2.2 Explain the aims, obstacles, and accomplishments of the explorers, sponsors, and leaders of key European expeditions and the reasons Europeans chose to explore and colonize the world (e.g., the Spanish Reconquista, the Protestant Reformation, the Counter Reformation).

Lesson 2

Who were the explorers and what did they find?

SET THE SCENE You have already learned why Europeans wanted to make voyages to Asia. But when they arrived in new lands, why might they have wanted to stay? What did they find there that encouraged more people to follow them?

Preview the Lesson

Vocabulary

cartographer *(n.)* a person who makes maps or charts

colony *(n.)* an area or place that is ruled by a distant country

reform *(v.)* to change

convert *(v.)* to change someone's or one's own beliefs

emperor *(n.)* the ruler of an empire

circumnavigation *(n.)* the act of sailing around something

Vocabulary Activity The word part *circum-* means "around." You have learned the word *navigation*. How does knowing what *circum-* means help you understand the meaning of *circumnavigation*? Write your answer below.

People

Amerigo Vespucci
Vasco Núñez de Balboa
Hernando Cortés
Francisco Pizarro
Henry Hudson
Jacques Cartier
Samuel de Champlain
Ferdinand Magellan

Reading: Cause and Effect

Reading Skill

Remember that a cause is what makes something happen and an effect is what happens as a result of the cause. As you read the lesson, circle the signal words that help you find causes and effects.

1495

1500

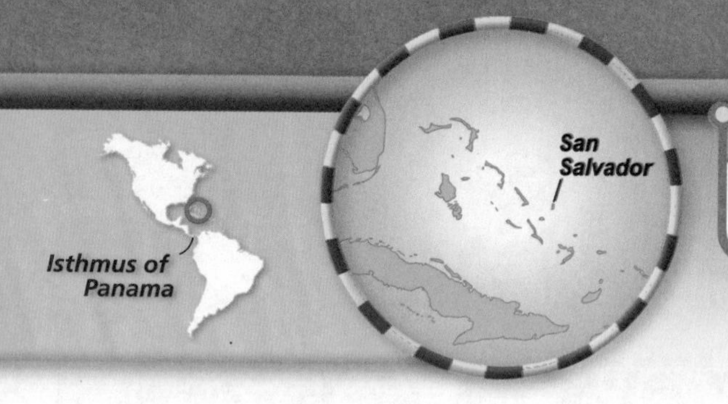

1492 Christopher Columbus lands on San Salvador.

The European Discovery of America

When Europeans set sail to find new trade routes to Asia, they had no idea of what lay to the west. In 1492 Christopher Columbus hoped to reach Asia by sailing west from Spain across the Atlantic Ocean. Instead, he landed on the island of San Salvador, off the southeast coast of North America. However, Columbus believed that he had reached islands in Asia called the Indies. He even called the native people he met "Indians." In 1497 John Cabot led an English expedition that reached the east coast of North America. Like Columbus, Cabot thought that he had reached Asia.

Europeans soon realized that these lands were not really part of Asia. In 1501 Amerigo Vespucci led a Portuguese expedition to lands south of where Columbus had landed. Vespucci came to believe that these lands were in fact unknown to Europeans. In a letter, Vespucci called these lands a "New World." In 1507 a **cartographer,** or person who makes maps or charts, suggested naming this land after Vespucci. Because of this, the New World became known as *America*. Then in 1513 Spanish explorer Vasco Núñez de Balboa crossed the Isthmus of Panama. He became the first European to see the Pacific Ocean from the west coast of the Americas.

1. Cause and Effect **How did Columbus's voyages affect European exploration?**

This map shows the *Novus Orbis*, or "New World." Over time, these lands become known as *America*, after Amerigo Vespucci.

The Goals of Exploration Change

When Europeans realized that new lands lay to the west, the goals of exploration changed. Countries began wanting not only new routes to Asia. They also wanted to claim land and resources in the Americas. Over time, European countries set up colonies to help secure their claims. A **colony** is an area or place that is ruled by a distant country.

Differences between religious groups also made Europeans want to explore and set up colonies in the Americas. For 400 years, Christians from Spain had been taking land in Europe from another religious group called Muslims. This period was called the *Reconquista*, or reconquest. As the Spanish began exploring the Americas, they wanted to make sure that these lands would be controlled by Christians too.

Differences between European Christian groups also led to exploration and colonization. Some Christians, called Protestants, broke away from the Roman Catholic Church in the 1500s. This period was known as the Protestant Reformation because these people wanted to **reform,** or change, parts of the Catholic religion. Catholic countries such as Spain soon began a Counter Reformation. *Counter* means "to go against." One of the goals of the Counter Reformation was to convert people in new lands to Catholicism. To **convert** is to change someone's or one's own beliefs. Because of their differences, Catholics and Protestants competed for power in Europe and the Americas during the Age of Exploration.

2. Cause and Effect **How did the Americas change the goals of European exploration?**

This Protestant was trying to convert American Indians.

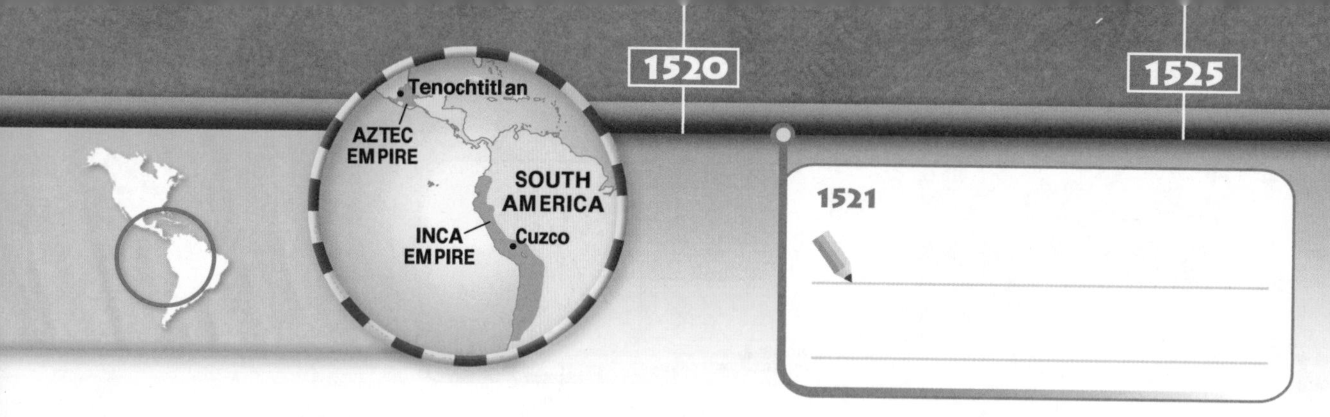

Spain Conquers Wealthy Empires

Spain and Portugal were among the earliest European countries to sponsor exploration. Portugal explored lands in eastern South America. However, because Vasco da Gama found an eastern route around Africa to Asia in 1497, Portuguese expeditions focused on those two continents. Spain chose to gain land and wealth in the New World.

In 1519 the Spanish conquistador, or conqueror, Hernando Cortés began taking over the wealthy Aztec Empire in what is now Mexico. Cortés and his army marched on Tenochtitlan, the Empire's capital city. His army consisted of Spanish soldiers and American Indians who did not like being ruled by the Aztecs. They quickly captured Moctezuma (mahk teh ZOO mah), the **emperor,** or ruler of an empire. The Aztecs fought back, but by 1521 Cortés controlled all Aztec lands.

Another Spanish conquest took place in South America. In 1530 Francisco Pizarro began conquering the Inca Empire in what is now Peru. The conquistador and a small army captured the Inca emperor Atahualpa (at tah HWAHL pah). The Incas gave Pizarro a room filled with gold and silver in exchange for their ruler's freedom, but he did not let Atahualpa go. By 1533 Pizarro had also captured the Inca's capital, Cuzco.

3. In what ways were the actions of Cortés and Pizarro examples of Spain's goals in the New World?
Draw Conclusions

The Pyramid of the Sun *(above)* is an example of the wealth and power of the people who were living in the Valley of Mexico. European weapons and armor helped Spanish soldiers *(left)* conquer the Empire.

1530	1535	1540

1534 Jacques Cartier explores the St. Lawrence River.

1533 Francisco Pizarro conquers the Inca Empire.

The Search for Western Routes to Asia

While Spain and Portugal explored Central and South America, other European countries sent expeditions to areas farther north. Many of these expeditions tried to find a water route through North America that would lead to the Pacific Ocean and thus to Asia. This route was called the Northwest Passage. No ship successfully sailed such a route until the 1900s, but the attempt to find it led European countries to explore and claim new land in North America. Henry Hudson tried to find the Northwest Passage when he led expeditions to North America for the Netherlands in 1609 and then for England in 1610. France also became interested in searching for a Northwest Passage. Jacques Cartier was looking for a Northwest Passage in 1534, but he found the St. Lawrence River instead. Samuel de Champlain sailed to the area in 1608 and claimed much of northeastern North America for France.

Eventually, Spain became the first country to reach Asia by sailing west. In 1519 Ferdinand Magellan began an expedition that sailed south around South America and west into the Pacific Ocean. He reached Asia in 1521, where he was killed in a battle with native people. His crew continued the journey and arrived back in Spain in 1522. Not only had they finally found a westward route to the riches of Asia, but they had completed the first circumnavigation of the world. **Circumnavigation** is the act of sailing around something.

4. Cause and Effect **In the text, underline the reason why some countries sent expeditions to North America.**

Magellan's expedition began with five ships and about 250 men. Only one ship and 18 men completed the nearly three-year voyage around the world.

Summary

Explorers set sail for a number of reasons. Of all the explorers and expeditions you have read about, which one do you think was the most important? Why?

Biography

Amerigo Vespucci, 1454–1512

Learn More Amerigo Vespucci was born in Florence, Italy. As a boy, he learned the newest European ideas in science and mathematics. In 1492 he went to Spain to help run a shipping business. While there, he met Christopher Columbus and helped him prepare for his trips across the Atlantic Ocean. In 1499 Vespucci himself went to sea as a navigator on an expedition for Spain. Like Columbus, he thought he was exploring the east coast of Asia.

Vespucci sailed west again in 1501, this time with an expedition for Portugal. He sailed far down the east coast of South America. However, Vespucci no longer thought that this land was Asia. He had figured out a way to measure the circumference of, or distance around, the Earth. He also knew how to find his longitude. With these two measurements, Vespucci realized that South America was too far east to be Asia.

Answer the questions below.

1. **Circle the names of the two countries for which Vespucci sailed.** *Identify*
2. **How do you think Vespucci's education helped him figure out that western lands were not part of Asia?** *Interpret*

____

____

____

____

Name:

H-SS 5.2.3 Trace the routes of the major land explorers of the United States, the distances traveled by explorers, and the Atlantic trade routes that linked Africa, the West Indies, the British colonies, and Europe.

Lesson 3

What explorations were made by land?

SET THE SCENE When Europeans first arrived in the Americas, they explored coastal areas. Over time, they wanted to gain control of lands deeper in the continent. Where did their desire for riches and new trade routes lead them, and what did they find?

Preview the Lesson

Vocabulary

mission *(n.)* a place set up by a religious group to teach religion and other ways of life to native people

trading post *(n.)* a place where people meet to trade goods

tributary *(n.)* a river that flows into a larger river or lake

slavery *(n.)* the practice of owning people and forcing them to work without pay

Vocabulary Activity Circle a vocabulary word in the list above that is related to the following words: *church, education*.

People

Juan Ponce de León
Hernando de Soto
Robert La Salle

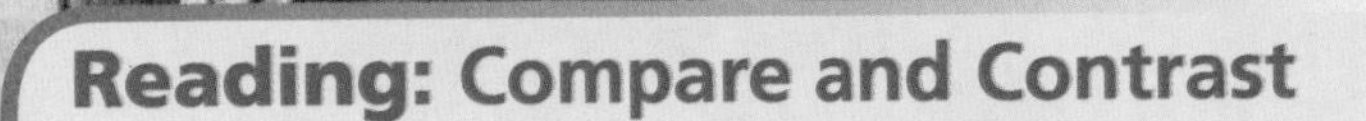

Reading: Compare and Contrast

To compare things, writers sometimes use the words *also* and *like*. As you read page 32, underline sentences that compare the expeditions of Juan Ponce de León, Hernando de Soto, and Francisco Vásquez de Coronado.

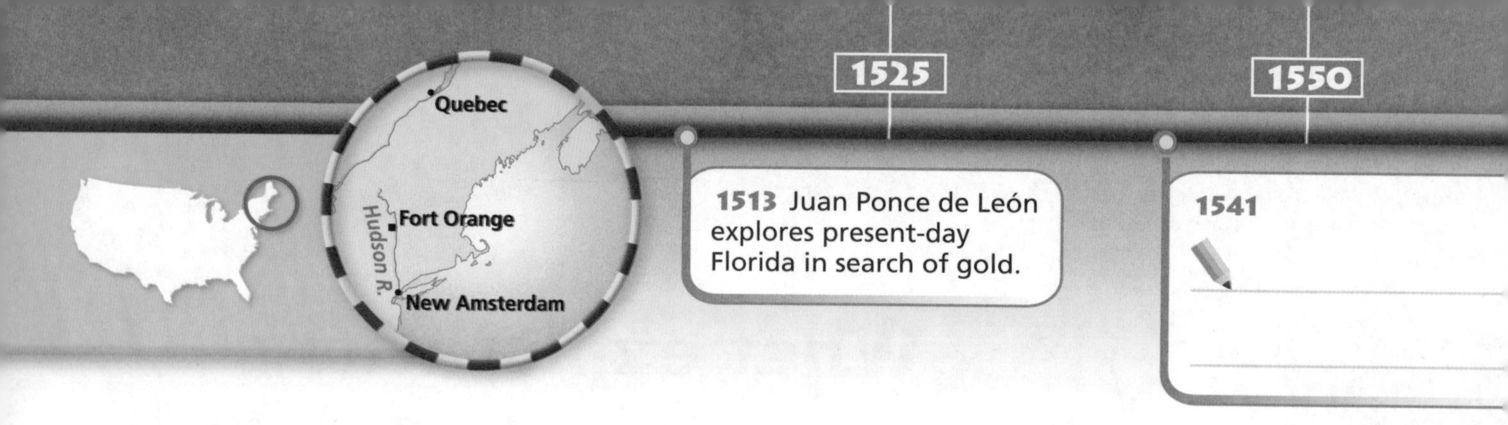

Spain Explores North America

Soon after exploring lands in Central and South America, the Spanish began to explore North America in search of riches. In 1513 Juan Ponce de León set out to explore present-day Florida. He mapped the coast, but attacks by American Indians kept him from moving deeper inland to find the gold he sought.

Hernando de Soto also explored land in North America for Spain. In 1539 he led an expedition that began in what is now Florida. Later, de Soto and his soldiers marched north and west from the region to look for riches. In 1541 they became the first Europeans to see the Mississippi River.

In 1540 Francisco Vásquez de Coronado explored what would become Mexico and the southwestern United States. He was seeking cities of gold that an earlier explorer had said were in the area. Like Ponce de León, Coronado never found what he was looking for. However, the Spanish later started missions in the areas they explored. A **mission** is a place set up by a religious group to teach religion and other ways of life to native people.

1. How were the expeditions of Ponce de León and Coronado alike? *Compare and Contrast*

The Spanish built many missions in areas claimed by early explorers. The Santa Barbara Mission was founded in 1782 in present-day California.

1575 1600 1625

1608 Samuel de Champlain founds trading post at Quebec.

1609 Henry Hudson explores present-day New York.

In the legend, circle the names of two explorers who travelled on or near the Mississippi River.

The Search for the Northwest Passage

As you have learned, France and the Netherlands sent expeditions to search for a Northwest Passage to Asia. Samuel de Champlain of France explored land along the St. Lawrence River. In 1608 he founded a trading post that became the city of Quebec. A **trading post** is a place where people meet to trade goods. Later, Robert La Salle of France traveled south along the Mississippi River to the Gulf of Mexico. In 1682 he claimed all the lands around the Mississippi River and its tributaries for France. A **tributary** is a river that flows into a larger river or lake.

Explorers from the Netherlands also searched for a Northwest Passage. In 1609 Henry Hudson traveled up the Hudson River in present-day New York. Later, the Netherlands built towns and forts along the river, including New Amsterdam and Fort Orange, where the present-day cities of New York and Albany are located.

2. Who helped France claim lands around the Mississippi River?

Main Idea and Details

Summary

In the 1500s, Europeans began exploring large areas of North America. What were some of the causes for their explorations?

Skill

Movement on Maps

Learn More One of the major reasons why Europeans colonized the Americas was to gain wealth from the lands' many natural resources. Europeans often used slavery to supply the many people needed to work this land. **Slavery** is the practice of owning people and forcing them to work without pay. Over time, trade routes developed for carrying goods and enslaved people between Africa, Europe, and the Americas. Europeans went to Africa to capture or trade for enslaved people and then shipped them to the West Indies. There, ships picked up goods and took many enslaved people on to North America. These routes created a triangle pattern across the Atlantic Ocean. The arrows on the map below show how European traders moved goods and enslaved Africans between Africa, Europe, and the Americas. Use the map to answer the questions below.

Try It

1. **On the map, number from one to three the places at the beginning, middle, and end of the journey of enslaved Africans to North America.** *Sequence*
2. **Circle goods that were shipped back to Africa from the colonies.** *Identify*
3. **How were products shipped from the colonies to England different from the manufactured goods shipped back to the colonies?** *Explain*

____

____

____

____

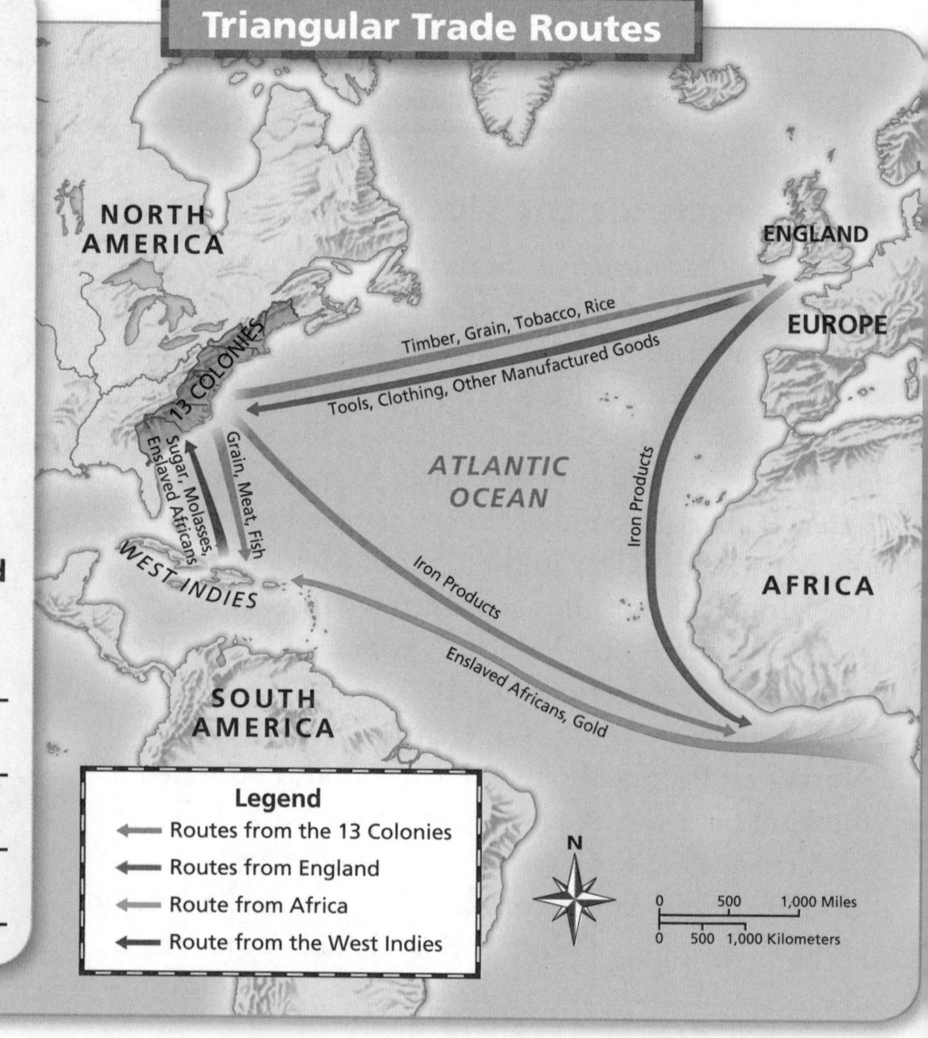

Name:

Lesson 4

H-SS 5.2.4 Locate on maps of North and South America land claimed by Spain, France, England, Portugal, the Netherlands, Sweden, and Russia.

Where in the Americas did European countries claim land?

SET THE SCENE Do you know who the first people were to live in your area? How long ago did they move there? People choose to go to new places for different reasons. As Europeans came to the Americas, where did they look for places to settle?

Preview the Lesson

Vocabulary

charter *(n.)* an official document from an authority to do something

settlement *(n.)* a place to live that is set up in a new area

Vocabulary Activity Word parts can be used to help you figure out the meaning of a word. In the vocabulary list above, circle the root word in *settlement.* Underline the suffix.

Reading: Make Generalizations

Generalizations are statements that are true most of the time. To signal a generalization, writers use words such as *often* or *usually*. As you read page 36, circle the words that signal generalizations about how Europeans set up colonies in the Americas.

European Land Claims

As European countries claimed land in North and South America, people began to move to and settle on this land. Forming colonies was part of the process of settling new land. Because most land claims were owned by a country's ruler, settlers usually had to get a charter from their king or queen in order to set up a colony. A **charter** is an official document from an authority to do something. Some charters also included information about the boundaries of the colony, how the colony would be ruled, and who could live there.

When settlers arrived in the Americas after sailing across the Atlantic Ocean, they had to decide where they would build settlements for their colony. A **settlement** is a place to live that is set up in a new area. People often chose to set up their settlements near the ocean or along rivers. This allowed them to use ships to move people and supplies easily. It also provided them with access to fish and other food sources.

The map on page 37 shows early land claims and settlements by European countries in the Americas. As you look at it, think about some of the explorers' routes that you have already learned. You may notice that a country's land claims and settlements often followed its path of exploration. For example, Spain controlled much of present-day Central America and South America. England, France, and the Netherlands started colonies in eastern North America. Portugal claimed eastern South America, near their African trade routes. Later, Sweden and Russia also started small colonies in North America.

1. Why did colonists in the Americas often build their homes near bodies of water?

Make Generalizations

This document is a later copy of the 1606 charter that established the English colony at Jamestown, Virginia.

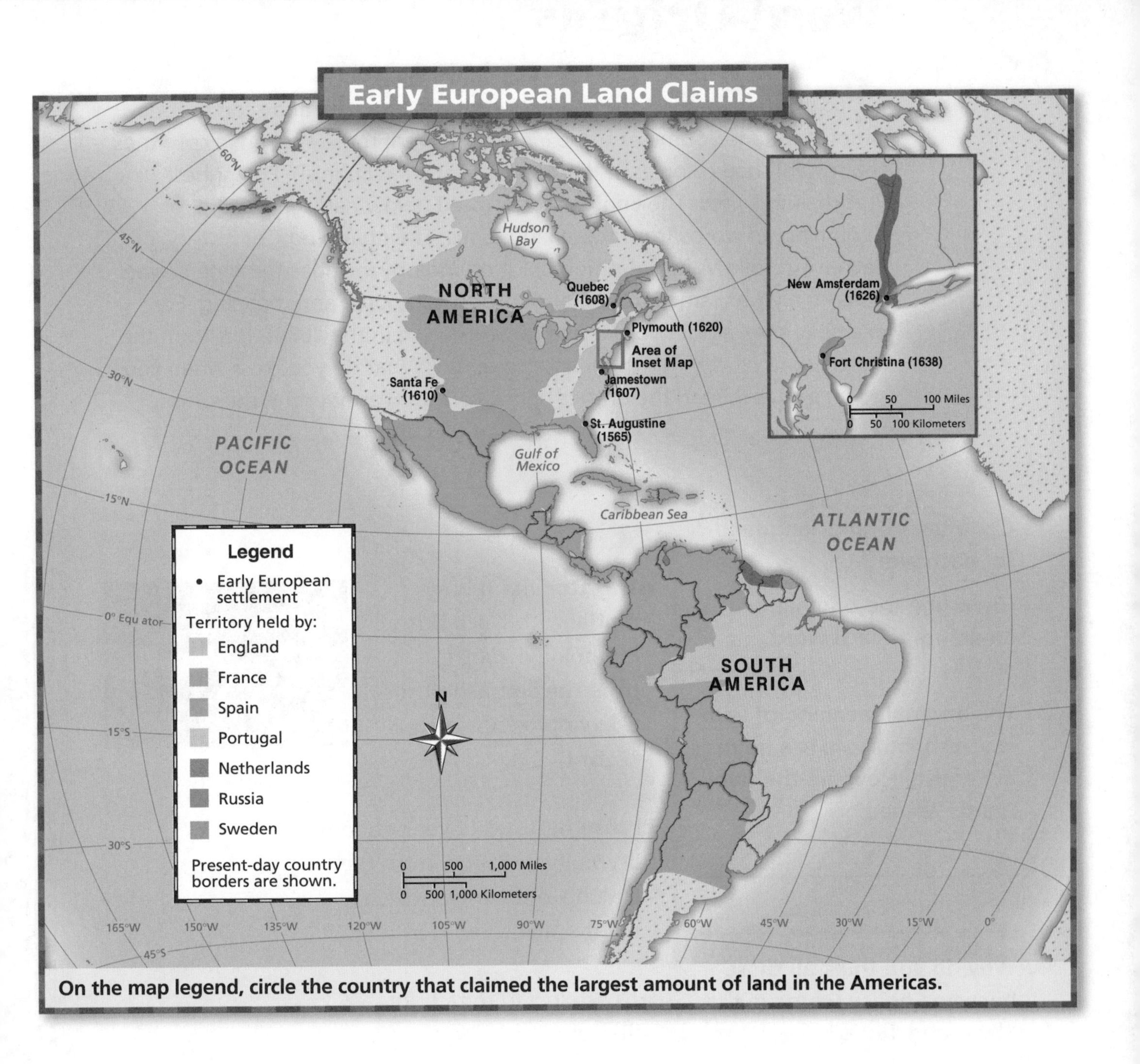

On the map legend, circle the country that claimed the largest amount of land in the Americas.

Summary

European countries began to build settlements in the lands they claimed. Describe where these countries claimed land in the Americas.

Skill

Word Origins

Learn More Many English words that we use today come from other languages. Some of these languages were those spoken in countries that established colonies in the Americas, such as Spanish, Portuguese, French, and Dutch. The English words listed below had their origin, or beginning, in words from these languages. The etymology, or history, of each word follows its definition. Each etymology includes the time period when the word came into use and its original source and meaning. For example, the English word *cruise* came into use in the 1600s. It is from the Dutch word *crucen*, which means "to cross." What do you cross when you go on a cruise? Read the entries below and then answer the questions.

Try It

1. **Circle the original language for each word.** Identify
2. **Underline the original meaning of each word.** Identify
3. **The original meaning of *yam* is a verb, but *yam* is a noun in English. How are the two words related?** Interpret

   ____

   ____

4. **Why do you think all these became English words in the 1500s and 1600s?** Analyze

   ____

   ____

   ____

alligator *(n.)* a large reptile with thick skin; Etymology: 1500s, from the Spanish phrase *el lagarto,* which means "lizard"

cruise *(v.)* to sail over or about; Etymology: 1500s, from the Dutch word *crucen,* which means "to cross"

parade *(v.)* to march for display; Etymology: 1600s, from the French word *parer,* which means "to prepare"

yam *(n.)* a type of sweet potato; Etymology: 1600s, borrowed by the Portuguese in the word *inhame,* from a West African word meaning "to eat"

Name:

Unit 3

Study Journal

In this unit you will learn how American Indians cooperated with each other and with European and American settlers. You will also learn about the problems that existed among these groups. Complete the activities on these pages as you read the unit.

What I know about . . .

interactions among American Indians and settlers:

Conflicts in North America

Classify information about each event in the chart below.

Event/Year	Who	Where	What Happened
Pequot War, 1637			
Beaver Wars, 1640s to 1701			
Treaty of Doak's Stand, 1820			
Sand Creek Massacre, 1864			
Wounded Knee, 1890			

Complete these sections as you read the unit.

Circle the name of a person below who interests you. Write a brief paragraph from his point of view about how his actions showed either cooperation or conflict among groups.

- Bartolomé de Las Casas
- Squanto
- John Marshall

Draw a picture of something Europeans traded with American Indians. Write one way it changed American Indians' way of life.

Write the events below the correct year on the time line below.

I have learned . . .

Name:

Lesson 1

H-SS 5.3.1 Describe the competition among the English, French, Spanish, Dutch, and Indian nations for control of North America.

Why did European nations and American Indians compete in North America?

SET THE SCENE Suppose that you found a place filled with valuable things. What if other people wanted those same things? What if someone else already lived there? This is what happened when Europeans and American Indians began to compete for land and resources in North America.

Preview the Lesson

Vocabulary

raw material *(n.)* something from the Earth, such as wood or metal, that is changed so that people can use it

conflict *(n.)* a struggle or disagreement

Vocabulary Activity *Synonyms* are words that have the same or almost the same meaning. Circle the word in the list above that is a synonym of the word *argument.*

People

Samuel de Champlain
Junípero Serra
Bartolomé de Las Casas

Reading: Sequence

Reading Skill

When you read history, looking for a *sequence* helps you keep events in order. Often a writer will include the dates of events to help you keep track of their sequence. As you read page 42, circle the dates to help you keep track of the sequence of events.

Quebec
New Amsterdam
Jamestown
St. Augustine

1565 Spain founds St. Augustine in present-day Florida.

Europeans Settle North America

During the Age of Exploration, Spain made the first and largest European land claims in the Americas. After conquering much of present-day Mexico and South America, Spain began claiming land and building settlements farther north. In 1565 Spain founded St. Augustine in present-day Florida, the first permanent European settlement in what is now the United States.

Other European nations also began building settlements in North America. In 1607 England founded Jamestown on the coast of present-day Virginia. After many French explorations, Samuel de Champlain founded Quebec, a trading post on the St. Lawrence River, in 1608. In 1624 settlers from the Netherlands began building New Amsterdam, where present-day New York City is located. In 1769 Father Junípero Serra built the first Spanish mission in present-day California, which later became the city of San Diego.

1. Sequence **List European settlements in the order in which they were founded. Include the countries that founded them.**

The Value of New Resources

Why did European nations build settlements in North America? They saw value in the continent's many raw materials. A **raw material** is something from the Earth, such as wood or metal, that is changed so that people can use it. Spain took gold and silver from the Aztecs in Mexico. England found tobacco to be a valuable crop. France and the Netherlands found great value in beaver furs. At trading posts that were built along rivers and land routes, Europeans traded raw materials and other goods with American Indians. Europeans also built forts to protect their land claims and raw materials from competition with others.

2. Circle the raw materials that became important to Spain, England, France, and the Netherlands. *Main Idea and Details*

Dutch traders worked with American Indian hunters to develop the North American fur trade.

1600

1620

1640

1607 England founds Jamestown in present-day Virginia.

1608 France founds Quebec on the St. Lawrence River.

1624

Land Claims Lead to Disagreements

The struggle to control land and resources in North America created many conflicts among European nations. A **conflict** is a struggle or disagreement. The movement of settlers from one country onto land claimed by another country often led to conflicts. For example, Spain did not want English or French settlers to move south onto Spanish lands in present-day Florida. Some conflicts occurred over attempts to control important locations along rivers or on the coast. As English colonies were established along the East Coast, they took over the Dutch colony of New Netherland and its important ports in 1664. Other conflicts were over land that had particularly rich resources. In 1754 competing French and English claims to the resource-rich Ohio and Mississippi River Valleys led to war between the two countries.

Conflicts also occurred because Europeans claimed lands already claimed by American Indians. In some areas, Spanish settlers moved onto American Indians' lands and enslaved the people who lived there. A Spanish priest named Bartolomé de Las Casas spoke out against this practice as early as 1514, but it continued. In 1680 a group of American Indians forced the Spanish out of present-day New Mexico in what became known as the Pueblo Revolt. This was only one of many conflicts between American Indians and European settlers that would occur throughout North America.

3. Sequence **Circle dates that help you put in order conflicts that occurred among European countries and American Indians.**

A good harbor and access to water routes allowed the Dutch settlement of New Amsterdam to grow into a trade center.

Summary

During the Age of Exploration, Europeans competed with each other and with American Indians for control of North America. What were the main reasons for conflicts among these groups?

Skill

Thematic Maps

Learn More A thematic map shows information about a specific theme, or topic. The thematic map below is about the North American fur trade. The colors show areas where trade occurred between a specific European country and the area's American Indians.

The fur trade was important because it brought wealth to Europeans and European goods to American Indians. However, the fur trade also led to conflicts as European nations competed for land claims. American Indian groups also competed with each other to control trade with European nations. Use the map to answer the questions below.

Try It

1. **The fur trade began in the 1500s with American Indians trading furs for European tools and weapons. In the legend, circle the first region to trade furs in North America.**
   Identify
2. **Circle an important trade center for the fur trade in New Netherland.**
   Identify
3. **Trade routes included major rivers and waterways. Draw a star next to a large bay in northern North America controlled by England.**
   Interpret
4. **In the 1700s, conflicts over trade began in the area between the Mississippi River and the Appalachian Mountains. Which European nations would have fought for control of this area?**
   Analyze

____

____

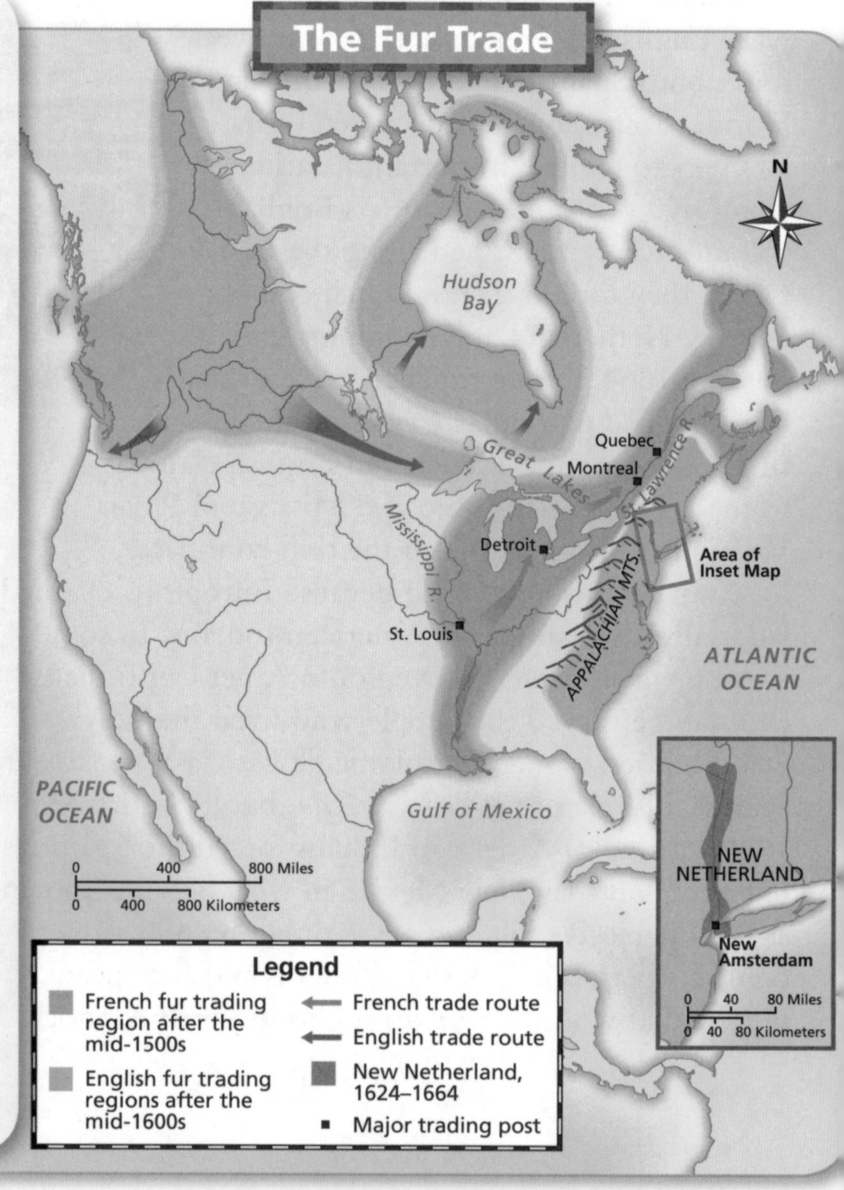

Name:

Lesson 2

H-SS 5.3.2 Describe the cooperation that existed between the colonists and Indians during the 1600s and 1700s (e.g., in agriculture, the fur trade, military alliances, treaties, cultural interchanges).

How did colonists and American Indians cooperate?

SET THE SCENE Playing on a team, working together on a school project, and helping with chores are all forms of cooperation. When European colonists came to North America, they needed to cooperate with American Indians to survive in a new land. How did cooperation affect both of these groups?

Preview the Lesson

Vocabulary

ally *(n.)* a person or group that helps another for a common purpose

treaty *(n.)* a written political agreement between two or more groups

Vocabulary Activity *Antonyms* are words that have opposite meanings. Circle the word above that is an antonym of *enemy*.

People

Squanto
Pocahontas
John Rolfe

Reading: Compare and Contrast

Remember that comparing and contrasting will help you see similarities and differences between two or more things. Writers use signal words such as *both* to compare things and *however* to contrast them. As you read the first paragraph on page 46, circle signal words that help you compare and contrast the relationships of European settlers with American Indians.

Cooperation in North America

You have learned that land claims in North America led to competition among European countries and American Indians. However, not all relationships between American Indians and Europeans involved competition. During the 1600s and 1700s, people from both groups often cooperated and influenced each other in positive ways. For example, French, English, and Dutch fur traders worked closely with American Indians. American Indian groups also became allies with Europeans during wars. An **ally** is a person or group that helps another for a common purpose. In order to end conflicts, competing groups often worked together to write **treaties,** or written political agreements between two or more groups.

1. What did French, English, and Dutch fur traders have in common? Compare and Contrast

American Indians Help English Settlers

The first English colonists in North America depended on help from American Indians in order to survive. Colonists at Plymouth had a difficult time adapting to life in their new settlement. A Wampanoag man named Squanto helped the settlers. He showed the colonists where to hunt and fish and how to grow crops. He also helped them set up peaceful relationships with other American Indian groups.

American Indians also helped English colonists in Virginia. Settlers at Jamestown traded European goods for badly needed food with the Powhatan Indians. According to legend, a young Powhatan woman named Pocahontas saved English leader John Smith from being killed by her father, Chief Powhatan. American Indians also taught colonists how to grow tobacco. In 1612 a settler named John Rolfe raised a successful tobacco crop in Virginia. By 1619 tobacco was Virginia's main crop grown for profit.

2. Sequence **Number in the text from one to three the events that led to tobacco becoming an important crop in Virginia.**

Squanto showed English settlers how to use fish to fertilize their crops.

The Effects of Interaction

When different groups interact, they also share ideas and learn from each other. Interaction between European settlers and American Indians introduced both groups to new goods and ways of doing things. Such sharing changed the ways of life of both groups.

American Indians influenced European colonists in many ways. They taught colonists how to grow crops in the New World and how to prepare food so that it would not spoil. They also showed the settlers which plants could be used as medicines. Even some words we use today in the English language come from American Indian languages. Words such as *squash* and *moccasin* and place names such as *Massachusetts* all come from American Indian languages.

American Indian groups were also influenced by their interaction with Europeans. Colonists introduced American Indians to useful animals that were not originally found in North America, such as horses. Other new animals, such as cattle and sheep, could be used for food. Some American Indians traded furs with the French, English, and Dutch for metal items, such as knives, kettles, needles, and axes. American Indians also began to use goods from Europeans, such as cloth for clothing and glass beads for new kinds of decorations. Over time, American Indians began to depend on these European goods and resources, which changed their way of life.

3. Underline sentences that show the effect that Europeans and American Indians had on the foods that each group ate.

Cause and Effect

European colonists traded metal items, such as knives *(top)*, for American Indian goods, such as corn and squash *(bottom)*.

Summary

American Indians and Europeans interacted in many ways. How did cooperation between American Indians and Europeans influence each group's way of life?

Primary Source

Journals: Christopher Columbus

Learn More A journal is a primary source because it is written by a person involved in an historical event. Christopher Columbus kept a journal when he sailed to the New World in 1492. In the passages below, Columbus wrote about trades he made with the native peoples. This was the beginning of an exchange of food, animals, and technology between Europeans and American Indians that would go on for many years. For example, American Indians taught Europeans about crops such as corn, sunflowers, tomatoes, tobacco, and potatoes. In return, Europeans brought to the Americas oats, rye, wheat, coffee, sugar, sheep, horses, and cows.

Remember that a primary source gives you just one person's point of view of a situation. As you read the first passage, think about how a native person might describe the same event. After reading both passages, answer the questions below.

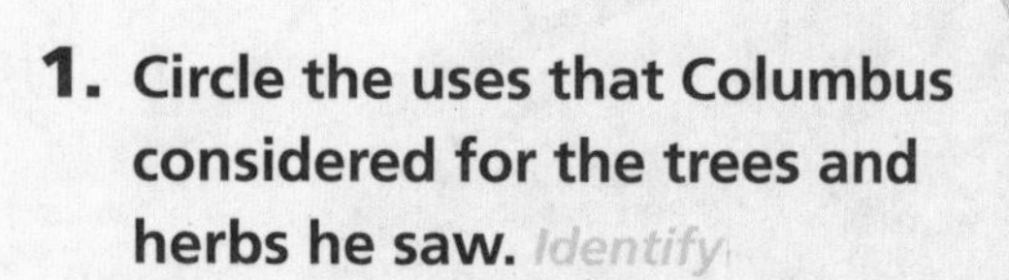

1. **Circle the uses that Columbus considered for the trees and herbs he saw.** *Identify*
2. **How might the point of view of a native person be different from Columbus's point of view in the first passage?** *Analyze*

____

____

____

____

____

____

____

". . . all night there were great numbers of canoes coming off to us, who brought us water and other things. I ordered each man [native person] to be presented with something, as strings of ten or a dozen glass beads apiece, and thongs of leather, all which they estimated [valued] highly . . ."

— Christopher Columbus,
October 16, 1492

"I have no doubt there are trees and herbs here which would be of great value in Spain, as dyeing materials, medicine, spicery, etc."

— Christopher Columbus,
October 19, 1492

Name:

Lesson 3

H-SS 5.3.3 Examine the conflicts before the Revolutionary War (e.g., the Pequot and King Philip's Wars in New England, the Powhatan Wars in Virginia, the French and Indian War).

What major conflicts did European colonists and American Indians have?

SET THE SCENE You have learned how American Indians and Europeans often shared the land and helped each other. What do you think happened when Europeans tried to take land in North America as their own?

Preview the Lesson

Vocabulary

massacre *(n.)* the cruel killing of many people

Vocabulary Activity Circle the word in the sentence below that could be replaced with the word *massacre*.

The killing in this battle was the highest of any conflict between Europeans and American Indians.

People

Metacom
Chief Tecumseh

Reading: Sequence

Time-order words can help you understand a sequence of events. As you read page 50, circle the following time-order words to help you understand the events that led to conflicts between English colonists and the Powhatan: *at first*, *soon*, and *then*.

1600

1650

Pequot War

King Philip's War

Powhatan Wars

1610 The Powhatan Wars begin in Virginia.

1637

English Conflicts with American Indians

Although European settlers and American Indians often cooperated and learned from each other, they had many conflicts too. As more Europeans arrived and pushed deeper onto American Indian lands, American Indians began to fight back.

In 1607 English colonists founded Jamestown, Virginia, in an area controlled by the Powhatan. At first, the colonists and the Powhatan traded goods and food. However, neither side really trusted the other. The Powhatan soon realized that the colonists wanted their land. Then, in 1610, the two sides began a series of conflicts called the Powhatan Wars. Both sides fought fiercely, but by 1646 the colonists had taken most of the Powhatan land.

In 1637 conflicts between English colonists and the Pequot over trade, land, and culture led to the Pequot War in New England. One night the colonists and their American Indian allies set fire to a Pequot village and killed hundreds of people. This is called a **massacre,** or the cruel killing of many people. Further attacks by colonists killed and displaced even more Pequot. Soon after, colonists moved onto the Pequot lands.

In 1675 a Wampanoag chief named Metacom brought American Indian groups together to fight back against English colonists in New England. The colonists called Metacom "King Philip." King Philip's War lasted about a year and caused great destruction to both sides. However, the colonists finally defeated Metacom and his allies and began moving onto American Indian lands throughout New England.

1. Sequence **List in order the important years from the Powhatan Wars and tell what happened in each year.**

English colonists long remembered the violence of King Philip's War. A colonist named Paul Revere made this engraving of Metacom in 1772, nearly 100 years after the war.

1700

1750

1800

1675 King Philip's War begins in New England.

1754 The French and Indian War begins.

1763 The Treaty of Paris ends the French and Indian War.

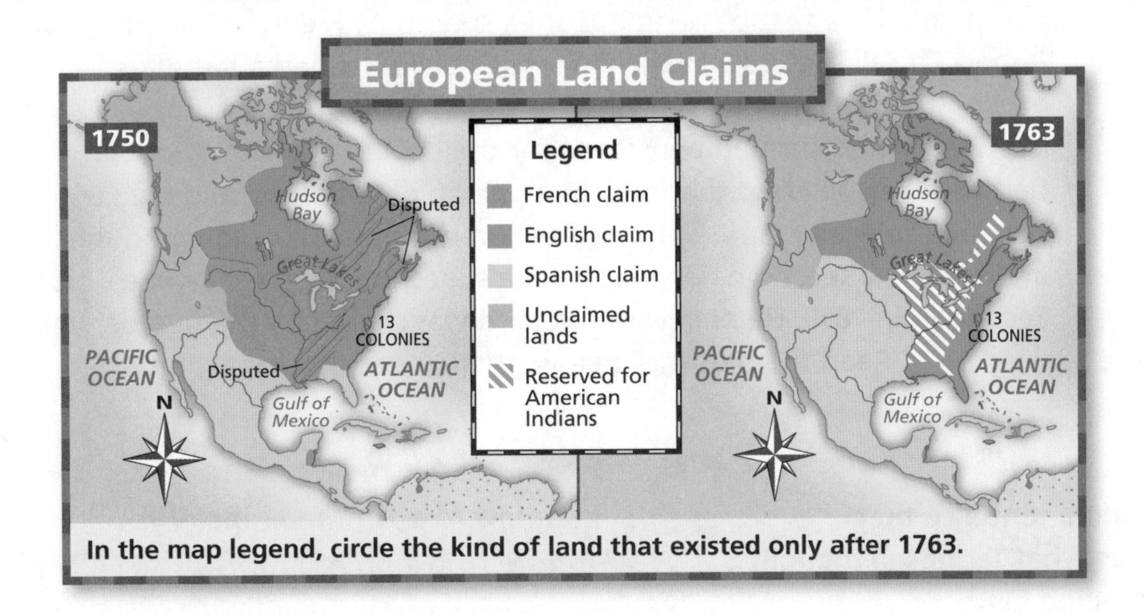

In the map legend, circle the kind of land that existed only after 1763.

The French and Indian War

In the 1700s, conflicts between European countries began occurring farther west in North America. American Indians became involved in these conflicts too. Both France and England (now known as Britain) claimed land in the Ohio River Valley. The French and their American Indian allies controlled the fur trade there, but British settlers also moved into the area. In 1754 the French and Indian War broke out. The French and their allies were winning the war until the British government sent more soldiers. In 1759 the Iroquois also joined the British side. By 1760 the British and their allies had driven the French out of the area.

The 1763 Treaty of Paris gave Britain control of Canada and all French lands east of the Mississippi River. American Indians hoped that in return for their help the British government would help keep settlers off of their land. However, British settlers soon began to move onto American Indian lands anyway.

2. Underline the sentence that explains what Britain's American Indian allies hoped to gain from the French and Indian War.
Cause and Effect

Summary

The movement of European settlers onto American Indian lands led to many conflicts. What were the major conflicts between Europeans and American Indians in the 1600s and 1700s and where did they occur?

Primary Source

Speeches: La Salle and Tecumseh

Learn More By studying historical speeches, you can get different points of view on a historical topic. The two primary sources below show how American Indians and Europeans thought differently about land. The first passage is from a speech by French explorer Robert La Salle in 1682. In the speech, La Salle claimed a large area around the Mississippi River for King Louis XIV of France. European explorers often claimed new lands for their country's king or queen because they believed that only one person or country could own a particular piece of land. They also believed that land could be bought and sold. The second passage is from a speech made by Shawnee Chief Tecumseh in 1810. He believed that land was shared by the people who lived on it. Read the passages below, then answer the questions.

1. **Underline a sentence that describes what Tecumseh thought about selling land.** Identify
2. **How was La Salle's idea about using the land different from Tecumseh's?** Analyze

____

____

____

____

____

"I . . . do now take, in the name of his His Majesty [the king of France] . . . possession of the country of Louisiana, the seas, harbours, ports, bays, adjacent straits, and all the nations, peoples, provinces, cities, towns, villages, mines, minerals, fisheries, streams and rivers, within the extent of the said Louisiana."

— Robert La Salle,
April 9, 1682

"Sell a country! Why not sell the air, the great sea, as well as the earth? Did not the Great Spirit make them all for the use of his children?"

— Chief Tecumseh,
August 11, 1810

Name:

H-SS 5.3.4 Discuss the role of broken treaties and massacres and the factors that led to the Indians' defeat, including the resistance of Indian nations to encroachments and assimilation (e.g., the story of the Trail of Tears).

Lesson 4

How were American Indians forced off their lands?

SET THE SCENE When you agree to something, other people expect you to keep your word. The United States government made many agreements with American Indian groups for their land. But did it keep its promises?

Preview the Lesson

Vocabulary

assimilate *(v.)* to become like the people around you

Vocabulary Activity The word *similar* means "the same." How does knowing the word *similar* help you understand the meaning of *assimilate*?

Reading: Sequence

Reading Skill

Remember that a sequence is a series of events presented in the order in which the events happened. Writers often use dates to help make a sequence of events clear. As you read page 54, circle important dates that help you sequence important events in the relationship between the United States and American Indians.

1800 1825

Wounded Knee
Sand Creek

1820 The Choctaw give up land in present-day Mississippi in the Treaty of Doak's Stand.

Agreements Are Broken

As European settlers moved onto more and more American Indian lands, conflicts occurred across North America. To ease these conflicts, European countries sometimes signed treaties with American Indian groups. These treaties described the boundaries of lands to be given to settlers and the rights of the American Indians who lived there. Soon after becoming an independent country, the United States also began to sign treaties with American Indian groups. Over time, the U.S. government signed hundreds of treaties with American Indians.

These treaties, however, were not always fair. Because of language differences, American Indian leaders often did not understand what they were signing. Other times, some leaders of a group would be paid to sign over lands without the approval of other groups' leaders.

The goal of many treaties was to remove American Indians from their lands. For example, in 1786 the United States began signing a series of treaties with the Choctaw, who lived in present-day Mississippi. In 1820 the United States and the Choctaw signed the Treaty of Doak's Stand. In this treaty, the United States agreed to give the Choctaw new lands west of the Mississippi River in exchange for part of their land. The United States also offered to build schools that would help assimilate the Choctaw. To **assimilate** is to become like the people around you. Many Choctaw did not want to sign this or other treaties. But they knew that if they did not, they would be forced off their land anyway.

1. Sequence **How many years after the United States began signing treaties with the Choctaw did the two groups sign the Treaty of Doak's Stand?**

Choctaw Chief Pushmataha signed the Treaty of Doak's Stand, which gave a large part of his people's land to the United States.

Circle the name of the American Indian group that received the largest area of land in the Indian Territory.

Struggles in the West

In the 1830s, the U.S. government began removing all American Indians from lands east of the Mississippi River. The Cherokee and other groups were forced to move to "Indian Territory" in present-day Oklahoma. During the Cherokee's journey west, many people died as a result of bad weather and disease. Their journey became known as the Trail of Tears.

Over time, settlers moved west of the Mississippi River too, and the U.S. government began taking more land from American Indians. However, some American Indian groups fought back. In 1864 a group of settlers led by Major John Chivington killed several hundred Cheyenne at Sand Creek, Colorado, even though the Cheyenne had agreed to return peacefully to their reservation. This became known as the Sand Creek Massacre. In 1890 hundreds of Lakota decided to stop fighting and return to lands given to them by treaties. Despite surrendering, they were killed by U.S. soldiers at Wounded Knee, South Dakota. This massacre was the last armed American Indian resistance to U.S. rule.

2. In the text, circle the names of two locations of massacres of American Indians.

Main Idea and Details

Summary

American Indians signed many treaties with the U.S. government. What effect did these treaties have on the American Indian groups who signed them?

Primary Source

Documents: The Treaty of Doak's Stand

Learn More A treaty is a primary source because it is a document written at the time an event took place. The passage below is from the Treaty of Doak's Stand, signed by the United States and the Choctaw in 1820.

This document shows what U.S. government leaders thought about American Indians. For example, the treaty states that the United States will move to new lands those Choctaw "who live by hunting and will not work." This wording shows that many Americans thought working meant having a job, such as farming or working in a factory. They did not think that hunting for food was a civilized, or proper, way to make a living. For many Choctaw, however, hunting was an important part of their traditional way of life. Such different ways of thinking often led to conflicts between the United States and American Indian groups. Read the passage, then answer the questions below.

Choctaw Chief Pushmataha

> ". . . [I]t is an important object with the President of the United States, to promote the civilization of the Choctaw Indians, by the establishment of schools amongst them; and to perpetuate [keep] them as a nation by exchanging, for a small part of their land here, a country beyond the Mississippi River, where all who live by hunting and will not work, may be collected and settled together."
>
> — The Treaty of Doak's Stand, 1820

1. **Underline the words that tell what the U.S. government would give the Choctaw in exchange for their land.** *Identify*

2. **How did the U.S. government hope to "civilize" the Choctaw?** *Analyze*

____

____

Name:

H-SS 5.3.5 Describe the internecine Indian conflicts, including the competing claims for control of lands (e.g., actions of the Iroquois, Huron, Lakota [Sioux]).

Lesson 5

What conflicts occurred among American Indians?

SET THE SCENE Even before the arrival of Europeans, American Indian groups had conflicts with each other over the control of their areas' natural resources. How do you think this changed when Europeans arrived and began taking land and resources for themselves?

Preview the Lesson

Vocabulary

rivalry *(n.)* a relationship in which people or groups compete for the same thing

Vocabulary Activity The suffix *-ry* means "the condition of being" something. Circle the suffix in the vocabulary word above and in these words: *misery*, *ordinary*.

People

Chief Powhatan

Reading: Main Idea and Details

Remember, a *main idea* is the most important idea about a topic. *Details* give more information about the main idea. As you read the first paragraph on page 58, underline the main idea.

American Indian Conflicts

You have learned about several conflicts between European settlers and American Indians. However, some American Indian groups had rivalries over land and resources too. A **rivalry** is a relationship in which people or groups compete for the same thing. For example, in the early 1600s, an American Indian leader named Chief Powhatan had rivalries with neighboring groups. He lived in what is now Virginia and wanted to control a large area of farmland along the coast. He eventually came to rule many groups, whom he forced to give his tribe food and other goods.

1. Write a detail that supports the main idea that American Indian groups had rivalries over land and resources. *Main Idea and Details*

Europeans Cause New Conflicts

The arrival of Europeans caused new rivalries between American Indian groups. During the early 1600s, the fur trade led American Indian groups in the Northeast to become allies with European countries. The Huron traded beaver furs with the French, while groups from the Iroquois Confederacy traded with the Dutch. However, by the 1640s, the Iroquois had killed off most of the beavers on their lands. To keep up trade, they needed to find new land with many beavers.

The Iroquois soon began fighting the Huron and their French allies for control of their lands. This series of conflicts is called the Beaver Wars. Over time, the Iroquois gained control of large areas to the north and west of their homeland. Struggles for control of the fur trade continued until 1701, when the Iroquois signed a peace treaty with the French and agreed to stop further attacks.

2. Sequence **In the text, circle important dates and periods of time related to the Beaver Wars.**

The guns that the Iroquois received through the fur trade gave them an advantage over their rivals in the Beaver Wars.

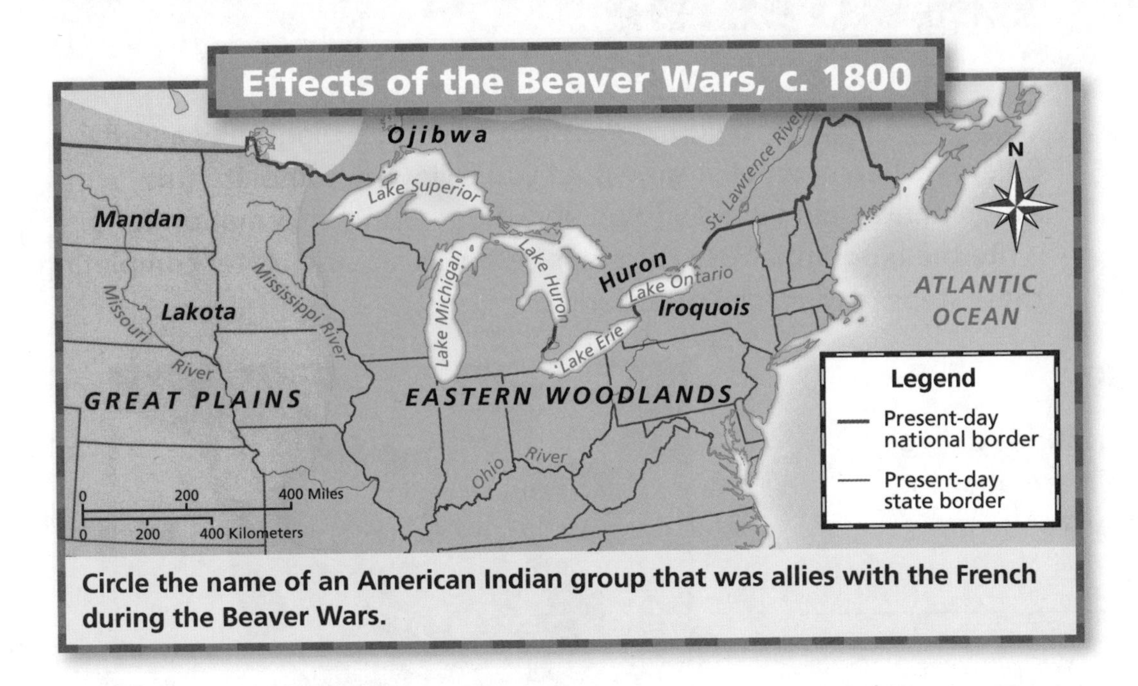

Circle the name of an American Indian group that was allies with the French during the Beaver Wars.

Conflicts Move Westward

The Iroquois' success in the Beaver Wars pushed other American Indian groups off their lands. Many of these groups moved farther west. As they moved into new western regions, they came into conflict with the groups that already lived there. For example, the Lakota lived in the Great Lakes region. When the Ojibwa moved west into this region, the two groups started a major rivalry. The Ojibwa had a strong advantage because of the guns they had received from Europeans in the fur trade. By the late 1700s, the Lakota had left the Great Lakes region and moved farther west, onto the Great Plains.

As the Lakota moved west, they then pushed other American Indian groups off of lands along the Missouri River. The Lakota also began to trade for European horses and weapons. These items helped them become skilled buffalo hunters and feared warriors. The Lakota continued to compete with other Great Plains groups until settlers began arriving in the region in the 1800s. This caused new concerns for the Lakota and the region's other American Indian groups.

3. In the text, circle two groups that came into conflict in the Great Lakes region following the Beaver Wars. *Main Idea and Details*

Summary

American Indian groups competed with each other for resources, but these conflicts grew worse after the arrival of Europeans. How did trade with Europeans affect rivalries between American Indian groups?

Skill

Researching

Learn More If you were asked to write a biography about Chief Powhatan, what steps would you follow to complete this assignment? How would you go about gathering information to write the biography? Use the steps below as a guide. After completing these steps, answer the questions.

1. Write down questions that you would like to answer, such as "Where in Virginia did Powhatan live? What were the major events of Powhatan's life?"
2. Go to your library or media center.
3. Determine the key words that you will use to search for answers to your questions, such as "Chief Powhatan," "Virginia," or "American Indians." Use these topics to search the following materials:
   - **Nonfiction Books** Look for these in the card catalog or database using your topic words.
   - **Reference Materials** Use encyclopedias and other materials in the reference section to find these topics.
   - **Internet** Use a search engine for your topics. Remember that Web sites ending in .org, .edu, and .gov have the most reliable and accurate information.
4. Group the information you found so that it helps you answer the questions you wrote.

Try It

1. **What questions did you write to learn about Powhatan?** *Pose Questions*

   ____

   ____

   ____

2. **Which topic gave you the most books in the card catalog or database?** *Apply*

   ____

3. **Which Web site was the most helpful?** *Analyze*

   ____

4. **What is the most interesting fact you learned about Powhatan?** *Explain*

   ____

   ____

   ____

   ____

   ____

   ____

Name:

Lesson 6

H-SS 5.3.6 Explain the influence and achievements of significant leaders of the time (e.g., John Marshall, Andrew Jackson, Chief Tecumseh, Chief Logan, Chief John Ross, Sequoyah).

Who were the leaders in the struggle for American Indian lands?

SET THE SCENE Have you ever been the leader of a group? Good leaders try to do what is best for the people they serve. What would you have done if you were a leader in the struggle between American Indians and settlers for control of land in North America?

Preview the Lesson

Vocabulary

act *(n.)* a law

Vocabulary Activity A *synonym* is a word that is similar in meaning to another word. Circle the word in the sentence below that is a synonym of *act*.

The committee passed a rule against wearing hats in school.

People

Chief Logan
Lord Dunmore
Sequoyah
Andrew Jackson
Chief John Ross
John Marshall

Reading: Sequence

Reading Skill

When you read about history, it is important to understand the *sequence*, or order in which events took place. Writers use time-order words such as *first*, *then*, *later*, and *finally* to signal that they are describing a sequence. They may also use dates. Circle all the dates and signal words in the lesson that help you understand the sequence.

1811 Tecumseh's followers are defeated at the Battle of Tippecanoe.

The Struggle for Unity

As settlers pushed west, some American Indian leaders brought groups together to oppose them. One such leader was Tahgahjute (TAH gah joot), also known as Chief Logan. At first, Logan helped settlers who moved into the Ohio River Valley. Then, in 1774, his family was killed by colonial traders. Later that year, Logan led the Mingo and their allies, the Shawnee, in attacks against settlers. Lord Dunmore, the governor of Virginia, sent troops to the area. Finally, Logan and his allies were defeated. The American Indian groups were forced to give up some of their lands in a treaty. However, Logan refused to sign the document.

In the early 1800s, a Shawnee leader named Chief Tecumseh attempted to bring American Indian groups together to oppose the migration of settlers into the Mississippi and Ohio River Valleys. Tecumseh was a great speaker and convinced many groups to become allies against the settlers. When some American Indian leaders signed a treaty giving up land in present-day Ohio, Tecumseh demanded that the land be returned. He said, "The white people have no right to take the land from the Indians because [the Indians] had it first." However, in 1811 U.S. troops defeated Tecumseh's followers in the Battle of Tippecanoe. Tecumseh was later killed fighting against the United States during the War of 1812.

1. Sequence **Use signal words and dates to explain the events that led to Chief Logan's refusal to sign a treaty with settlers.**

Tecumseh *(left)* helped unite American Indian groups against settlers.

1820 | 1830 | 1840

1830

1832 U.S. Supreme Court Chief Justice John Marshall rules in favor of Cherokee rights.

1838 U.S. troops force the Cherokee to move west on the Trail of Tears.

The Struggle for Justice

By the 1820s, some southeastern groups, such as the Cherokee, had assimilated in some ways due to contact with settlers. A Cherokee named Sequoyah had even developed an alphabet for the Cherokee language. However, settlers in search of good farmland and gold then began moving onto Cherokee lands. In 1830 President Andrew Jackson asked Congress to pass the Indian Removal Act. An **act** is a law. This law let the President force the Cherokee and other groups to move west of the Mississippi River, to what is now Oklahoma.

Cherokee leader Chief John Ross decided to seek justice without violence. He asked the U.S. Supreme Court to stop the state of Georgia from taking control of Cherokee lands. In 1832 Chief Justice John Marshall ruled in favor of the Cherokee. However, President Jackson refused to support the court's decision. As a result, in 1838 U.S. troops forced the Cherokee to move west on what became known as the Trail of Tears.

2. In the text, underline President Jackson's response to Chief Justice Marshall's decision about Cherokee rights.

Main Idea and Details

President Andrew Jackson *(above)* wanted to move American Indian groups to lands west of the Mississippi River. Chief John Ross *(left)* asked the U.S. Supreme Court to allow the Cherokee to keep control of their lands.

Summary

American Indian leaders used different methods in the struggle to keep their lands. How were the ways Tecumseh and John Ross opposed the loss of their lands different?

Skill

Point of View

Learn More Sometimes there are different primary sources available about one historical event. These primary sources often provide different points of view about the event. The three sources below are reactions to the Indian Removal Act: a court document from Chief Justice John Marshall, the spoken words of President Andrew Jackson, and a letter from Chief John Ross. Read the quotes, and then answer the questions below.

Try It

1. **Which of these three men disagreed with the Indian Removal Act? Circle their names.** *Interpret*
2. **Underline the conditions under which Georgia citizens could enter Cherokee territory, according to Marshall.** *Identify*
3. **Underline what Ross said the Cherokee would have to do if removed from their lands.** *Identify*
4. **According to Ross, why did the Indian Removal Act upset the Cherokee?** *Summarize*

____

____

____

____

____

"The Cherokee Nation . . . is a distinct community, occupying its own territory . . . which the citizens of Georgia have no right to enter but with the assent [consent] of the Cherokees themselves or in conformity with treaties and with the acts of Congress."

— Chief Justice John Marshall, in his decision of the U.S. Supreme Court case *Worcester V. Georgia,* 1832

"John Marshall has made his decision, now let him enforce it."

— U.S. President Andrew Jackson, in response to Marshall's ruling, 1832

"Little did [the American Indians] anticipate, that when taught to think and feel as the American citizen, and to have with him a common interest, they were to be despoiled [stripped of their possessions] by their guardian, to become strangers and wanderers in the land of their fathers, forced to return to the savage life, and to seek a new home in the wilds of the far west, and that without their consent."

— Cherokee Chief John Ross, in a protest letter to the U.S. Congress, 1836

Name:

Unit 4

Study Journal

In this unit you will learn about how European colonists began their settlements in North America, focusing on the English colonies. You will also understand colonial governments and economic systems and the religious and social movements taking place at that time. Complete the activities on these pages as you read the unit.

What I know about . . .

European colonies in North America:

English Colonial Regions

Classify information about the English colonies in the chart below.

Colonial Region	Resources	Early Leaders	Religious Groups	Economic Activities
New England Colonies				
Middle Colonies				
Southern Colonies				

Complete these sections as you read the unit.

Fill in facts to support the generalization below:

Fact

Fact

The First Great Awakening had many effects on the colonies.

Fact

Fact

List two ways slavery changed life in the Americas. Use two words from the list below in your responses:

- auction
- cash crop
- economy
- indentured servant
- plantation
- proponent
- proprietor
- rebel

1. ______________________________

2. ______________________________

Fill in the time line below with the correct events.

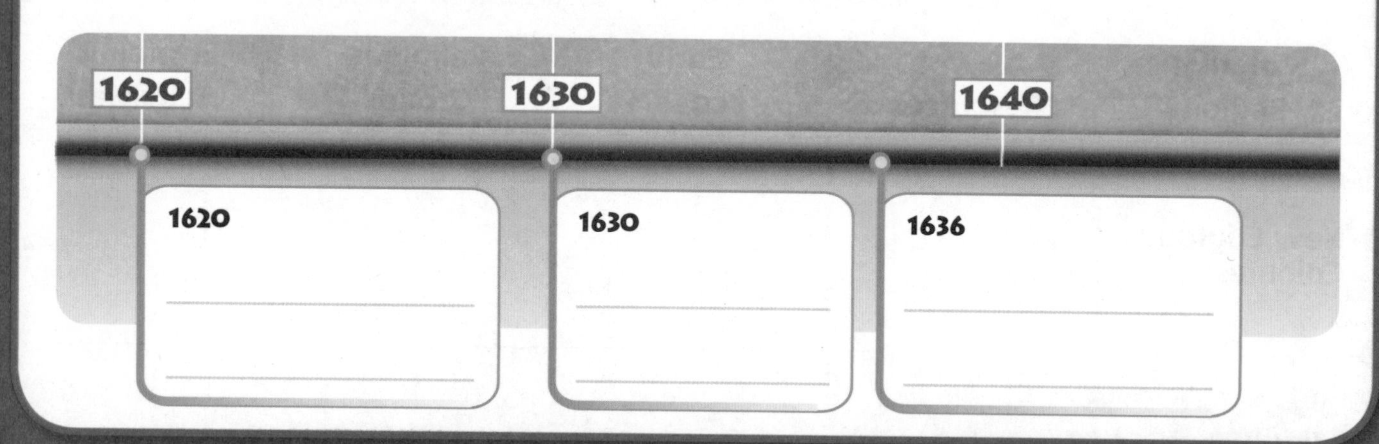

I have learned . . .

Name:

Lesson 1

H-SS 5.4.1 Understand the influence of location and physical setting on the founding of the original 13 colonies, and identify on a map the locations of the colonies and the American Indian nations already inhabiting these areas.

What influenced where Europeans settled in North America?

SET THE SCENE What would make you and your family leave home and move to a new place? European explorers began arriving in North America in the late 1400s. When other Europeans heard their stories of rich land and large forests, many people decided to move to North America.

Preview the Lesson

Vocabulary

plantation *(n.)* a large farm with many workers who lived on the land they worked

cash crop *(n.)* a crop that is grown to be sold for profit

proprietor *(n.)* an owner

indentured servant *(n.)* a person who agreed to work for an amount of time in exchange for the cost of housing, food, and the voyage to North America

self-sufficient *(adj.)* having the ability to produce most everything that one needs

grant *(v.)* to give something formally to someone

Vocabulary Activity The root word in *proprietor* is related to the root word in *property*. The suffix *-or* means "one who." Circle the suffix in the vocabulary word above. How does knowing these word parts help you understand the meaning of the word?

People

Eliza Lucas Pinckney

Reading: Make Generalizations

Reading Skill

A *generalizations* is a statement that is true most of the time. It is based on facts. As you read the first section on page 68, underline facts that will help you make the generalization that many English settlers came to North America to seek a better life.

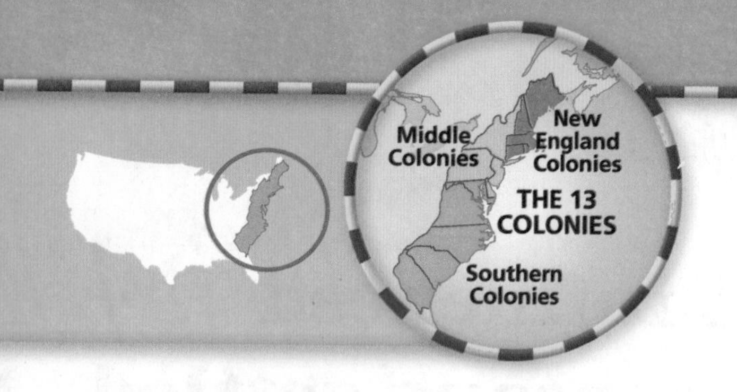

English Settlers Arrive

In the 1600s, English settlers began founding successful colonies along the Atlantic coast of North America. When people in England heard about this land's many resources, more people began moving to the colonies. Many did so to own their own land, to seek gold and silver, and to make money from the fur trade. Over time, different colonial regions developed based on the area's climate and resources.

1. Make Generalizations **What facts lead to the generalization that people came to the colonies to seek a better life?**

The Southern Colonies

The warm climate and rich soil of the Southern Colonies were well suited for agriculture. Settlers throughout the colonies established small farms, but settlers in the South realized that their region would also support **plantations,** or large farms with many workers who lived on the land they worked. On plantations, farmers grew cash crops, such as tobacco and rice. **Cash crops** are crops that are grown to be sold for profit. In 1744 Eliza Lucas Pinckney raised the colonies' first successful crop of indigo, a plant that can be made into a blue dye. Indigo soon became another important plantation cash crop.

To work in their fields, **proprietors,** or owners, brought workers from England. Many of these workers were **indentured servants,** or people who agreed to work for an amount of time in exchange for housing, food, and the cost of the voyage to North America.

2. How did the land and climate of the Southern Colonies affect agriculture? *Cause and Effect*

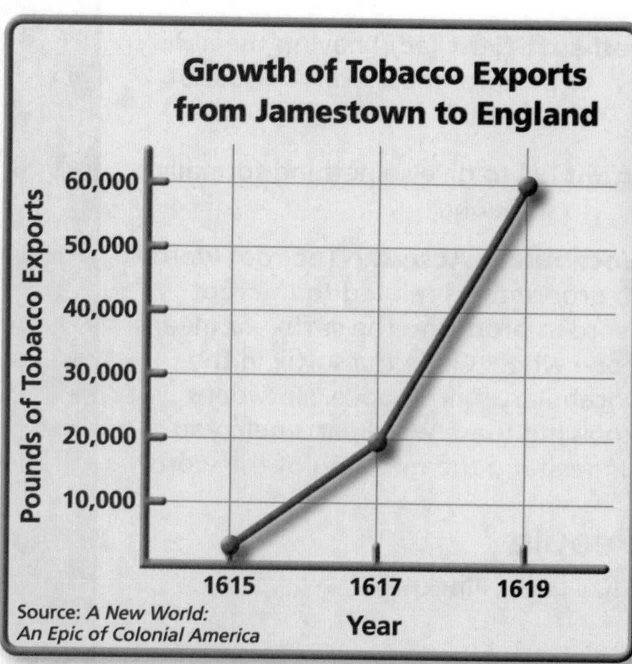

In the Southern Colonies, cash crops such as tobacco, indigo, and rice were grown on large plantations.

The New England Colonies

Unlike the Southern Colonies, the cold climate and rocky soil of the New England Colonies could not easily support large plantations. Instead, colonists there used the region's other natural resources to meet their needs. Shipbuilders used tall, white pine trees to build ship masts. Colonists also fished for cod and mackerel.

Many people in New England were self-sufficient farmers. To be **self-sufficient** is to have the ability to produce most everything that one needs. Many families lived on small farms. They grew crops, raised livestock, and hunted animals for food. They cut lumber from trees to build homes and make tools.

3. How were farms in New England different from farms in the Southern Colonies?

Compare and Contrast

Cod and other fish became important resources to the New England colonies.

The Middle Colonies

The Middle Colonies also offered settlers many important resources. The Dutch first settled New Netherlands and profited from the fur trade. England later took over the area and granted some people large areas of land to settle. To **grant** is to give something formally to someone. Some colonists established farms and grew wheat as a cash crop. Because of the many good harbors, the Middle Colonies also became important for shipping. Philadelphia harbor became a seaport and a shipbuilding center. New Amsterdam, later renamed New York City, also became an important seaport.

4. Underline a sentence that tells why shipping became important in the Middle Colonies.

Cause and Effect

Summary

Early colonists used their area's resources to live. How did geography and climate affect where people settled in North America?

Skill

Resource Maps

Learn More A resource map shows the resources of an area. The resource map below shows the resources in the New England Colonies, the Middle Colonies, and the Southern Colonies of North America. It also shows the major American Indian groups of the area. In most cases, the resources of an area determined what kinds of economic activities developed there. As you have learned, resources also affected relationships between Europeans and American Indians. Use the map legend below to identify the major crops and goods produced in colonial America. Then answer the questions.

Try It

1. **Underline the cash crops in the map legend.** *Identify*
2. **Circle the name of the colonial region where fish were most plentiful.** *Identify*
3. **Place a check mark next to an American Indian group that lived in the Middle Colonies.** *Identify*
4. **In the map legend, circle the resource found in all three colonial regions.** *Analyze*

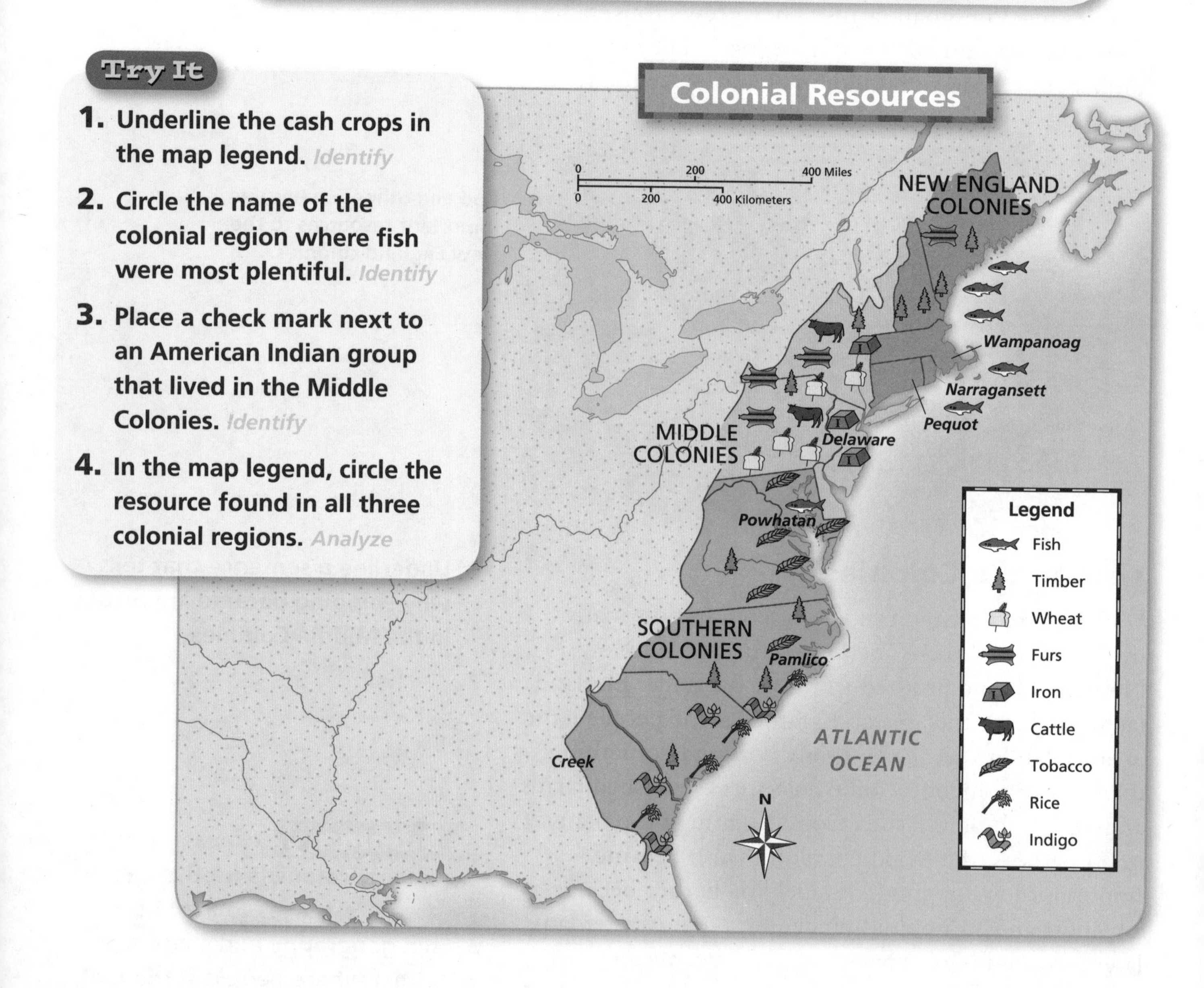

Name:

H-SS 5.4.2 Identify the major individuals and groups responsible for the founding of the various colonies and the reasons for their founding (e.g., John Smith, Virginia; Roger Williams, Rhode Island; William Penn, Pennsylvania; Lord Baltimore, Maryland; William Bradford, Plymouth; John Winthrop, Massachusetts).

Lesson 2

Who founded the colonies and why?

SET THE SCENE Why do people move to new areas? As you have learned, the resources and opportunities in North America attracted many settlers from Europe. But people moved to North America for other reasons too. What other reasons might Europeans have had for founding new colonies?

Preview the Lesson

Vocabulary

persecution *(n.)* unjust treatment

Separatists *(n.)* a group of people from England who wanted to separate themselves from the Church of England

pilgrim *(n.)* a person who travels to a place for religious reasons

Puritan *(n.)* a person from England who wanted to improve the Church of England

dissenter *(n.)* a person whose views are different from those of his or her leaders

Vocabulary Activity Circle the word above that has *pure* as its root word. Underline the word that has *separate* as its root word.

People

John Smith
Lord Baltimore
James Oglethorpe
William Bradford
John Winthrop
Thomas Hooker
Roger Williams
Duke of York
William Penn

Reading: Compare and Contrast

When you *compare* two or more things, you look for their similarities. When you *contrast* them, you look for their differences. Writers use signal words such as *like* and *similar to* compare things. They use signal words such as *unlike* and *different* to contrast them. As you read the lesson, circle the compare and contrast signal words.

The English Establish Colonies

European countries and settlers had many reasons for building colonies. Countries wanted to gain wealth through land and natural resources. Like their home countries, some settlers also hoped to grow rich by owning their own land. In addition, some settlers came to the colonies to escape persecution for their religious beliefs. **Persecution** is unjust treatment. Others wanted the chance to start a new life.

In the late 1500s, English monarchs, or rulers, began giving people charters to form different kinds of colonies in North America. In corporate colonies, the monarch gave control of the land and its settlers to a business. In proprietary colonies, control was given to a proprietor or group of proprietors. In royal colonies, the monarch kept control, usually through appointed officials. By 1752 monarchs had changed many corporate and proprietary colonies into royal colonies.

English businesses sought to profit by founding corporate colonies such as Jamestown.

1. How were corporate colonies different from royal colonies?
Compare and Contrast

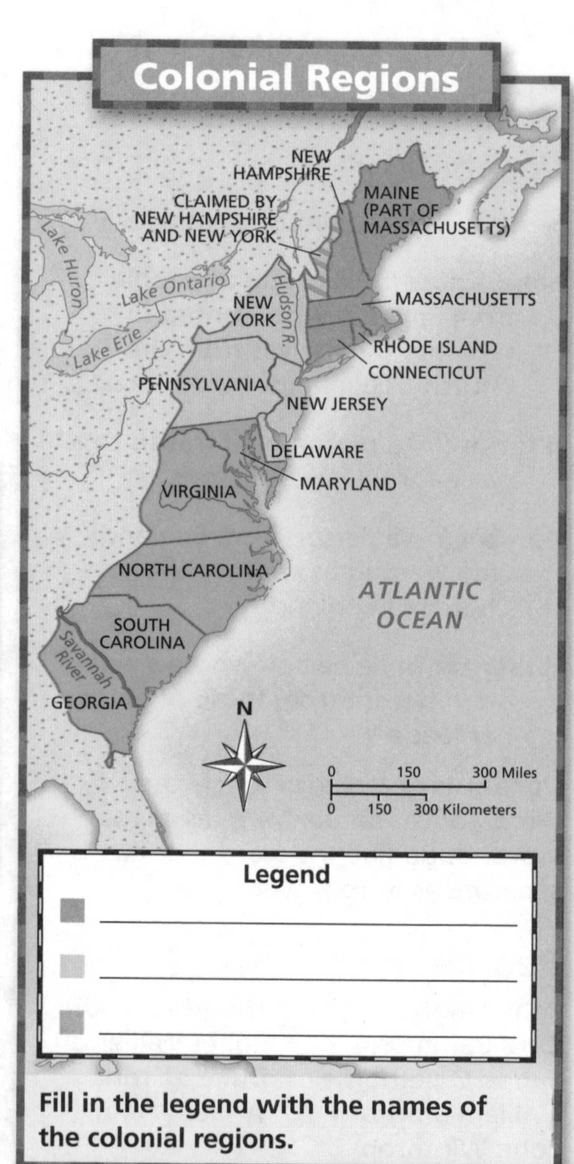

Fill in the legend with the names of the colonial regions.

1630 1640 1650

1630

1636 Thomas Hooker founds Connecticut. Roger Williams founds Rhode Island.

1634 Lord Baltimore founds Maryland.

Founding the Southern Colonies

Many Southern Colonies were started as corporate colonies. John White founded a colony on Roanoke Island as a trading center in 1587. After starting the colony, White returned to England for supplies. When he returned to Roanoke in 1590, all the colonists had disappeared. No one knew what had happened to them.

In 1607 the Virginia Company founded the Jamestown Colony. Illness, poor food, and lack of discipline caused many hardships for the colonists. Less than half of the original colonists survived their first year at Jamestown. Then a new leader named John Smith created a strict rule that food should be given only to people who worked. Working together, the colonists built houses and learned to use the area's resources. After the colonists planted their first successful tobacco crop in 1612, the colony began to thrive.

Other Southern Colonies were founded as proprietary colonies. Lord Baltimore founded Maryland in 1634 as a place for Catholics, who were persecuted in England. Like colonists in Virginia, some colonists in Maryland built large tobacco plantations.

The colony of Carolina was founded by a group of proprietors in 1663. Over time, the region's rich soil and good harbors attracted many settlers. In 1712 the colony divided into North Carolina and South Carolina. These became official royal colonies in 1729.

James Oglethorpe founded Georgia in 1733 for a different reason. He wanted to give English debtors, or people who owed money, a new start as farmers. Few debtors came, but skilled workers and others settled in Georgia.

2. How was Maryland different from other Southern Colonies? How was it similar? *Compare and Contrast*

The development of tobacco crops attracted many colonists and was key to the success of Virginia and other Southern Colonies.

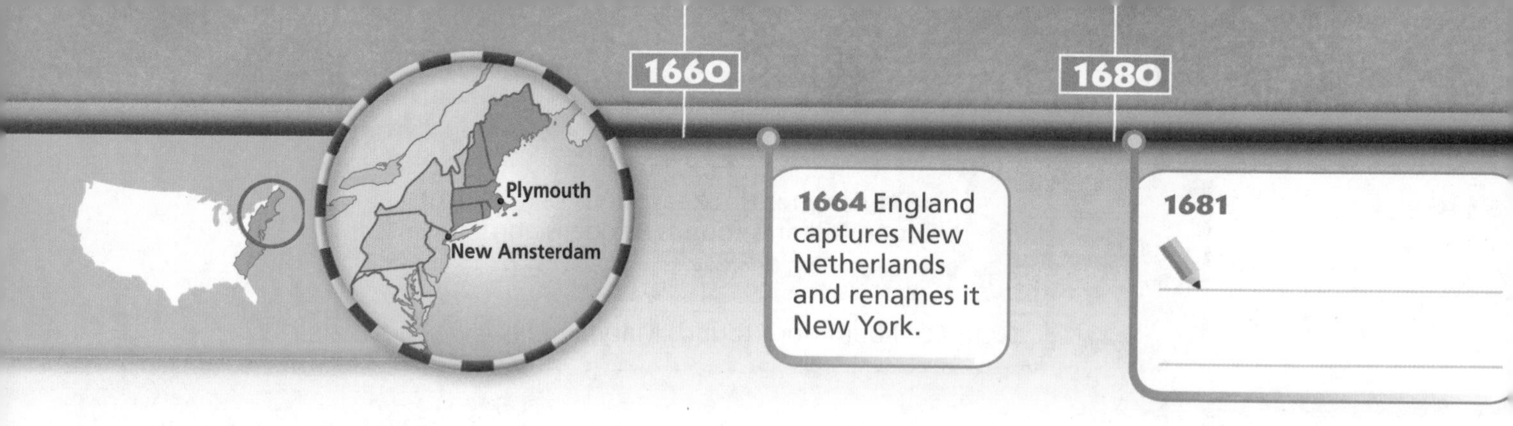

Founding New England Colonies

Unlike most Southern colonists, many colonists came to New England to escape religious persecution. The first of these colonists were **Separatists,** or people who wanted to separate themselves from the Church of England. In 1620 a group of Separatists landed in the area that is now Massachusetts. They founded Plymouth Colony and elected William Bradford as their governor. This first group of New England colonists came to be known as Pilgrims. A **pilgrim** is a person who travels to a place for religious reasons.

In 1630 another group came to New England in search of religious freedom. This group, known as the Puritans, was led by John Winthrop. A **Puritan** was a person from England who wanted to improve the Church of England. Winthrop hoped to start a colony where Puritans could worship as they wanted and be an example to others. He said, "We shall be a City upon a hill, the eyes of all people are on us." The Puritan colony was called the Massachusetts Bay Colony. Its main settlement was the city of Boston.

Although many early colonists came to Massachusetts hoping to escape religious persecution, religion within the colony was strictly controlled. Because of this, people left Massachusetts to start their own colonies. In 1636 Thomas Hooker founded Hartford. Later, the area would become the colony of Connecticut. Roger Williams was known as a **dissenter,** or person whose views are different from those of his or her leaders. He was forced to leave Massachusetts and founded the settlement of Providence in 1636. Later, this area would become the colony of Rhode Island.

3. Make Generalizations **What facts help you make the generalization that most of the New England colonies were founded for religious reasons?**

Some Separatists first sought religious freedom in the Netherlands. In 1620 a group of Separatists sailed from England to North America on the *Mayflower*.

1700 | 1720 | 1740 | 1760

1729 North and South Carolina become royal colonies.

1733 James Oglethorpe founds Georgia colony.

Founding the Middle Colonies

The founding of the Middle Colonies was different than that of New England and the Southern Colonies. The area was first claimed by the Netherlands and Sweden. In 1624 the Dutch named their colony New Netherlands. They built a trading post called New Amsterdam that became a center for the fur trade.

The area did not stay under Dutch control, however. England already had colonies to the north and south of New Netherlands. King Charles II of England wanted to combine these colonies and to control New Netherlands' rich resources. In 1664 England captured the Dutch colony. The king gave a large part of the colony to his brother James, the Duke of York. The Duke renamed the colony New York, and New Amsterdam became New York City. The Duke then gave part of the land to his friends, who renamed it New Jersey. To pay off a debt, the king also gave William Penn land along the Delaware River. Penn belonged to a religious group called the Quakers. In 1681 he founded the colony of Pennsylvania as a "holy experiment," where people of all religions could live together.

4. In the text, underline the reason why England took over New Netherlands. *Main Idea and Details*

New York City became a valuable colonial trade center because of its important location and good harbor.

Summary

People from England began founding North American colonies in the 1500s. What reasons did people have for founding these colonies?

Skill

Classifying and Sorting

Learn More When you classify information, you sort it into categories. Classifying information makes it easier to compare and contrast it. The chart below classifies information about the thirteen English colonies. In this chart, the colonies are classified and sorted alphabetically by name. The headings at the top of each column can be used to classify the information by other categories. Study the chart, then answer the questions below.

Try It

1. **How many colonies are classified alphabetically by the letter *N*?** Identify

____

2. **Which category would you use to create a time line of when the colonies were founded?** Analyze

____

3. **If you classified the colonies according to the year they were founded, which colony would be listed first? Draw a star next to it.** Interpret

4. **Circle the colonies that could be classified as being founded for religious reasons.** Analyze

Colony	Year	Early Leaders	Reasons for Founding
Connecticut	1639[2]	Thomas Hooker	Farming, trade, political freedom
Delaware	1704[2]	William Penn	Trade, farming
Georgia	1733[1]	James Oglethorpe	Refuge for debtors, colony between Carolinas & Florida
Maryland	1634[1]	Lord Baltimore	Refuge for Catholics in North America
Massachusetts	1620[1]	William Bradford, John Winthrop	Escape religious persecution in England
New Hampshire	1729[2]	John Wheelwright	Trade, fishing
New Jersey	1664[2]	John Berkeley, George Carteret	Build colony on land captured from Dutch
New York	1664[2]	Duke of York	Build colony on land captured from Dutch
North Carolina	1653[1]	William Berkeley	Farming
Pennsylvania	1682[1]	William Penn	Establish Quaker colony in North America
Rhode Island	1636[1]	Roger Williams	Establish colony for people of all religions
South Carolina	1670[1]	Anthony Ashley-Cooper	Farming
Virginia	1607[1]	John Smith	Establish English colony in North America, search for gold

[1] Settled [2] Charter granted

Name:

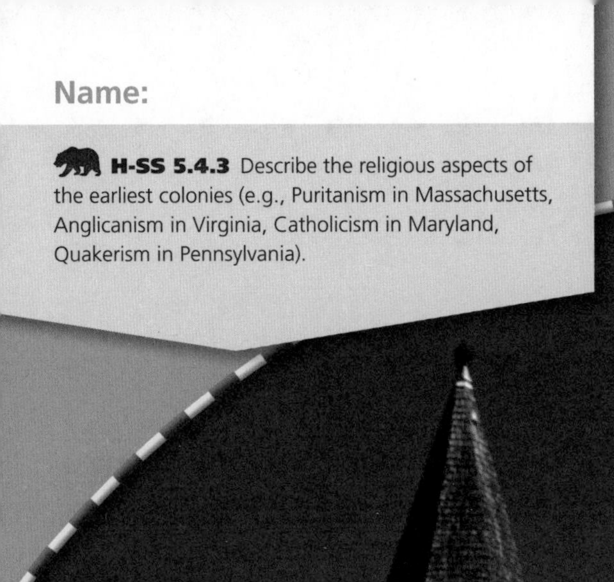

H-SS 5.4.3 Describe the religious aspects of the earliest colonies (e.g., Puritanism in Massachusetts, Anglicanism in Virginia, Catholicism in Maryland, Quakerism in Pennsylvania).

Lesson 3

How did religion affect the founding of the colonies?

SET THE SCENE One thing many early colonists had in common was a strong religious faith. However, the colonists practiced religion in different ways.

Preview the Lesson

Vocabulary

intolerant *(adj.)* to be not accepting of ideas or behaviors different from one's own

Vocabulary Activity The prefixes *in-* and *un-* mean "not." Circle the prefix in the vocabulary word above. Then write a definition for the root word based on what you know about the meaning of the prefix.

People

Anne Hutchinson

Reading: Make Generalizations

Reading Skill

Remember that to *make generalizations* you use facts from a text to write statements that are true most of the time. As you read the first paragraph on page 78, place check marks next to sentences that contains facts about religious laws in the colonies.

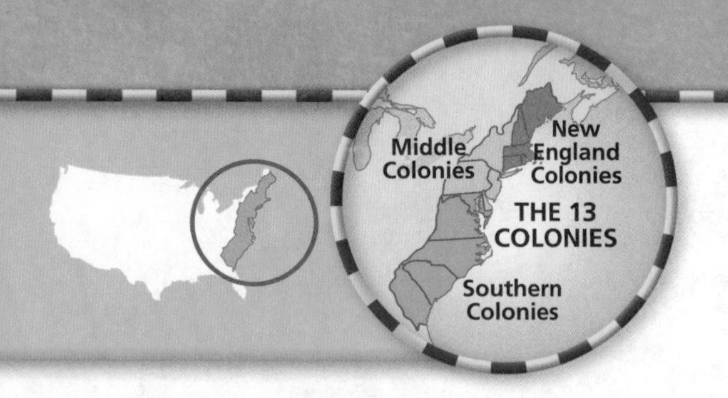

Religion in the Colonies

You have learned that some people came to North America to find a place to worship freely. In fact, every colony had laws that officially allowed freedom of religion. However, most colonies had established churches too. An established church is a religious group that is supported by the government. Laws said that even people who did not belong to this group had to pay taxes to support it. The conflict between religious freedom and established churches played a key role in the development of some colonies.

1. Make Generalizations **Underline a sentence in the text that makes a generalization about the role of religion in the development of the colonies.**

The New England Puritans

The colony of Massachusetts began as a place for Puritans to practice their religion freely. However, only Puritan church members could vote and church leaders called ministers held a lot of power. Some of these leaders were **intolerant,** or to be not accepting of ideas or behaviors different from their own.

People who disagreed with Puritan leaders began to leave Massachusetts. Thomas Hooker, a minister, did not agree that only church members should rule. He left the colony and founded Hartford, which later became part of the colony of Connecticut. Roger Williams was forced to leave Massachusetts for his beliefs too. As a result, he founded the colony of Rhode Island, whose charter stated that no one could be punished "for any differences in opinion in matters of religion." Anne Hutchinson also challenged the power of Puritan leaders when she began leading her own religious meetings. Like Williams, Hutchinson was forced to leave the colony and moved to Rhode Island.

2. What caused people to leave the Massachusetts Bay colony?

Cause and Effect

After disagreements with Puritan leaders in Massachusetts, Roger Williams received a charter to start the colony of Rhode Island.

Religion in the Southern Colonies

Established churches played an important role in the Southern Colonies too. Anglicanism, or the Church of England, was the established church of Virginia. John Smith recalled that, from the earliest days, "[We] had daily Common Prayer morning and evening, every Sunday two Sermons." Lord Baltimore founded Maryland as a place where Catholics who were persecuted in England could live in peace. However, many non-Catholics also moved there, and leaders soon passed a law giving religious freedom to all Christians.

Religion in the Middle Colonies

Unlike the other colonial regions, people from many religions lived in the Middle Colonies. People from a variety of countries, cultures, and religions settled in the colony of New York. Pennsylvania and Delaware did not have established churches, so people from many different religious groups settled there too. In Pennsylvania a group called the Quakers welcomed people of all religions and backgrounds. The Quakers believed in leading a simple life. They preferred simple styles of clothing and buildings and opposed war and other acts of violence.

3. How was the founding of Maryland like the founding of Rhode Island? *Compare and Contrast*

4. Underline a sentence that gives details about the beliefs of Pennsylvania Quakers.
Main Idea and Details

Quakers "go to meeting" but have no regular services or ministers. Instead, they believe people should pray in a way that feels right to them.

Summary

Religion was an important part of life in the English colonies. Describe the effect of religion in the three colonial regions.

Biography

Anne Hutchinson, 1591–1643

Learn More Anne Hutchinson spent her life in pursuit of religious freedom. Her religious beliefs were greatly influenced by a minister named John Cotton and by her father, who was also a minister. Hutchinson's father was not afraid to speak his mind. He was twice sent to prison in England for speaking out against the Church of England. In 1633 John Cotton was forced to leave England because of his beliefs. Hutchinson and her family followed Cotton to Boston.

In Boston, Hutchinson spoke freely about her beliefs. She held meetings in her home, where she taught that faith was more important than following the rules of the established church. Some colonial leaders disapproved of Hutchinson's beliefs. They took her to court, and she was forced to leave the colony. She moved first to Rhode Island, which had been founded on the promise of religious freedom, and later to New York. The risks taken by Hutchinson and others like her helped establish the freedom of religion in the United States today.

Answer the questions below.

1. **Underline the events in Hutchinson's father's life and in John Cotton's life that taught her about standing up for her beliefs.** *Identify*
2. **Why do you think church leaders disapproved of Hutchinson's actions?** *Interpret*

____

____

____

____

____

Name:

H-SS 5.4.4 Identify the significance and leaders of the First Great Awakening, which marked a shift in religious ideas, practices, and allegiances in the colonial period, the growth of religious toleration, and free exercise of religion.

Lesson 4

How did the First Great Awakening affect the colonies?

SET THE SCENE Have you ever changed the way you thought about something? Ideas and beliefs can change over time. In the 1700s, many colonists began to change how they thought about religion. These changes led colonists to practice their religion in new ways.

Preview the Lesson

Vocabulary

preacher *(n.)* a person who gives speeches about religious subjects

Vocabulary Activity As you know, the suffix *-er* means "one who." For example, a *teacher* is one who teaches. Circle the suffix in the vocabulary word above. Then write a definition for the root word below.

People

Jonathan Edwards
George Whitefield

Reading: Main Idea and Details

A *main idea* is a statement that tells you what a paragraph is generally about. *Details* can be found in sentences that support or explain the main idea. As you read the second paragraph on page 82, circle the names of three people that support the paragraph's main idea.

1730

1735

Middle Colonies

New England Colonies

THE 13 COLONIES

Southern Colonies

1734 Jonathan Edwards starts religious revivals in New England.

Religious Changes in the Colonies

As you have learned, religion was an important part of many American colonists' lives. However, in the 1730s, some Protestants began to develop new ideas about religion. They wanted religion to be about strong emotions that could be felt by anybody instead of about difficult ideas that were understood by few people. This was the beginning of a period known as the First Great Awakening.

The First Great Awakening

The First Great Awakening spread throughout the colonies. In 1734 Jonathan Edwards began holding religious meetings called revivals in New England. At revivals, preachers gave emotional speeches warning people about the dangers of a weak faith. A **preacher** is a person who gives speeches about religious subjects. In the Middle Colonies, Gilbert Tennent and his family held large revivals. Samuel Davies brought this new kind of religious service to the Southern Colonies in 1748.

One of the most important people in the First Great Awakening was a traveling preacher from Britain named George Whitefield (WIT feeld). In 1739 Whitefield began traveling throughout the colonies. He often preached in open fields to large crowds. These crowds often contained a wide variety of people, including men, women, and children, rich and poor, and members of different religions. Many of these people felt more strongly about their faith after hearing Whitefield speak. He also inspired many new preachers, who imitated his dramatic speaking style.

1. How did some colonists' ideas about religion begin to change?
Main Idea and Details

2. In the text, underline the sentence in each paragraph that gives the main idea.
Main Idea and Details

"Ever since the great work of God [a revival] that was wrought [happened] here . . . there has been a great abiding [lasting] alteration [change] in this town in many respects. There has been vastly more religion kept up in the town, among all sorts of persons, in religious exercises and in common conversation than used to be before."

— Jonathan Edwards,
in a letter dated December 12, 1743

1740 | 1745 | 1750

1739

1748 Samuel Davies brings revivals to the Southern Colonies.

Effects of the Great Awakening

The First Great Awakening increased many colonists' interest in religion. However, some people disagreed with the changes it brought. Many Puritans did not agree with these new ideas. Among a group called the Presbyterians, colonists split into groups called "old lights," who disagreed with the revivals, and "new lights," who favored them.

Despite this resistance, the First Great Awakening influenced people throughout the colonies in many ways. Thousands of people joined new religious groups, such as the Baptists or Methodists. Some of these groups reached out to African Americans. Religious groups also set up many new schools, including universities that still exist today. The growth and spread of such groups led to greater acceptance of people of different faiths throughout the colonies. Many colonists also began to believe that they could stand up to authority on important issues like religion. Finally, these changes brought many colonists together behind a common set of ideas, which had a lasting effect on the role of religion and politics throughout the colonies.

3. In the text, circle two religious groups that grew as a result of the First Great Awakening.

Main Idea and Details

Princeton University and many other schools were founded by religious groups during the First Great Awakening.

Summary

In the 1700s, religious ideas in the colonies began to change. How did the First Great Awakening change the way many colonists practiced their religion?

Skill

Circle Graphs

Learn More Circle graphs use percentages or fractions to compare information. The size of each section of the graph represents a portion of the whole. If you add the pieces together, the total will equal 100 percent.

As the population of the United States grows and changes, so does the variety of religions practiced here. The circle graph below shows some of the religions practiced in the United States based on a survey. Each section represents a part of the population that belongs to a particular religion. Use the graph to answer the questions.

Try It

1. **Underline the religion that is practiced by 1.3% of the people in the United States.** *Identify*

2. **Circle the names of two religions that are practiced by about the same percentage of people.** *Identify*

3. **What is the total percent of people who practice a religion or set of beliefs other than Christianity?** *Interpret*

____

4. **If someone chose not to practice any religion, where would they be included on this graph?** *Apply*

____

Religions in the United States

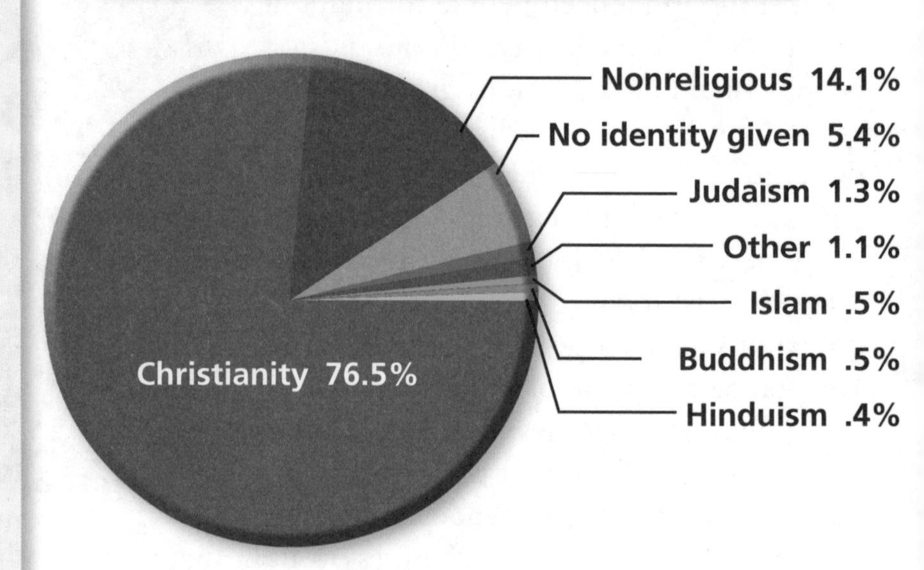

Major Christian groups:		
	Catholic	24.5%
	Baptist	16.3%
	Methodist	6.8%
	Lutheran	4.6%
	Presbyterian	2.7%

Source: American Religion identity Survey, 2001

Name:

H-SS 5.4.5 Understand how the British colonial period created the basis for the development of political self-government and a free-market economic system and the differences between the British, Spanish, and French colonial systems.

Lesson 5

What systems developed in the colonies?

SET THE SCENE Suppose you moved to a new town or city. You would have to figure out new ways of doing things, such as getting to school. In the 1500s, colonists from Spain, France, and England began arriving in North America. How did life change for them once they arrived?

Preview the Lesson

Vocabulary

artisan *(n.)* a skilled worker who makes things by hand

apprentice *(n.)* a person who learns a skill or trade from an experienced worker

town common *(n.)* an open space in the center of a town where cattle and sheep could graze

free-market economy *(n.)* a system in which prices are not controlled by the government

Vocabulary Activity Draw an arrow to connect the two vocabulary words above that describe people who might work together. Which one would learn from the other? Circle that word.

Reading: Compare and Contrast

Comparing and contrasting ideas can help you see how ideas are related. As you read the first paragraph on page 86, underline details about New Spain and New France that you could compare in order to better understand how people in both colonies worked with American Indians.

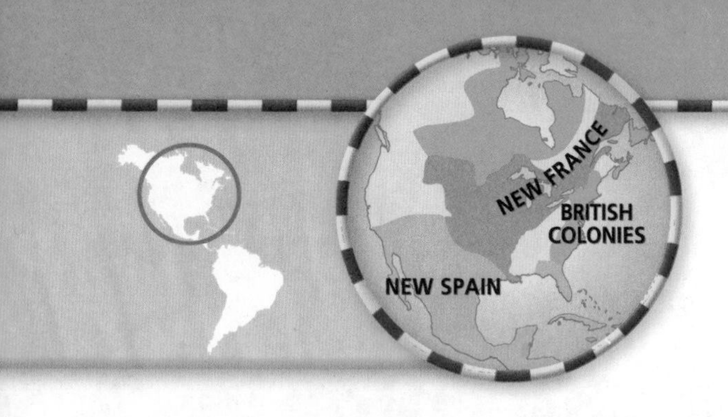

Spanish and French Colonies

In the 1500s and 1600s, France and Spain began to found and settle colonies in North America. As you have learned, the French developed trade relationships with several American Indian groups. The fur trade brought huge profits to the French, who built trading posts throughout New France. Settlements in New Spain, however, focused on agriculture. Plantations were an important part of the Spanish colonies, but the hot, dry climate in some areas of New Spain did not allow crop farming. In areas with grasslands, sheep and cattle ranches were developed instead. On both plantations and ranches, much of the work was done by enslaved American Indians and Africans.

1. Compare the ways in which Spanish and French colonists interacted with American Indians. *Compare and Contrast*

Life in the English Colonies

The English colonies attracted more people than the French and Spanish colonies did. These colonists came for many different reasons but worked hard once they got here. In the New England and Middle Colonies, most people lived in small towns or on family farms. All family members, including children, worked together to make or grow what the family needed.

Soon, other work roles developed. **Artisans** were skilled workers who made things by hand. They made goods such as barrels for storage and iron goods, such as nails and horseshoes. Artisans often hired apprentices to help them. An **apprentice** is a person who learns a skill or trade from an experienced worker.

2. How did family farms become self-sufficient? *Cause and Effect*

Tools, brought mostly from England, allowed artisans to practice trades such as carpentry.

Economic Systems Develop

Different kinds of settlements and economic systems formed in the English colonial regions. In the Southern Colonies, wealthy farmers ran large plantations that depended on enslaved people to work in the fields. The crops they grew were shipped to other colonies and to England.

Small towns developed throughout New England and the Middle Colonies. Many New England towns had a **town common,** which was an open space in the center of a town where cattle and sheep could graze. Families also owned small plots of land for farming. Towns in the Middle Colonies often served as busy trading centers, where farmers from the area came to sell their crops and buy items like clothing and tools. Meeting needs through trade allowed free-market economies to develop in these towns. In a **free-market economy,** prices are not controlled by the government.

Cities developed throughout the colonies and served as major trading centers. From coastal cities, merchants exported goods such as flour and wheat. They also imported goods the colonies did not produce, such as sugar and spices, as well as manufactured goods, such as tools and cloth.

3. What role did cities play in all three colonial regions? *Compare and Contrast*

The economy of the Southern Colonies focused on exporting tobacco and other cash crops.

Government Systems Develop

For the most part, the colonies governed themselves and acted independently of England. Colonial governments handled most of the everyday decisions. However, England did set laws on how goods could be traded to and from the colonies. These laws sometimes went against the idea of a free-market economy. This issue would later lead to conflicts between the colonists and England.

4. Underline a sentence that tells one way England governed the colonies. *Main Idea and Details*

Summary

France, Spain, and England each developed different systems for their North American colonies. Summarize how different ways of life developed in the French, Spanish, and English colonies.

Citizenship

Rules of Civility

Learn More Education was an important part of life in the colonies. There were few formal schools, but people learned in different ways. Apprentices learned skills from artisans. In 1636 Puritans founded Harvard College in Cambridge, Massachusetts. In 1642 Massachusetts passed a law that required parents to teach their children to read.

Much of the reading students did was about religion and good manners. While still a young student, a Virginia colonist named George Washington copied 110 "rules of civility," or polite behavior, into his notebook. These rules helped teach young people proper behavior so that they would become good citizens and valuable members of society. Many of the rules are still useful today.

Read the rules of civility listed to the right. Then answer these questions.

1. Circle the numbers of two rules that would be most useful to remember when you are in a quiet place, such as a library. *Interpret*

2. Which of these rules do you think is most important? Rewrite it in your own words. *Apply*

____

____

____

____

____

____

____

Rule 1: Every Action done in Company, ought to be with Some Sign of Respect, to those that are Present.

Rule 4: In the Presence of Others Sing not to yourself with a humming Noise, nor Drum with your Fingers or Feet.

Rule 5: If You Cough, Sneeze, Sigh, or Yawn, do it not Loud but Privately; and Speak not in your Yawning, but put Your handkercheif or Hand before your face and turn aside.

Rule 6: Sleep not when others Speak, Sit not when others stand, Speak not when you Should hold your Peace, walk not on when others Stop.

Name:

Lesson 6

H-SS 5.4.6 Describe the introduction of slavery into America, the responses of slave families to their condition, the ongoing struggle between proponents and opponents of slavery, and the gradual institutionalization of slavery in the South.

What was the role of slavery in colonial America?

NOTICE

NEGROES FOR SALE AT AUCTION THIS DAY AT 1 O'CLOCK

SET THE SCENE When we do work, we usually receive something in return for our effort. As you have learned, American colonists needed many people to help do their work. However, enslaved people lived lives of hardship and received no pay in return.

Preview the Lesson

Vocabulary

auction *(n.)* a public sale in which something is sold to the person who offers the most money

proponent *(n.)* a person who supports something

rebel *(v.)* to resist or fight against authority

Vocabulary Activity *Opponents* are people who fight or speak against something. Circle the vocabulary word above that is an antonym for *opponent.*

People

Olaudah Equiano

Reading: Make Generalizations

Reading Skill

A *generalization* is a broad statement about people or places that is true most of the time. As you read the second paragraph on page 90, underline a sentence that makes a generalization about slavery in the Southern Colonies.

1700

1725

Jamestown

WEST AFRICA

1700 Samuel Sewell argues against slavery.

Slavery in the Americas

Early Spanish settlers were the first Europeans to enslave people in the Americas. In the 1500s, Spanish settlers forced many American Indians to work in mines and on plantations. Many of these workers died, so the Spanish began bringing enslaved Africans to the Americas. In the early 1600s, the first enslaved Africans were brought to the English colonies.

The growth of plantations in the Southern Colonies caused slavery to increase. Early colonial farmers used indentured servants to work on their small farms. However, large plantations needed many people to work the fields to produce cash crops. This need was so great that the population of some areas included more enslaved Africans than colonists.

A Life of Hardship

Enslaved Africans faced many hardships. The journey to the English colonies often began in the present-day West African country of Benin. There European traders forced captured Africans to board ships. In 1789 an African named Olaudah Equiano (OL uh dah EH kwee AH noh) wrote that when he was taken aboard a ship, "I saw myself deprived of all chance of returning to my native country." During the voyage, he and other Africans were kept in chains. Many of them died.

1. Make Generalizations **Which details in the first paragraph support the generalization that many settlers enslaved other people?**

2. In the text, circle the present-day country where many enslaved Africans began their voyage to the Americas. *Main Idea and Details*

Overcrowded ships, cruel treatment, hunger, thirst, and disease caused many enslaved Africans to die on the voyage across the Atlantic Ocean.

1750

1775

1800

1739

1789 Olaudah Equiano writes about his life as an enslaved African.

The hardships of enslaved Africans continued when the ship reached the colonies. Traders sold them as property at auctions. An **auction** is a public sale in which something is sold to the person who offers the most money. Sometimes family members were sold to different owners. After they were purchased, most enslaved people worked in plantation fields. They often worked many hours under the hot sun. Others worked in the owner's house. They cooked and took care of the family's children. Whatever they did, enslaved people faced punishment if they disobeyed their owner. In most cases, they were enslaved for life.

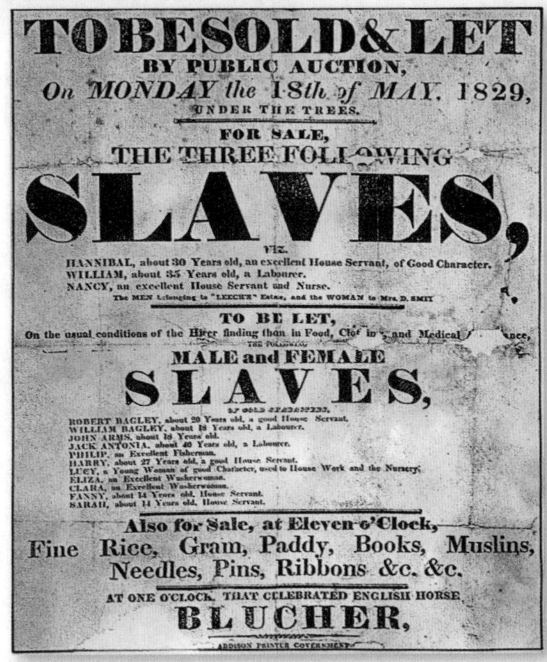

Auctions for enslaved people were announced by posters such as this.

Resistance to Slavery

Many colonists and enslaved people resisted slavery. In 1700 colonist Samuel Sewall wrote, "[A]ll Men . . . have equal Rights unto Liberty." Many Quakers also opposed slavery. However, other colonists were proponents of slavery. **Proponents** are people who support something. In the South, many colonists supported slavery and encouraged its spread.

Enslaved people often rebelled against their owners in many ways. To **rebel** is to resist or fight against authority. Some people rebelled by working slowly or running away. Others, such as Equiano, saved money and bought their freedom. Sometimes they even rebelled by fighting. The Stono Rebellion took place in South Carolina in 1739. In this rebellion, about 100 enslaved people tried to escape but were later recaptured. Even those people who did not openly rebel resisted slavery by keeping their African culture alive through music, dance, and stories.

3. Underline ways in which enslaved people resisted their owners.
Main Idea and Details

Summary

The growth of colonial plantations led to the use of enslaved people as workers. How did slavery affect life in the American colonies?

Primary Source

Autobiographies: Olaudah Equiano

Learn More An autobiography is a primary source in which a person tells his or her life story. Olaudah Equiano was born in the West African country of Nigeria. At the age of eleven, he was kidnapped, sold into slavery, and shipped to Barbados. Over time he was sold again and again to owners in Virginia and Philadelphia. Equiano was twenty-one years old before he was able to buy his freedom. He moved to Britain and wrote the first autobiography by a freed enslaved African, *The Interesting Narrative of the Life of Olaudah Equiano, or Gustavus Vassa, the African,* which was published in 1789. Read the passage from Equiano's autobiography and then answer the questions.

1. **In the passage, circle the name that Equiano had chosen for himself.** Identify
2. **Underline the information that explains what happened when Equiano refused to answer to the name Gustavus Vassa.** Identify
3. **Why do you think enslaved people, like Equiano, were not allowed to keep their African names?** Analyze

____

____

____

____

____

____

"While I was on board this ship, my captain and master named me Gustavus Vassa. I at that time began to understand him a little, and refused to be called so, and told him as well as I could that I would be called Jacob; but he said I should not, and still called me Gustavus: and when I refused to answer to my new name, which I at first did, it gained me many a cuff [hit]; so at length I submitted, and by which I have been known ever since."

Name:

H-SS 5.4.7 Explain the early democratic ideas and practices that emerged during the colonial period, including the significance of representative assemblies and town meetings.

Lesson 7

What brought on democratic ideas in colonial America?

SET THE SCENE Have you and your friends ever taken a vote? Asking for everyone's opinion is one way to settle problems in a fair, organized way. When the colonists created governments, they wanted people to have a voice in making the laws. How did these ideas come about?

Preview the Lesson

Vocabulary

democracy *(n.)* a government that is run by the people

citizen *(n.)* a member of a country

representative *(n.)* a person who is chosen to act for others

assembly *(n.)* a gathering of elected representatives for a specific purpose

town meeting *(n.)* a gathering of people who live in a town to discuss issues

county seat *(n.)* a place where a county government is located

Vocabulary Activity Words we do not know often contain parts that we do know. Circle a familiar word with at least 8 letters in the vocabulary word *representative*. Write a definition for that word below.

Reading: Make Generalizations

Generalizations are broad statements that are true for many people, places, or events. As you read the first section on page 94, underline a sentence that makes a generalization about the purposes of early colonial governments.

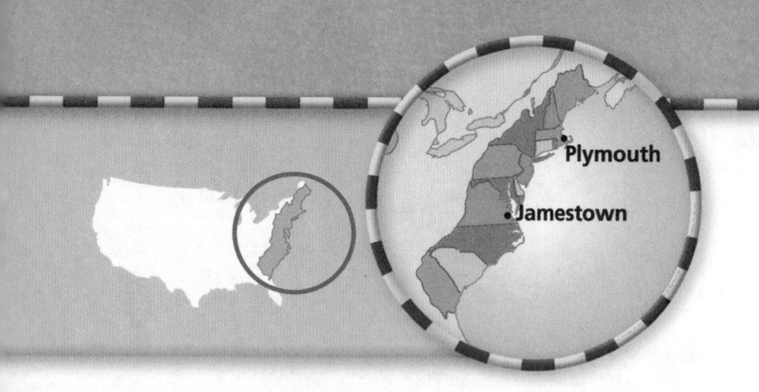

Early Colonial Government

Early American settlements needed governments to help solve problems and make rules. For example, in its first years, the Jamestown colony struggled for survival until governor Thomas Dale took charge and created strict new rules. Settlers were punished if they came late to work or broke tools. Before the Pilgrims landed in Plymouth, they drew up a document called the Mayflower Compact. In 1620 forty-one men signed the Compact, swearing to make "just and equal laws . . . for the general good of the Colony." This document became the basis of their government.

1. Make Generalizations **What generalization can you make about the Mayflower Compact?**

Government by the People

Many colonies formed governments based on the ideas of democracy. A **democracy** is a government that is run by the people. In a democracy, members of a country, called **citizens,** rule themselves. They can vote for and serve as representatives. **Representatives** are people who are chosen to act for others.

The idea of having representatives was similar to a part of government the colonists had known in England. The House of Commons was a group of elected representatives that passed laws and advised the king. Members of the House of Commons represented landholders and other property owners in England.

2. **How were many colonial governments like the government the colonists had known in England?** Compare and Contrast

Pilgrim men signed a document that set up a government for their colony while still at sea aboard their ship, the *Mayflower*.

Colonial Democracy

Throughout the colonies, people set up colonial governments in which they could have a voice in making the laws. Many colonies had an **assembly,** or a gathering of elected representatives for a specific purpose. At colonial assemblies, representatives made laws. The first colonial assembly, the House of Burgesses, met in Jamestown, Virginia, in 1619. Each settlement in Virginia sent two representatives to the assembly. There, "all matters [were] decided, determined and ordered by the greater part of the voices present."

Colonists also formed local governments. In New England, a gathering of people who lived in a town discussed issues at a **town meeting.** In the Southern Colonies, local representatives met at the **county seat,** the place where the county government was located.

3. Make Generalizations **Underline a generalization in the first paragraph about the kind of governments people set up in the colonies.**

Twenty-two representatives from eleven settlements met in Virginia's first colonial assembly.

The Limits of Colonial Democracies

Colonial governments were not complete democracies. There were limits on who could help run the government and what an assembly could do. Only white men who owned property could vote or be elected representatives. In addition, the British government could pass laws for the colonies without asking the opinions of the colonists. This last issue would cause serious problems in the years to come.

4. Underline ways that colonial governments were not complete democracies. *Main Idea and Details*

Summary

Early American colonies set up governments called democracies. How did democracies develop throughout the colonies?

Citizenship

Colonial and U.S. Governments

Learn More The system of government in the English colonies combined control by a king or queen with representative democracy. The king of England was the official ruler of the colonies. However, because he ruled from so far away, the king appointed governors to each colony to carry out his orders. Many colonial governments also had assemblies of elected representatives. These assemblies represented the interests of the colonists rather than those of the king.

Today, the United States is an independent country. Our system of government is a representative democracy that allows citizens to become more involved in their government. Unlike colonial government, our national government allows the people to help elect their President, who heads the country. The elected assemblies of the U.S. government, however, are similar to those in the colonies. Then and now, citizens elect representatives to serve their interests in governments.

The diagram below compares and contrasts colonial and U.S. governments. Complete the chart using these directions.

1. Complete the diagram by filling in the blanks. *Apply*

2. Circle the name of the government in which people could be more involved. *Analyze*

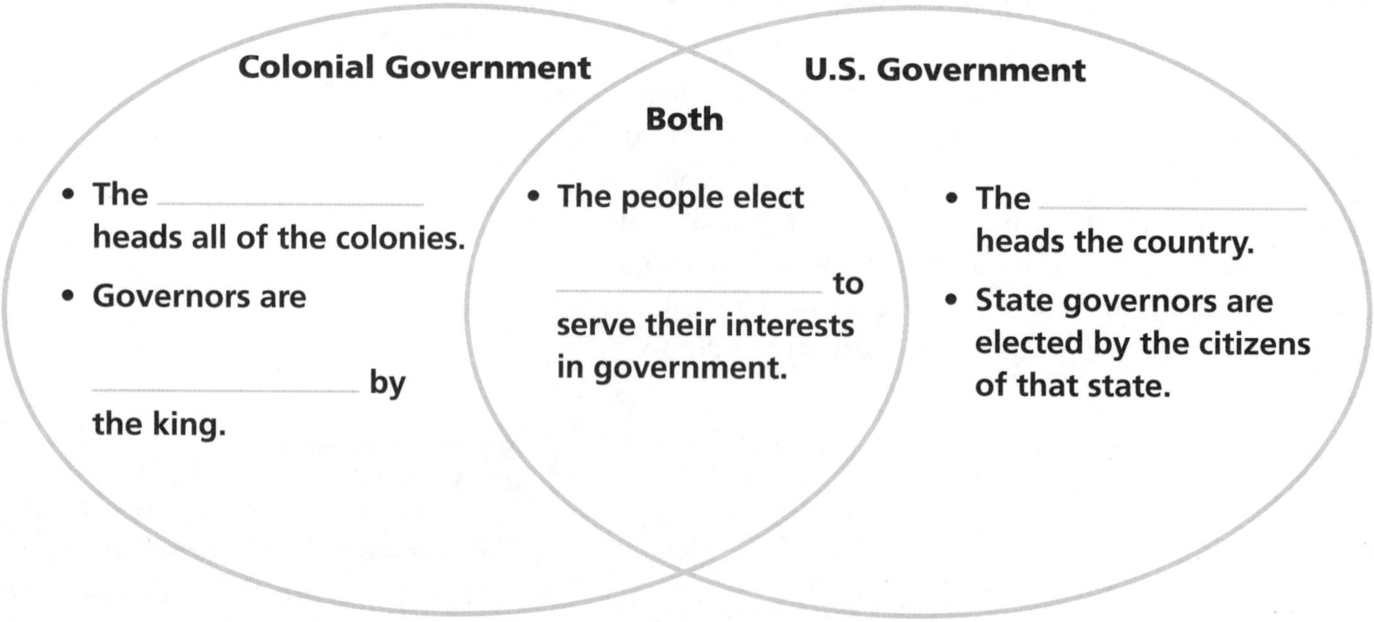

Colonial Government

- **The ________________ heads all of the colonies.**
- **Governors are ________________ by the king.**

Both

- **The people elect ________________ to serve their interests in government.**

U.S. Government

- **The ________________ heads the country.**
- **State governors are elected by the citizens of that state.**

Name:

Unit 5

Study Journal

In this unit you will learn about the political and economic causes of the American Revolution. Complete the activities on these pages as you read the unit.

What I know about . . .

causes of the American Revolution:

British Acts Before the Revolution

What effect did each act have on the movement toward independence?

Act of Parliament	Effects
Stamp Act, 1765	
Townshend Acts, 1767	
Coercive Acts, 1774	

Complete these sections as you read the unit.

For each pair of words below, write a sentence that uses both words:

Parliament – repeal

boycott – protest

Patriot – militia

List the colonial meeting and its purpose for each year below:

1754

1765

1775

1776

Draw a line from each statement to the Patriot who said or wrote it.

"A government of our own is our natural right."	Benjamin Franklin
"All men are created equal."	Patrick Henry
"We must all hang together, or most assuredly we shall all hang separately."	James Otis
"Taxation without representation is tyranny."	Thomas Paine
"Give me liberty or give me death."	Thomas Jefferson

I have learned . . .

Name:

H-SS 5.5.1 Understand how political, religious, and economic ideas and interests brought about the Revolution (e.g., resistance to imperial policy, the Stamp Act, the Townshend Acts, taxes on tea, Coercive Acts).

Lesson 1

What events led to the American Revolution?

SET THE SCENE Do you like to be involved in decisions that affect you? After the French and Indian War, the British government made decisions that affected the colonists without asking their opinion. What do you think the colonists did?

Preview the Lesson

Vocabulary

Parliament *(n.)* Great Britain's lawmaking assembly

tariff *(n.)* a tax on imported goods

protest *(v.)* to speak out against something

petition *(n.)* a document that people sign that formally asks leaders to do or change something

repeal *(v.)* to do away with

boycott *(n.)* an organized refusal to buy goods or services

Vocabulary Activity Circle the vocabulary word in the list above that is a proper noun.

People

Pontiac
George III
Crispus Attucks
Paul Revere

Reading: Cause and Effect

Reading Skill

Writers include causes and effects to help you see the connections between events. A *cause* is what makes something happen. An *effect* is what happens. Writers often use words and phrases to signal causes and effects, such as *because* and *as a result.* As you read page 100, circle words and phrases that signal causes and effects.

1763 George III issues the Proclamation of 1763.

The Benefits and Costs of War

By 1763 Great Britain had finally won the French and Indian War. This victory gave Britain many benefits, such as control of resource-rich land west of the Appalachian Mountains. However, it also caused new problems. The British had borrowed and spent a lot of money on soldiers and supplies. As a result, they now faced a huge debt.

More problems developed when settlers began moving onto Britain's new western lands. The British government could not easily control settlers who lived far from the colonies. Because of this, some settlers moved into new areas, which caused conflicts with American Indians who already lived there. In 1763 an Ottawa leader named Pontiac led a rebellion against British settlers and soldiers. Although the British eventually won Pontiac's War, they realized that protecting western settlers would cost even more money. How would Britain pay for both its debt and the cost of protecting western settlers?

To help solve these problems, King George III of Britain issued the Proclamation of 1763. It said that colonists were not allowed to settle on land west of the Appalachian Mountains. The British hoped that this would keep colonists in areas that were easier to control, which would lower the cost of protecting the colonies. However, this rule angered some colonists. They wondered why they had helped fight for this land but could not move there.

1. Cause and Effect **How did victory in the French and Indian War cause British debts?**

Because of the Proclamation of 1763, settlers could not move west of the Appalachian Mountains.

1764

1765

1764

1765 Britain passes the Stamp Act.

Britain Taxes the Colonies

King George and **Parliament,** Britain's lawmaking assembly, wanted the colonists to help pay the debt from the French and Indian War. Britain had gone to war to protect the colonies, so British leaders felt it was fair to have the colonies pay part of the debt through taxes and tariffs. A **tariff** is a tax on imported goods, or products that come from another country. The Sugar Act of 1764 said colonists must pay a tariff on goods such as molasses and sugar. The Stamp Act followed in 1765. This act placed a tax on every kind of printed material, including newspapers, legal documents, and even playing cards. When the colonists bought such items, they had to get the item stamped to show that they had paid the tax.

The colonists had paid taxes before the new acts, but those taxes they paid had been passed by their colonial assemblies. The Sugar Act and the Stamp Act were passed by Parliament, which had no representatives from the colonies. Many colonists did not think it was fair to force them to pay taxes that had been passed without their consent, or approval.

2. List some of the items that were taxed by the Stamp Act of 1765.
Main Idea and Details

Under the Stamp Act, different kinds of printed materials were taxed at different rates. Each of these stamps shows a different amount of money paid as tax.

1766 Parliament repeals the Stamp Act.

1767

Colonists Respond to the Stamp Act

The Stamp Act made many colonists angry. Some of them decided to **protest,** or speak out against it. A group of men called the Sons of Liberty became active protestors. They burned stamps and threatened the stamp agents who collected the taxes. Other colonists protested by making speeches or sending petitions to Parliament. A **petition** is a document that people sign that formally asks a leader to do or change something.

Anger over the Stamp Act caused the colonies to unite. Leaders from nine colonies met in New York City in 1765 to discuss how to resist Britain's attempts to tax and control them. This meeting became known as the Stamp Act Congress. This congress wanted Parliament to **repeal,** or do away with, the Stamp Act. Its leaders wrote to Parliament and said that the British government had no right to tax people who had no voice in the decision. The slogan "No taxation without representation" became a popular way to show resistance to Britain's new laws.

The Stamp Act Congress was the first time the colonists took action against authority as an organized political group. During the Great Awakening, many colonists had learned to question authorities on important issues such as religion. Now the colonists' protests and petitions showed what they could do when they worked together to solve political problems. Because of the colonists' organized resistance, Parliament repealed the Stamp Act in 1766.

3. How did the Sons of Liberty protest the Stamp Act?
Main Idea and Details

Protests by colonists, such as tarring and feathering, made British stamp agents fearful of collecting the stamp taxes.

1770 Five colonists, including Crispus Attucks, are killed in the Boston Massacre.

The Townshend Acts Are Passed

After the Stamp Act was repealed, King George insisted that Britain still had the right to tax the colonies, no matter what the colonists said. So in 1767 Parliament passed the Townshend Acts. These acts taxed imported goods, such as glass, paint, and tea.

The Townshend Acts caused new protests in the colonies. Many colonists began a boycott of British goods. A **boycott** is an organized refusal to buy goods or services. These colonists would not buy anything that came from Britain. Colonial women played an important role in the boycott. Groups of women called the "Daughters of Liberty" wove cloth and made other goods to replace imported British goods. Over time, the boycott hurt British businesses and showed the strength of the colonists' resistance to British control. As a result, Britain sent more soldiers to the colonies to enforce the tax laws.

4. How did some colonial women protest the Townshend Acts? *Main Idea and Details*

Tension in Boston Turns Violent

The growing number of British soldiers in the colonies led to tension between soldiers and colonists. In Boston angry words and violence between soldiers and colonists became common. Finally, on the evening of March 5, 1770, things got out of control. A crowd gathered during an argument between a British soldier and a colonist. The crowd shouted insults at the troops, then surrounded them and began throwing snowballs, rocks, and oyster shells at the soldiers. The British fired into the angry crowd. An African American named Crispus Attucks was the first of five colonists who were killed. This event became known as the Boston Massacre.

5. In the text, number from 1 to 5 the events of March 5, 1770, that led to the Boston Massacre. *Sequence*

The Boston Massacre led to new concerns about the number of British troops in the colonies.

1771

1772

1773

1773 Colonists protest the Tea Act with the Boston Tea Party.

The Boston Tea Party

In 1770 Parliament repealed all the taxes in the Townshend Acts, except the tax on tea. Then in 1773 Parliament passed the Tea Act. This act did not raise taxes, but it did try to get the colonists to buy tea from only one British company. Again, the colonists protested Parliament's continued attempts to control them. Colonial leaders declared that ships bringing British tea to the colonies would not be allowed to unload. On December 16, 1773, colonists dressed as Mohawk Indians took over British ships in Boston Harbor and dumped all the tea into the water. This event became known as the Boston Tea Party.

6. Cause and Effect **What caused the Boston Tea Party?**

Britain Punishes Boston

In 1774 Parliament passed the Coercive Acts as punishment for the Boston Tea Party. Some colonists called them the "Intolerable Acts" because they were so severe. The acts closed the port of Boston until the colonists paid for the tea they had dumped. They sent even more British soldiers to Boston and forced colonists to house and feed them. Also, the entire colony of Massachusetts was put under the control of a British general.

The Coercive Acts angered many colonists but also made them more united. Other colonies began sending food, supplies, and money to Boston. Colonial leaders voted to stop all trade with Britain and to create volunteer armies.

7. Cause and Effect **How did colonists respond to the Coercive Acts?**

The Boston Tea Party showed the colonists' anger at the Tea Act of 1773.

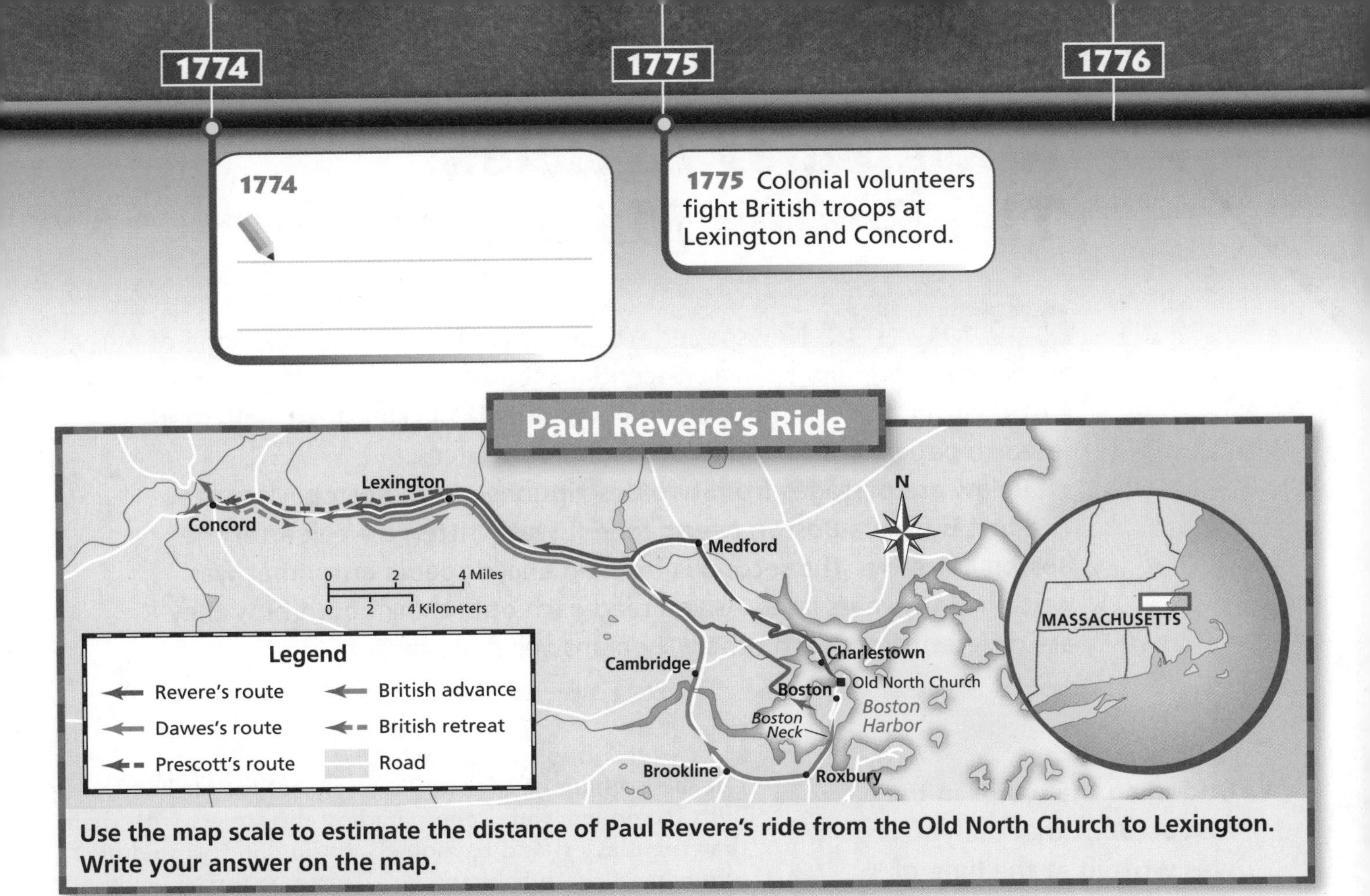

Use the map scale to estimate the distance of Paul Revere's ride from the Old North Church to Lexington. Write your answer on the map.

The Fighting Begins

In April 1775, colonists learned of secret British plans to destroy weapons that colonists had stored in the towns of Lexington and Concord, Massachusetts. On the night of April 18, colonists Paul Revere and William Dawes rode out from Boston to warn the towns that British troops were coming. The men were stopped after they reached Lexington, but another rider, Dr. Samuel Prescott, rode on to warn colonists in Concord.

The warnings worked. When British troops arrived in Lexington the next morning, a small group of colonists gathered to fight them. The British quickly defeated the colonists. However, when the British arrived in Concord, they were met by a larger group of colonists. These colonists fought well and forced the British back to Boston. The colonists continued to fire at the British along the way and caused heavy losses.

No one knows who fired the first shot at these battles, but people later called it "the shot heard 'round the world." From that point on, there would be no turning back. The American colonies had started the fight for independence.

8. Cause and Effect **In the text, underline what happened when colonists fought British troops at Concord.**

Summary

The American Revolution was caused by changes in political, religious, and economic ideas. What specific events led Americans to decide to fight for independence?

Primary Source

Newspaper Articles: The Boston Massacre

Learn More Newspaper articles written at or about the time of an event are primary sources. Secondary sources are accounts that are written after an event happened. Encyclopedia articles, textbooks, and research papers are examples of secondary sources.

Below are passages from two descriptions of the Boston Massacre. The first is from a Boston newspaper. It was written a week after the Boston Massacre. The second is from an encyclopedia entry that was written many years later. As you read each one, think about how they are different from each other. Then answer the questions.

1. Underline the words in the first account that tell you it was written at the time of the event. *Identify*

2. Underline a sentence from the encyclopedia article that tells about events that led up to the Boston Massacre. *Identify*

3. Who does the writer of the newspaper article seem to blame for this event? How is this point of view different from that of the encyclopedia? *Analyze*

____

____

____

____

____

____

On the evening of Monday, several soldiers of the 29th Regiment were seen parading the streets with their drawn cutlasses[1] and bayonets[2], abusing and wounding numbers of the inhabitants. . . . Thirty or forty persons, mostly lads . . . gathered in King Street, [and British] Capt. Preston with a party of men . . . came . . . crying, make way! They took their place by the custom house and, continuing to push to drive the people off, pricked some in several places, on which [the colonists] were clamorous[3] and, it is said, threw snow balls. On this, the Captain commanded [the troops] to fire.

— Excerpt from the *Boston Gazette and Country Journal,* March 12, 1770

[1]swords [2]knives attached to rifles [3]disorderly

Boston Massacre

(March 5, 1770), skirmish between British troops and a crowd in Boston . . . The incident was the climax of a series of brawls [fights] in which local workers and sailors clashed with British soldiers quartered [housed] in Boston. Harassed by a mob, the troops opened fire. Crispus Attucks, a black sailor and former slave, was shot first and died along with four others.

— Excerpt from *Encyclopaedia Britannica,* 2003

Name:

H-SS 5.5.2 Know the significance of the first and second Continental Congresses and of the Committees of Correspondence.

Lesson 2

How did the colonists work together?

SET THE SCENE Have you ever worked in a group or as part of a team? People who work together as a group are often more effective than one person who works alone. The American colonists realized they had to work together in order to cause change. What groups did they form in their move toward freedom?

Preview the Lesson

Vocabulary

delegate *(n.)* a person chosen to represent others

committee *(n.)* an organized group that meets to make decisions

correspond *(v.)* to communicate by writing letters

unify *(v.)* to come together or unite

militia *(n.)* a civilian army that is used only in emergencies

Vocabulary Activity The word part *uni-* means "one." Circle the vocabulary word above that uses the prefix *uni-*. Do you know other words that have this word part?

People

Samuel Adams
Benjamin Franklin
George Washington

Reading: Sequence

When you read history, dates can often help you follow the sequence of events. As you read the lesson, circle the dates to help you follow the sequence of events that brought the colonists together in the cause of independence.

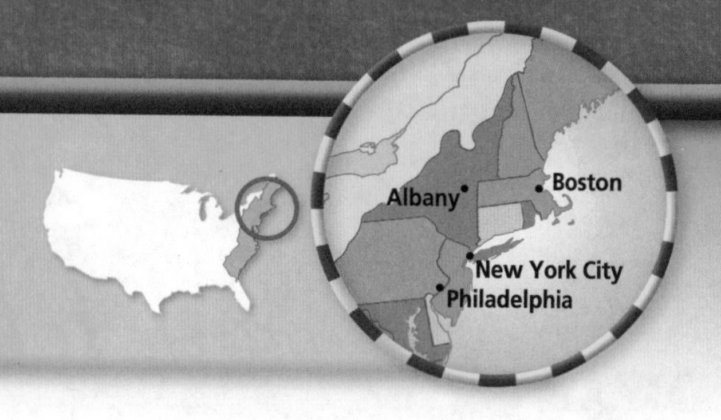

1755 1760

1754 The Albany Congress meets.

The Colonies Decide to Meet

For the most part, the thirteen British colonies were independent of one another and felt little reason to meet. However, in 1754 the need for representatives of the colonies to meet together finally came. As the French and Indian War approached, Britain wanted to improve relations with the Iroquois. Why? Britain hoped to gain the Iroquois as allies if war broke out. To achieve this goal, delegates from seven colonies and from the Iroquois Confederacy met in Albany, New York. A **delegate** is a person chosen to represent others. The Albany Congress, as it was called, helped the colonists realize how important it was for them to work together.

1. What events led to the Albany Congress? *Sequence*

The Colonists Come Together

As you have learned, colonial delegates met again in 1765 to respond to the Stamp Act. Although the Congress was successful, conditions in the colonies did not improve over time. As a result, Samuel Adams and other colonial leaders started groups called Committees of Correspondence in 1772. A **committee** is an organized group that meets to make decisions. To **correspond** is to communicate by writing letters. Adams felt that the colonies needed to **unify,** or unite. To do this, committees were formed throughout the colonies. Letters with news from each committee were carried from town to town by riders on horseback. In this way, leaders in each colony were made aware of what was going on in the other colonies.

2. What was the purpose of the Committees of Correspondence? *Main Idea and Details*

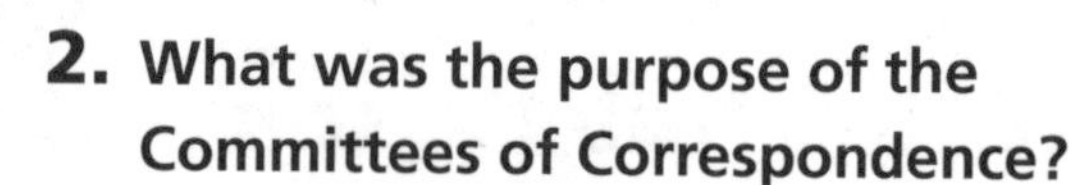

Benjamin Franklin created this cartoon to symbolize the need for the colonies to work together.

1765 1770 1775

1772 Samuel Adams forms the first Committee of Correspondence.

1774

Leaders Meet in Philadelphia

Although the colonists convinced Britain to repeal some taxes, Parliament was still making decisions for the colonies. This made many colonists angry because the colonies had no representation in Parliament. In response to the Coercive Acts, colonial leaders decided it was time to meet. The First Continental Congress met in Philadelphia in 1774. Every colony but Georgia sent delegates. The delegates decided to stop trading with Britain until the Coercive Acts were repealed. Each colony also agreed to start training militias to protect itself. A **militia** is a civilian army that is used only in emergencies. Delegates agreed to meet again in one year if relations with Britain had not improved.

3. **What were the results of the First Continental Congress?** *Main Idea and Details*

A Final Plea Is Made to the King

Relations with Britain did not improve, so the Second Continental Congress met in Philadelphia in May 1775. The Battles of Lexington and Concord had been fought just a month earlier, and many important decisions needed to be made. The Congress formed a Continental Army and made a Virginia plantation owner and former British soldier named George Washington its commander. The Congress also made a final attempt to avoid war. They sent a letter called the Olive Branch Petition to King George. This petition said that the colonists were still loyal to Britain and that war could be avoided if the colonies were given more freedom to govern themselves. The king never answered. As you will soon learn, this Congress would finally decide that there was only one thing left to do—declare independence from Britain.

4. **In the text, underline the actions taken by the Second Continental Congress.** *Main Idea and Details*

Summary

As conflicts came about with Britain, the colonies realized the importance of working together. How did the colonists work together to cause change?

Skill

Map Scales

Learn More A map scale is a set of lines on a map that help you figure out the actual distance between two places on Earth. To do this, line up the edge of a piece of paper between two places on the map. Mark both places with points on the paper. Then hold the marked edge to the scale, lining up the zero with the point farthest to the left. Use the scale to figure the distance between the two places.

The map below shows the thirteen colonies around the time of the First Continental Congress in 1774. When the colonists needed a meeting place for the Congress, they decided that Philadelphia was the best choice. Use the map and map scale to answer the questions below.

Try It

1. **One reason why colonists chose Philadelphia as a meeting place was its central location. Circle the colony in which Philadelphia was located.** *Identify*
2. **Some delegates still had to travel long distances to Philadelphia. Use the map scale to estimate the distance in miles from Charleston to Philadelphia. Write your answer between the two cities on the map.** *Apply*
3. **If a delegate stopped in Baltimore on his way from Charleston to Philadelphia, about how many miles would he have yet to travel? Write the answer on the map near Baltimore.** *Analyze*
4. **In colonial America, people could travel about 60 miles a day on horseback. Use the map scale to estimate the distance between Boston and Philadelphia. Then figure out about how many days it would take a delegate on horseback to travel that distance. Write the travel time on the map.** *Analyze*

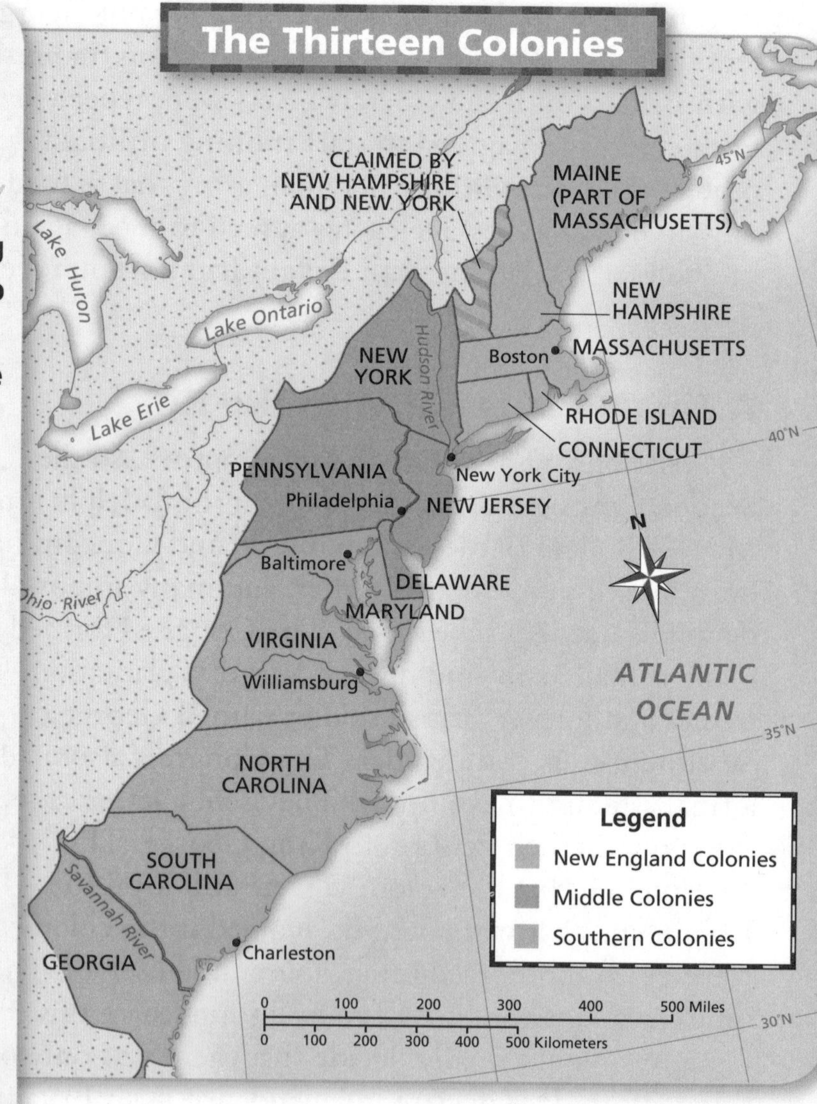

Name:

H-SS 5.5.3 Understand the people and events associated with the drafting and signing of the Declaration of Independence and the document's significance, including the key political concepts it embodies, the origins of those concepts, and its role in severing ties with Great Britain.

Lesson 3

Why did the colonists declare independence?

SET THE SCENE What does it mean to declare independence? The Declaration of Independence is one of our country's most important documents. Why was it written?

Preview the Lesson

Vocabulary

Patriot (n.) someone who felt the colonies should separate from Britain

Loyalist *(n.)* someone who felt the colonies should remain loyal to Britain

propaganda *(n.)* information written to persuade others to change their way of thinking

Vocabulary Activity The suffix *-ist* means "one who." Circle the vocabulary word above that uses the suffix *-ist*. Then write a new definition for that word starting with "one who."

____

____

People

Thomas Paine
Thomas Jefferson
John Hancock

Reading: Main Idea and Details

Remember that the *main idea* is the most important idea of a paragraph. *Details* give information that support the main idea. As you read the first paragraph on page 112, underline the sentence that states the main idea. Place check marks at the beginning of the sentences that support the main idea.

1776

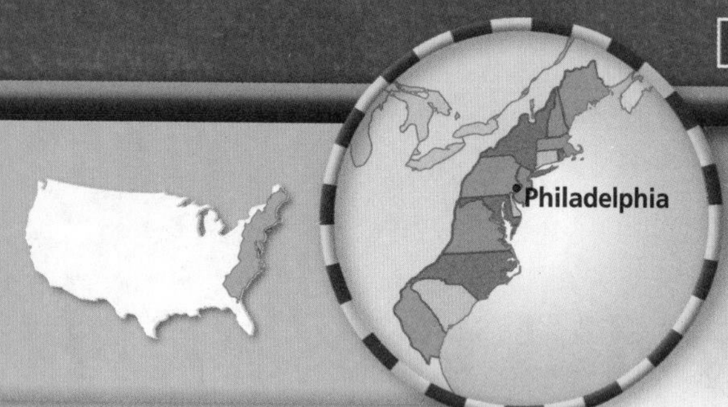

January 1776 Thomas Paine publishes *Common Sense.*

Making Common Sense

As conflicts arose between Britain and the colonies, colonists began to disagree about how the colonies should be governed. Someone who felt the colonies should separate from Britain was called a **Patriot.** Someone who felt the colonies should remain loyal to Britain and King George was called a **Loyalist.** By the spring of 1776, after one year of fighting, many Patriots felt that the time had come for a complete break from Britain.

The Patriots felt that they had many reasons to declare independence. Although they were British citizens, American colonists did not have the same rights as citizens who actually lived in Great Britain. For example, the colonies were not allowed to send representatives to Parliament. Therefore, they could not vote on issues and taxes directly affecting them. Also, the colonists had asked many times for greater freedom to govern themselves, but Britain had always refused.

Many Patriots wrote propaganda to support their cause. **Propaganda** is information written to persuade others to change their way of thinking. In January 1776, Thomas Paine published a booklet called *Common Sense.* Paine argued that people have the right to govern themselves rather than be ruled by a king. He stated, "A government of our own is our natural right." His powerful words convinced many colonists that it was time to declare independence.

1. In the text, number four reasons why Patriots felt the colonies should declare independence from Great Britain.
Main Idea and Details

COMMON SENSE:
ADDRESSED TO THE
INHABITANTS
OF
AMERICA,
On the following interefting
SUBJECTS.
I. Of the Origin and Defign of Government in general, with concife Remarks on the Englifh Conftitution.
II. Of Monarchy and Hereditary Succeffion.
III. Thoughts on the prefent State of American Affairs.
IV. Of the prefent Ability of America, with fome mifcellaneous Reflections.

Written by an ENGLISHMAN.
By Thomas Paine

Man knows no Mafter fave creating HEAVEN,
Or thofe whom choice and common good ordain.
THOMSON.

PHILADELPHIA, Printed
And Sold by R. BELL, in Third-Street, 1776.

The first copies of *Common Sense* said only that the author was "an Englishman." The words "by Thomas Paine" on this copy were written in later.

The Colonies Declare Independence

In June 1776, the Second Continental Congress met in Philadelphia, Pennsylvania. A vote was called for independence. Then Congress created a committee to prepare a document stating its goals. This committee chose Thomas Jefferson to write the document with the help of others.

2. In the text, underline the sentence in each paragraph that gives the main idea.
Main Idea and Details

This document was called the Declaration of Independence. In it, Jefferson included key political ideas to explain why the colonies wanted freedom. These ideas came from a long tradition of British self-government. Jefferson wrote that "all men are created equal" and have "unalienable rights" that governments cannot deny. He explained that government exists to protect those rights, and that it gets its power from the people. If a government does not protect the rights of its citizens, the people have the right to change or get rid of that government. Jefferson went on to list how the British government had abused the rights of the American colonists. Finally, he declared the colonies to be "free and independent states."

Fifty-six delegates to the Second Continental Congress signed the Declaration of Independence, which was written by Thomas Jefferson *(in red vest)* and others.

Congress approved the Declaration of Independence on July 4, 1776. The colonists could now rally around these ideas in their fight to free themselves from Britain. The United States and other countries around the world would be inspired by these ideas long into the future.

Summary

Writing the Declaration of Independence was a key event for the colonists. Why was the signing of the Declaration of Independence important to the colonists?

The Risks of Freedom

Learn More Sometimes being a good citizen involves risk. When the founders of our country signed the Declaration of Independence, they knew they were taking a risk. The document publicly blamed George III for "repeated injuries" and said that the colonists no longer owed loyalty to him. This made the signers guilty of treason, or being disloyal to one's country. The punishment for treason was death by hanging. Benjamin Franklin said, "We must all hang together, or most assuredly we shall all hang separately."

As president of the Continental Congress, John Hancock was the first person to sign the document on July 4, 1776. The other members did not begin signing until August 2. Their names were kept secret for about six months, but each man knew the risks of signing. The last sentence of the document reads, "And for the support of this Declaration . . . we mutually [together] pledge our Lives, our Fortunes, and our sacred Honor."

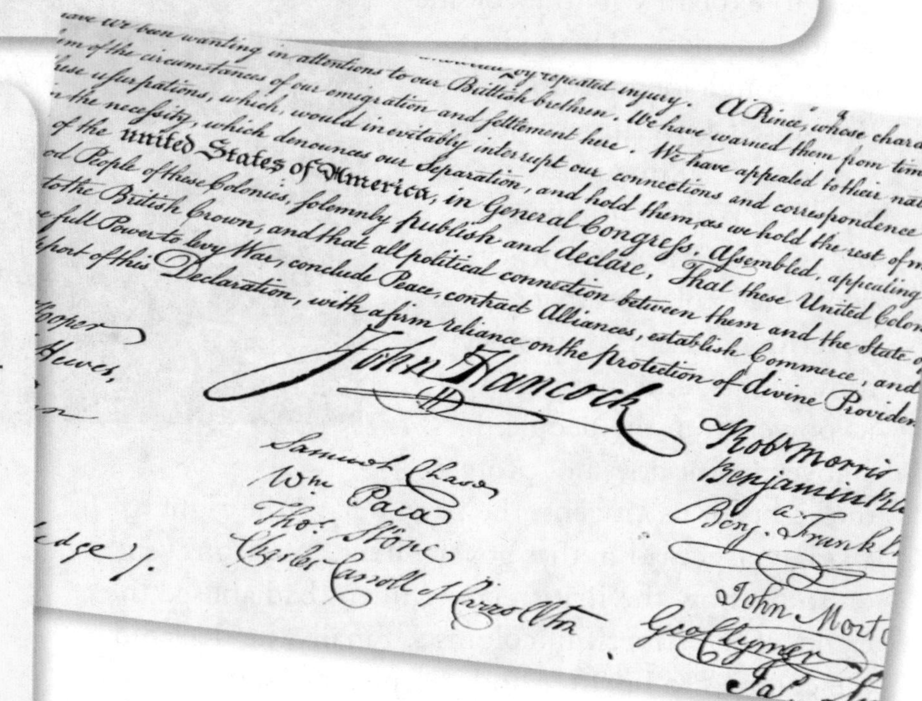

Answer the questions below.

1. **Who was the first signer of the Declaration of Independence?** *Identify*

____

2. **How do we know that the signers of the Declaration of Independence knew that they were taking a risk by signing the document?** *Analyze*

____

____

____

____

____

Name:

H-SS 5.5.4 Describe the views, lives, and impact of key individuals during this period (e.g., King George III, Patrick Henry, Thomas Jefferson, George Washington, Benjamin Franklin, John Adams).

Lesson 4

Who caused change in the colonies?

SET THE SCENE Have you ever tried to persuade others to see your point of view? Some colonists convinced others to push for independence from Britain. What effect did these important people have in the colonies?

Preview the Lesson

Vocabulary

orator *(n.)* someone who gives speeches

Vocabulary Activity The suffix *-or* means "one who." Circle it in the word above. The four letters that remain are part of the word *orate*. Given your understanding of the suffix *-or* and the definition of *orator* above, what do you think the word *orate* means?

People

James Otis
Patrick Henry
John Adams

Reading: Cause and Effect

Reading Skill

You have learned that a *cause* is why something happens and an *effect* is what happens as a result. Remember that words such as *because* and *since* can signal cause and effect. Circle the words that signal cause and effect on page 116.

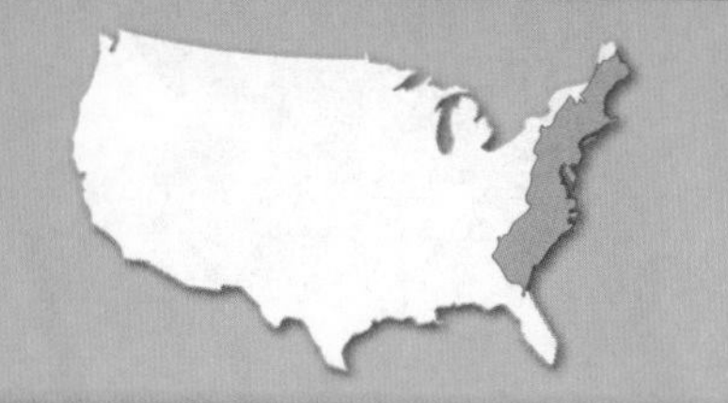

1765 Patrick Henry speaks out against the Stamp Act.

An Early Opponent of British Rule

George III of Britain believed that Parliament should be able to make laws for the colonies. Since the colonists were British citizens and received protection from Britain, he felt that they should be subject to laws enacted by Parliament.

James Otis, a colonist from Massachusetts, was one of the first people to oppose this idea. In 1761 Otis declared that a law allowing British soldiers to search the homes of colonists for illegal goods was unfair. Otis also thought that colonists should not have to pay taxes to Britain if they did not have a representative in Parliament. He said, "Taxation without representation is tyranny." Tyranny means an unjust use of power. Because of Otis's persuasive words, many colonists listened to and agreed with his views.

1. Cause and Effect **Fill in the effect to complete the chart below.**

Cause	Effect
James Otis said, "Taxation without representation is tyranny."	

Patriots Spread the Word

People throughout the colonies began to spread the idea of independence. Patrick Henry of Virginia was known as a great **orator,** or someone who gives speeches. In 1765 he gave an emotional speech to the Virginia House of Burgesses that convinced many Virginians to oppose the Stamp Act. In 1775 Henry declared, "Give me liberty or give me death." Samuel Adams of Massachusetts helped create the Committees of Correspondence. Henry and Adams both helped unite colonists in the cause of independence.

2. What generalization can you make about Patrick Henry and Samuel Adams? *Make Generalizations*

James Otis is often referred to as "the first Patriot" for being one of the first colonists to speak out against Britain.

1770 | 1775 | 1780

1775 George Washington becomes commander of the Continental Army.

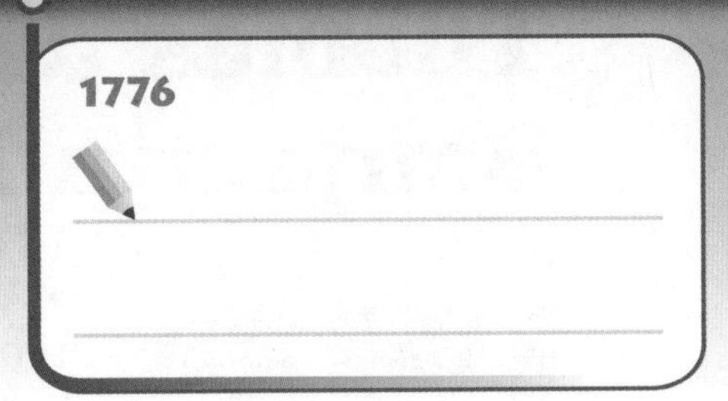

Patriots with Principles

American Patriots felt strongly about their cause. They also felt strongly about doing what was right. John Adams was a Patriot from Massachusetts. As a writer and orator, he spoke out against the Stamp Act in 1765 and the Townshend Acts in 1767. Yet he helped defend British soldiers in the trial following the Boston Massacre. Even though Adams was a Patriot, he felt the soldiers had the right to a fair trial. In 1775 George Washington became the commander of the Continental Army. Washington had fought in the British army during the French and Indian War. However, he came to oppose how Britain ruled the colonies. Both Adams and Washington believed that doing what was right was more important than going along with what others thought.

The Writers of the Declaration

Individual members of the Continental Congress helped bring about change in the colonies too. Thomas Jefferson owned a plantation in Virginia. He studied many new ideas about how government should work. In 1776 he led the committee that wrote and edited the Declaration of Independence. This committee also included John Adams and Benjamin Franklin. Franklin helped Jefferson make a final draft of the document. He was a publisher and scientist from Pennsylvania. Franklin and Jefferson convinced many colonists that they had the right to form their own government.

3. In the text, underline George Washington's military experience before serving as commander of the Continental Army. *Sequence*

Thomas Jefferson, John Adams, and Benjamin Franklin all helped write the Declaration of Independence.

4. In the text, underline the ways Jefferson and Franklin made their living. *Main Idea and Details*

Summary

It took many individuals to push for the cause of independence. How did the Patriots mentioned in this lesson contribute to American independence?

Biography

Thomas Jefferson, 1743–1826
Benjamin Franklin, 1706–1790

Learn More Thomas Jefferson was the third President of the United States, but he is known for more than his political achievements. He was also a scientist and an inventor. For example, he created a cipher wheel that helped put words into secret code and back again. He made a copying press that was portable, or easily carried. Jefferson was also interested in architecture. He enjoyed designing and working on Monticello, his home in Virginia. When he founded the University of Virginia, he designed its campus and selected books for its library.

Benjamin Franklin was another important colonial leader who was successful in other areas. Like Jefferson, Franklin was interested in both science and education. His inventions include the wood-burning stove and bifocal glasses. Franklin opened the first public library where people could borrow books, and he founded the University of Pennsylvania. He wrote and printed a book called *Poor Richard's Almanack* every year from 1732 to 1757. People still quote sayings from these books today.

Answer the questions below.

1. **Underline a sentence that tells how Thomas Jefferson and Benjamin Franklin were alike.** *Identify*
2. **Explain what you think are Jefferson's and Franklin's most important contributions.** *Apply*

____

____

____

____

____

Thomas Jefferson

Benjamin Franklin

Name:

Unit 6

Study Journal

In this unit you will learn about the people, events, and effects of the Revolutionary War. Complete the activities on these pages as you read the unit.

What I know about . . .

the Revolutionary War:

Revolutionary War Turning Points

Fill in the dates and explain what happened at each of the following events:

Siege of Boston	Battle of Trenton
Date: **What happened:**	**Date:** **What happened:**
Battle of Saratoga	**Battle of Yorktown**
Date: **What happened:**	**Date:** **What happened:**

Complete these sections as you read the unit.

Write a paragraph about the problems Americans faced during the Revolution. Use the following vocabulary words:

- **inflation**
- **profiteer**
- **hoard**
- **mutiny**

Choose one of the following and explain how the Revolution affected it.

- **State constitutions**
- **Settlement of western land**
- **Views toward slavery**

Fill in the name of a person that best fits each category below. Then explain that person's role in the Patriot cause.

Foreign Soldier	Patriot Woman	Patriot Commander
Name:	Name:	Name:
Role:	Role:	Role:

I have learned . . .

Name:

H-SS 5.6.1 Identify and map the major military battles, campaigns, and turning points of the Revolutionary War, the roles of the American and British leaders, and the Indian leaders' alliances on both sides.

Lesson 1

How did the American colonies defeat Great Britain?

SET THE SCENE Sometimes we have to do what we think is right, even when it is very difficult. By 1775 the Patriots' resistance to British rule had turned to war. But how could Americans stand up to the world's strongest army and win their independence?

Preview the Lesson

Vocabulary

retreat *(v.)* to stop fighting and move away from the enemy

siege *(n.)* the surrounding of a place by an army in order to capture it

campaign *(n.)* a series of battles to achieve a specific purpose

mercenary *(n.)* a soldier from one country who is paid to fight for another country

turning point *(n.)* a time when important changes occur

Vocabulary Activity When you know the meaning of the words that make up a word, you can often figure out its meaning. How might this help you understand the meaning of the term *turning point*?

People

Ethan Allen
Benedict Arnold
George Rogers Clark
John Paul Jones
Francis Marion
Nathanael Greene

Reading: Sequence

Reading Skill

Sequence is the order in which events take place. Dates can help you understand a sequence of events. As you read page 122, circle the years and underline the months of the early battles of the Revolutionary War.

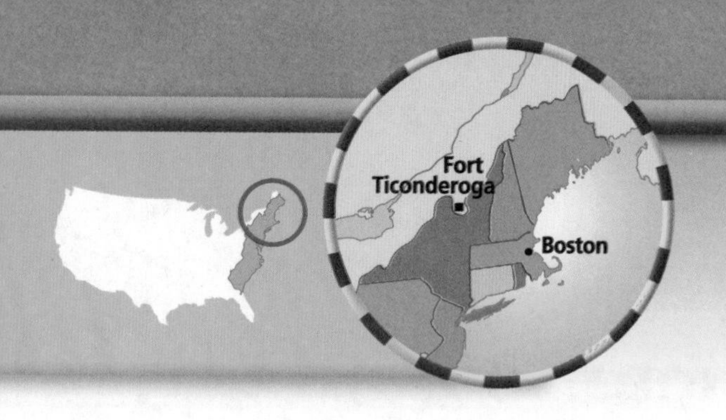

April 1775 Patriot militias battle the British at Lexington and Concord.

The Revolutionary War Begins

After many years of conflicts, the Revolutionary War, or American Revolution, began in Massachusetts in 1775. You have already learned about the Patriots' first victory. In April militias drove back British troops at Concord. The Patriots soon won another important battle. In May militias led by Ethan Allen and Benedict Arnold defeated British troops at Fort Ticonderoga and captured many badly needed cannons.

The Patriots then wanted to take control of Boston from the British. In June 1775, British troops attacked American forces setting up positions near Bunker Hill, just outside the city. The militias fought bravely but had to retreat. To **retreat** is to stop fighting and move away from the enemy. Still, the Patriots were proud. They had stood up to the mighty British army.

In July General George Washington arrived in Boston as the leader of the colonies' new Continental Army. He quickly set up a siege of the city. A **siege** is the surrounding of a place by an army in order to capture it. Washington's troops surrounded Boston for almost a year, but the British would not surrender. However, things changed in March 1776, when the cannons captured at Fort Ticonderoga nearly a year earlier finally arrived in Boston. With the cannons, Washington could destroy the British forces. The British soon realized the danger and retreated by sea to what is now Canada. Yet despite the British retreat, the war was far from over.

1. Sequence **List the early Revolutionary War battles in the correct sequence. Use the dates you circled to help you put them in order.**

Many Americans left their families and homes behind to fight in militias.

June 1775

March 1776 British troops retreat from Boston after a nearly year-long siege.

Allies and Enemies

When fighting began, American and British leaders both knew they needed allies to help them win the war. American Indians became important allies for both sides. Groups such as the Mohawks fought for the British. In exchange, Britain promised to keep settlers off their lands. Other American Indian groups aided the Americans. Members of the Stockbridge Mohican group had served in colonial militias even before the war began. They later took part in the siege of Boston. Other groups did not want to fight at all. "We are unwilling to join on either side," an Oneida leader explained, "for we love you both, old England and new." However, by 1776 the Oneida had decided to help the Americans in the fight against Britain.

Both sides also wanted help from African Americans. In 1775 the Loyalist governor of Virginia promised to free enslaved men who left Patriot owners to fight for the British. Thousands of enslaved people gained their freedom in this way. Many enslaved Africans were freed in exchange for fighting on the American side as well. At Bunker Hill, an enslaved African named Peter Salem fatally wounded the British commander, allowing the American forces to escape. James Armistead was an important spy for the Patriots in the Southern Colonies. Both men became free after the war. Overall, about 5,000 free and enslaved African Americans served in the Continental Army.

2. How did American Indians help the Patriots? *Main Idea and Details*

Service in the Continental Army allowed some African Americans to earn freedom from slavery.

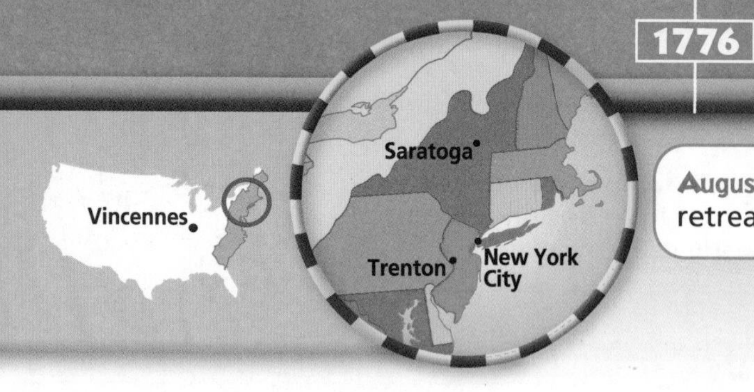

1776

1777

August 1776 American troops retreat from New York City.

December 1776 Washington captures Hessian mercenaries at Trenton.

Challenges in the Middle Colonies

After their losses in New England, the British began a new campaign in the Middle Colonies. A **campaign** is a series of battles to achieve a specific purpose. The British hoped to capture the region's important ports and separate New England from the other colonies. In August 1776, British troops attacked New York City and forced Washington's army to retreat to Pennsylvania. However, Washington struck back. In December he led troops into Trenton, New Jersey, and captured a group of German mercenaries called Hessians. A **mercenary** is a soldier from one country who is paid to fight for another country.

Then in the fall of 1777, there was a turning point in the war. A **turning point** is a time when important changes occur. British forces from Canada and New York City planned to meet in Albany, New York. From there, they believed they could cut off New England from the other colonies. Their plan failed. In October American forces captured more than 5,000 British troops near Saratoga, New York. This victory ended the British campaign in the Middle Colonies. Also, the defeat of a strong British army showed that the United States had a chance to win the war. As a result, France agreed to join the fight against Britain, their longtime enemy.

Even after Saratoga, Patriots faced many challenges. Britain still had thousands of well-trained troops. The small, poorly supplied Continental Army faced a cold winter at their camp in Valley Forge, Pennsylvania. From December 1777 to the spring of 1778, General Washington struggled to hold the army together as many soldiers died from hunger, cold, and disease.

3. Why was the Battle of Saratoga a turning point in the war?
Cause and Effect

Nathan Hale *(left)* was a school teacher who served in the Continental Army. He was captured while spying on the British near New York City and sentenced to death by hanging. Before the sentence was carried out, Hale inspired other Patriots to fight on by declaring, "I only regret that I have but one life to lose for my country."

October 1777

February 1779 George Rogers Clark recaptures the fort at Vincennes.

War in the West and at Sea

Not all the fighting in the American Revolution took place in the East. Fighting also occurred on the colonies' western frontier and at sea. A frontier is an area at the edge of where most people live.

In 1778 George Rogers Clark led an American militia west to seize British land in present-day Indiana and Illinois. The area was controlled by Britain, but the settlers there were French. The French settlers did not like being ruled by Britain, so when Clark arrived at the forts at Vincennes (vihn SENZ) and Kaskaskia, they let him take control without a fight. However, in December the British attacked and recaptured the fort at Vincennes. Clark refused to give up. He led his troops through miles of swamplands during the cold February of 1779. They surprised the British and won back the fort. British troops and their American Indian allies continued to attack frontier lands throughout the war. However, they were never able to launch a campaign against the colonies from the western frontier.

Although it was much smaller than the British navy, the American navy played an important role during the war. American ships captured supplies, moved troops, and helped defend port cities. John Paul Jones was one of the heroes in the fight against the British navy on the Atlantic Ocean. When the British demanded that Jones surrender his ship during a battle in 1779, he shouted back, "I have not yet begun to fight." True to his word, he and his troops fought until the British surrendered.

4. Sequence **What sequence of events led to Clark's finally taking control of the fort at Vincennes in February 1779?**

George Rogers Clark *(center)* and his troops marched through miles of freezing swampland to recapture the fort at Vincennes.

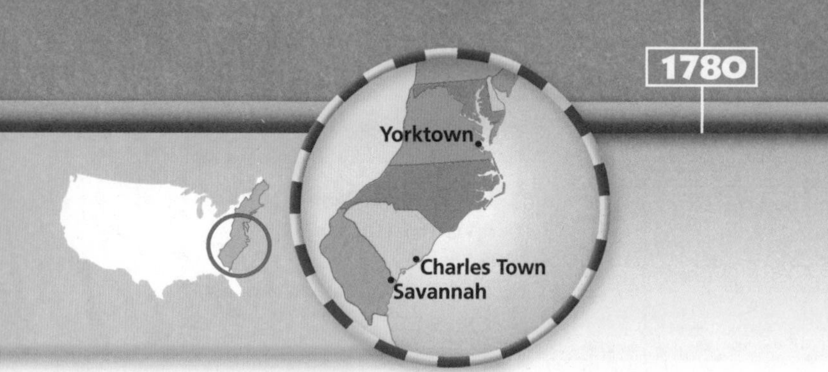

May 1780 More than 5,000 Patriots surrender to the British at Charles Town.

The Southern Campaign

In 1778 the British began a new campaign in the Southern Colonies. They had two goals. First, they planned to capture the Southern Colonies with help from the area's many Loyalists. Second, they planned to move north to take back the Middle Colonies and New England.

At first, the plan worked. In December 1778, British troops captured Savannah, Georgia, and returned the colony of Georgia to British rule. In May 1780, more than 5,000 American troops surrendered at Charles Town, South Carolina. A short time later, the British won another major battle at Camden, South Carolina.

Despite many victories, Britain's Southern campaign did not always go as planned. Some Loyalists grew angry at the damage caused by British troops and began to support the Patriots. Also, American forces repeatedly attacked and damaged British armies. Francis Marion led attacks against British troops and then quickly withdrew to hide in the marshes of South Carolina. His fighting style earned him the nickname the "Swamp Fox." General Nathanael Greene was especially important. He split his army into two smaller forces and made the British chase them back and forth across North and South Carolina. He would order his men to fight only when he saw a good opportunity.

5. How did American commanders fight the war in the Southern Colonies? *Make Generalizations*

General Nathanael Greene used small, quick forces to frustrate the British army. In this engraving, Greene's troops cross the Dan River in North Carolina, just ahead of the British.

1782 | 1783 | 1784

October 1781

September 1783 The Treaty of Paris officially ends the American Revolution.

Yorktown and Victory

You have learned that Britain's Southern campaign had two goals. The first was to secure Loyalist lands. The second was to move north and recapture the other colonies. The first part of the plan failed, but British General Charles Cornwallis decided to go ahead with the second part of the campaign anyway. In April 1781, Cornwallis's troops moved north into Virginia. They raided cities and nearly captured Virginia's Patriot governor. Yet Cornwallis knew that to keep winning he needed a larger army. In August he moved to the seaport of Yorktown so more troops could arrive by sea.

Meanwhile, General Washington, who was in New York, received news that French ships could help attack the British at Yorktown. He quickly moved a large army about 400 miles south to Virginia. His army and the French navy both reached Yorktown by September. Cornwallis was trapped. Washington's army had surrounded him, and French ships blocked an escape by sea. Cornwallis surrendered on October 19, 1781. Some fighting continued, but Yorktown was the final turning point of the war. The Treaty of Paris in 1783 officially ended the American Revolution. Finally, Britain accepted the independence of the United States.

6. In the text, underline the reason why Cornwallis surrendered at Yorktown. *Cause and Effect*

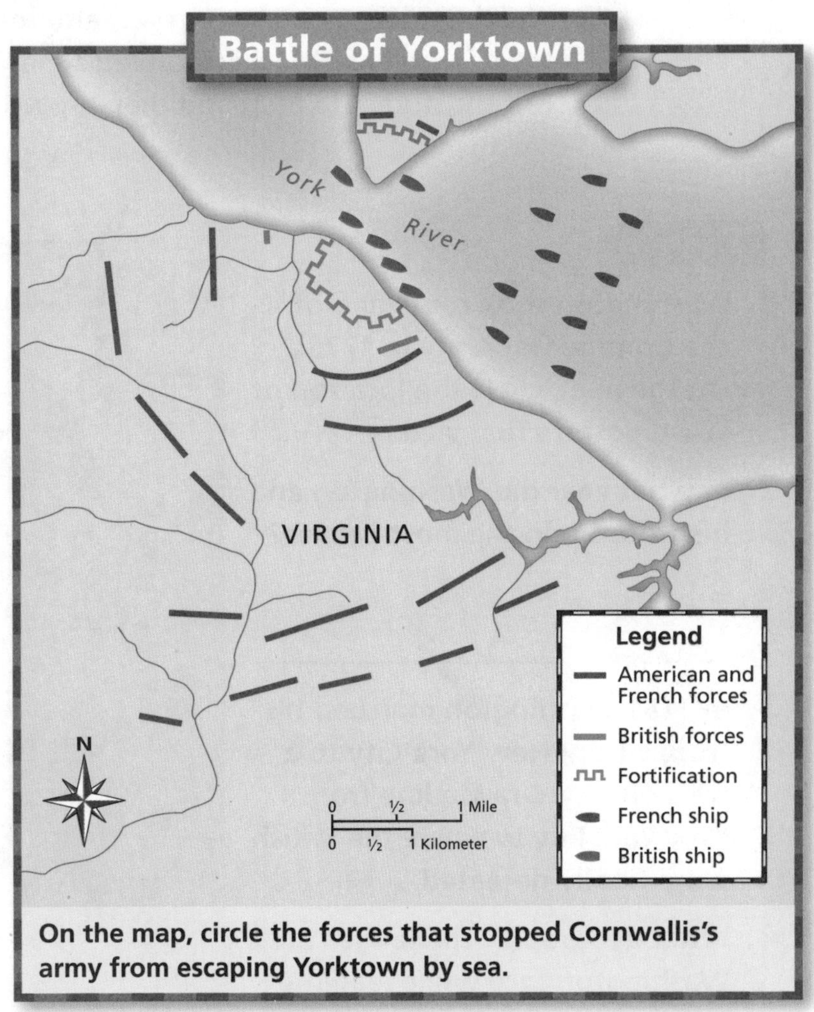

On the map, circle the forces that stopped Cornwallis's army from escaping Yorktown by sea.

Summary

Important turning points helped the Patriots defeat Britain in the American Revolution. What were some of the major turning points in the war, and why were they important?

Skill

Movement on Maps

Learn More Labels and dates on a map can be used to show someone's movement over time. The map below shows the major Revolutionary War battles that General George Washington fought in from 1775 to 1781. The map labels show that Washington experienced many victories and defeats during the fight for independence. The map also shows the many miles that he and his troops traveled during the war. They often traveled on foot while carrying heavy supplies. Bad weather, rivers, and poor roads also made travel difficult. Yet despite these problems, Washington led American troops to victory over the British. Study the map and then answer the questions below.

Try It

1. **Washington took command of the Continental Army in 1775. On the map, circle the location of Washington's first victory.** *Identify*
2. **In what year did Washington and his troops win the most battles?** *Analyze*

   ____

3. **In 1781 Washington marched his troops from New York City to a final victory. Draw a line from New York City to where the British were finally defeated.** *Apply*
4. **What geographic challenges did Washington face while leading the Continental Army?** *Interpret*

   ____

   ____

   ____

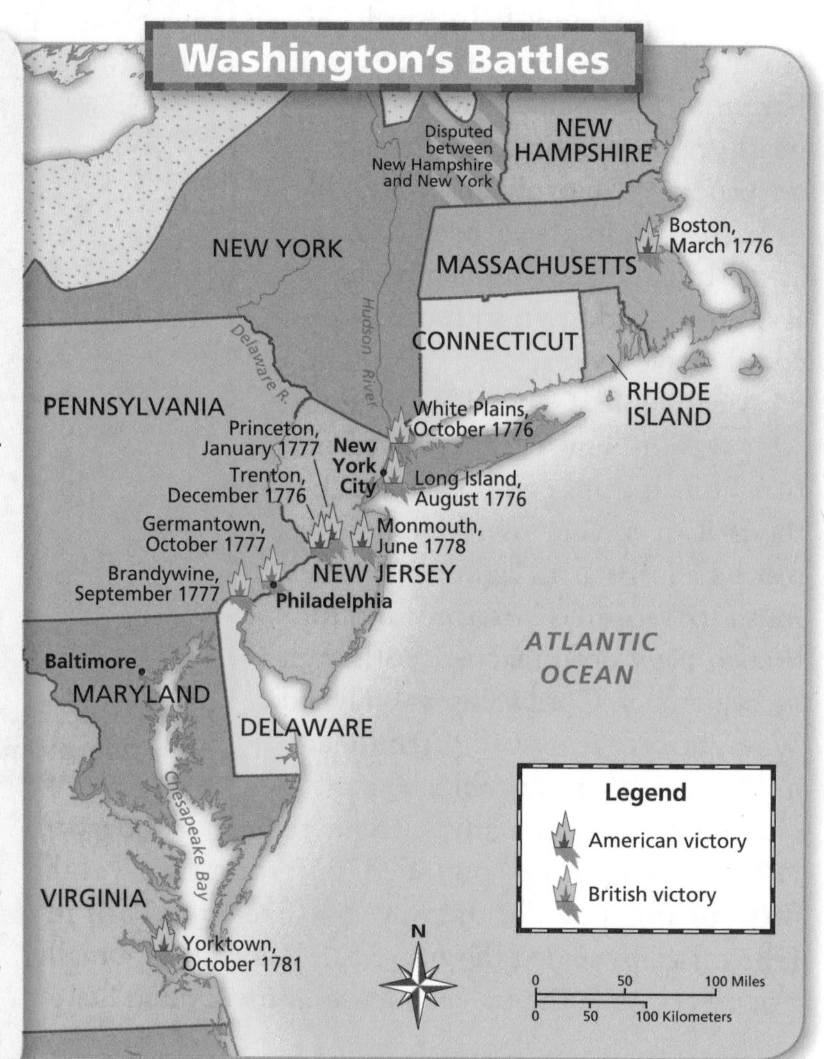

Name:

Lesson 2

H-SS 5.6.2 Describe the contributions of France and other nations and of individuals to the outcome of the Revolution (e.g., Benjamin Franklin's negotiations with the French, the French navy, the Treaty of Paris, The Netherlands, Russia, the Marquis Marie Joseph de Lafayette, Tadeusz Kósciuszko, Baron Friedrich Wilhelm von Steuben).

How did other nations help the Patriots?

SET THE SCENE What would you do without friends to help you through hard times? The Patriots could not have won the Revolutionary War alone. Many nations and individuals helped them. How did Americans and people from other nations work together to defeat Britain?

Preview the Lesson

Vocabulary

ambassador *(n.)* a representative sent by one government to another

negotiate *(v.)* to talk about something in order to reach an agreement

finance *(v.)* to provide money for

Vocabulary Activity If you wanted to stay up later on a weekend night, what vocabulary word above describes what you might do? Circle that word.

People

Tadeusz Kósciuszko
Marquis Marie Joseph de Lafayette
Baron Friedrich Wilhelm von Steuben

Reading: Make Generalizations

Generalizations are statements that are true for most people, places, or events. As you read the first paragraph on page 130, underline a generalization about why some European nations offered aid to the Patriots.

Support from Europe

During the Revolution, getting aid from European nations was a key part of the American war effort. Without it the small, poorly supplied Continental Army stood little chance against British military power. But how could Americans convince European nations to help them? The Continental Congress knew that some nations had conflicts with Britain over land claims and trade. To gain support, Congress tried to convince these nations that helping them would hurt Britain.

Congress sent ambassadors to European nations to ask for this support. An **ambassador** is a representative sent by one government to another. Benjamin Franklin, an ambassador to France, successfully negotiated for money, supplies, and troops. To **negotiate** is to talk about something in order to reach an agreement. Congress also sent ambassadors to or made agreements with Spain, the Netherlands, and Russia.

1. Place check marks next to sentences that support the generalization that European nations were willing to help the Patriots. *Make Generalizations*

Benjamin Franklin *(left)* helped get foreign support for the American Revolution as an ambassador to France.

French Support

France gave more support to the Patriot cause than any other European nation. The French government secretly helped **finance,** or provide money for, the war against Britain from the start. After the American victory at Saratoga, the French increased their support by sending their own troops and navy ships to help in the fight. France also helped convince the Netherlands and Spain to give money and supplies to the Patriots.

2. Underline the support that France gave to the United States after the Battle of Saratoga. *Cause and Effect*

Foreign Soldiers

Foreign soldiers had important roles in the war. At the Battle of Saratoga, Tadeusz (tad DA us) Kósciuszko (kahs ee US koh) of Poland built defenses that helped lead to the important American victory. Marquis (mahr KEE) Marie Joseph de Lafayette of France led French troops against the British. Baron Friedrich Wilhelm von Steuben of Germany trained the Continental Army at Valley Forge and helped make them into a strong fighting force. Both Lafayette and von Steuben played key roles at the Battle of Yorktown as well.

3. **Circle the names of battles in which foreign soldiers had key roles.** *Main Idea and Details*

Baron von Steuben *(right)* drilled American soldiers to increase their discipline and fighting skills.

The Treaty of Paris

After the war, the United States and its allies signed peace treaties with Britain. American leaders John Jay, John Adams, and Benjamin Franklin negotiated very skillfully. In the Treaty of Paris of 1783, Britain gave the United States a large area of land south of Canada and east of the Mississippi River. European negotiators were not as successful. In their treaties with Britain, France and Spain received much smaller amounts of land than the United States.

4. **In the text, underline the names of the Americans who negotiated the 1783 Treaty of Paris with Britain.** *Main Idea and Details*

Treaty of Paris, 1783

Mississippi River
ATLANTIC OCEAN
Gulf of Mexico
N

Legend
- United States
- British territory
- French territory
- Spanish territory
- Present-day national border
- Present-day state border

0 250 500 Miles
0 250 500 Kilometers

Write the names of the countries in the areas they controlled after the war.

Summary

The Patriots could not have defeated Britain without help from other nations. How did some European nations and individuals help the United States win independence?

Citizenship

The United Nations

Learn More Like people, nations can often accomplish more when they work together than when they work alone. During the American Revolution, the United States defeated Britain with help from other nations. Over a century and a half later, the United States and its allies worked together to win World War II, which affected many nations.

After World War II, fifty nations decided to create an organization of countries that would work together to solve problems. This organization, called the United Nations (UN), was founded on October 24, 1945. Its charter says that the UN's purpose is to prevent war, protect human rights, promote justice and respect, and improve life for people all over the world. Today, the UN has more than 190 members who meet at its headquarters in New York City. Nations that are members vote on issues that affect individual countries and the entire world.

Answer the questions below.

1. **In the text, underline the purposes of the United Nations.** *Identify*

2. **How is being a member of the United Nations like being a citizen of the world community?** *Interpret*

____

____

____

Name:

Lesson 3

H-SS 5.6.3 Identify the different roles women played during the Revolution (e.g., Abigail Adams, Martha Washington, Molly Pitcher, Phillis Wheatley, Mercy Otis Warren).

What role did women play in the Revolutionary War?

SET THE SCENE You have learned that the Patriots received aid from European allies to help in the fight against Britain. Women also had important roles in the war. How do you think Patriot women helped the United States gain independence?

Preview the Lesson

Vocabulary

activist *(n.)* a person who works for change

Vocabulary Activity The suffix *-ist* means "one who is or does" something. Circle the root word in *activist* above. How does knowing the suffix help you understand the word's meaning?

People

Mercy Otis Warren
Phillis Wheatley
Martha Washington
Molly Pitcher
Deborah Sampson

Reading: Draw Conclusions

To *draw conclusions,* you use facts from a text to identify information that is implied, or not clearly stated. As you read the first paragraph on page 134, circle names that will help you draw the conclusion that many women believed strongly in the Patriot cause.

Women Show Support

During the American Revolution, some women became activists in support of the Patriot cause. An **activist** is a person who works for change. Mercy Otis Warren wrote popular poems and plays that made fun of British laws she opposed. African American writer Phillis Wheatley wrote a poem to George Washington in support of the Revolution. Abigail Adams voiced her opinions in letters to her husband John Adams.

Women also organized groups to support the Patriot cause. Many women showed their opposition to British tariffs by not buying British cloth. Instead, they gathered together to make their own clothes by hand. Women in Edenton, North Carolina, an important Southern port, staged their own "tea party" in 1774. Fifty-one women signed an agreement to boycott British tea until Britain agreed to stop taxing the colonists without their consent.

1. Underline sentences describing two groups of women that came together to protest British taxes. *Draw Conclusions*

"We, the Ladys of Edenton, do hereby solemnly engage [agree] not to conform to that Pernicious [harmful] custom of drinking tea . . . until such time that all Acts which tend to Enslave our Native Country shall be Repealed."

— Resolution signed in Edenton, North Carolina, October 1774

Women Take on New Roles

During the war, women took on important new roles in the economy. In colonial times, men controlled land and businesses by law, even when the property belonged to their wives. Most women participated in the economy by raising children and doing housework such as sewing and cooking. These household skills played an important role in the Patriots' boycotts before the Revolution. However, when men went off to fight in the war, some women filled their husband's roles in the economy as well as their own. Planters' wives took charge of farms and plantations. Merchants' wives ran their husbands' businesses. By taking on these roles, women helped keep the economy going during a time of great difficulty.

2. Underline the effect that women had on the economy during the Revolution. *Cause and Effect*

This engraving shows a female shopkeeper helping a customer. Some women ran shops and other businesses during the Revolution.

Helping Behind the Lines

Some women aided the Patriot cause by helping the troops. They traveled with the army and did important tasks such as nursing the wounded and repairing uniforms. Even Martha Washington, George Washington's wife, lived with the army at times. She joined her husband and his troops at Valley Forge during the winter of 1778 and helped raise the spirits of the cold, hungry soldiers. Some women also acted as messengers and spies for the Patriots. Sybil Ludington, a sixteen-year-old from New York, rode her horse about 40 miles to alert the local militia about a British attack. She became known as "the female Paul Revere."

3. Why were women who traveled with the army important to the Patriot's cause? *Draw Conclusions*

Women on the Battlefield

Some women fought alongside men during the Revolution. According to legend, Mary Ludwig Hays helped fire cannons at the British during the Battle of Monmouth in New Jersey. She became known as "Molly Pitcher," a name given to women who brought water to soldiers during battles. Deborah Sampson disguised herself as a man to serve in the Continental Army. She served for about two years until she was found out and released from duty.

4. Underline examples of how women fought alongside the men of the Continental Army. *Main Idea and Details*

Although Deborah Sampson *(right)* was released from duty, Congress later granted her retirement pay for her military service.

Summary

Women helped the Patriot cause in many ways. What roles did women have during the American Revolution?

Primary Source

Letters: Abigail Adams

Learn More A letter is a primary source because it is written by a person who lived at the time an event happened. By reading letters from a certain time period, we can learn about people's thoughts and opinions about historical events.

During the American Revolution, Abigail Adams and her husband John wrote many letters to each other. Abigail often wrote about her political opinions and the difficulties of home life during wartime. Below is an excerpt from a letter that Adams wrote to her husband while he was attending the Second Continental Congress. It was written months before the signing of the Declaration of Independence. Read the passage below and then answer the questions.

"I long to hear that you have declared an independency—and by the way in the new code of laws which I suppose it will be necessary for you to make I desire you would remember the ladies..."

— Abigail Adams, March 1776

1. **Underline the parts of the text that describe how Abigail Adams felt about independence.** Identify
2. **How does Adams's letter hint at her feminist beliefs?** Analyze

____

____

____

____

____

____

Name:

H-SS 5.6.4 Understand the personal impact and economic hardship of the war on families, problems of financing the war, wartime inflation, and laws against hoarding goods and materials and profiteering.

Lesson 4

What was life like in the colonies during the Revolution?

SET THE SCENE What would happen if the price of food suddenly doubled? What if it cost four times as much? American soldiers and families faced these and other kinds of hardships during the Revolutionary War.

Preview the Lesson

Vocabulary

inflation *(n.)* an increase in prices

hoard *(v.)* to gather for one's own future use

profiteer *(n.)* a person who charges unfairly high prices for goods

mutiny *(n.)* an open rebellion against authority, especially by sailors or soldiers

Vocabulary Activity The suffix *-eer* means "one who does something." For example, a *puppeteer* makes puppets move. Circle the root word in *profiteer* above. Write another definition below for the vocabulary word using what you know about the root word.

____

____

Reading: Main Idea and Details

You have learned that writers use a topic sentence to show the main idea in a paragraph. You also have learned that writers use details in the other sentences to explain or support the main idea. As you read the first paragraph on page 138, underline the main idea.

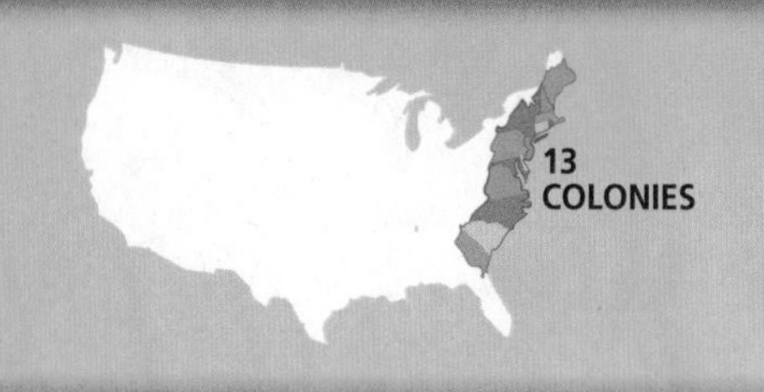

Paying for the War

The Continental Congress had a hard time paying for the war. The colonies provided some money and supplies, but it was not enough. In 1775 Congress began printing and spending paper money that became known as Continentals. The new money was supposed to allow the government to buy supplies quickly. Congress also asked for large loans from European countries.

1. What are three ways the colonies tried to pay for the war? *Main Idea and Details*

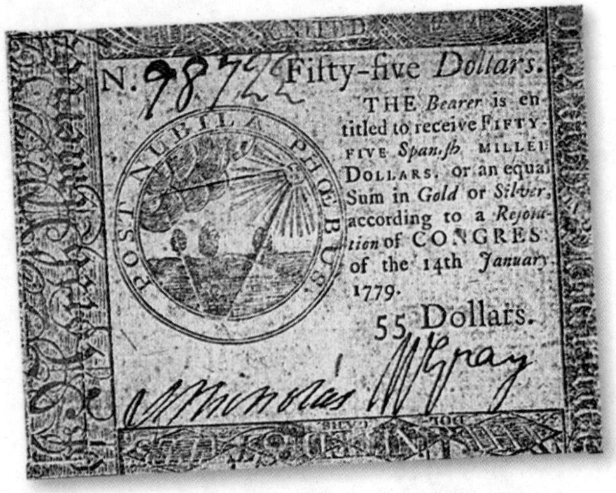

This Continental contains the motto *Post nubila phoebus,* which is Latin for "After dark clouds comes the sun."

Inflation and Profiteering

As the war went on, Congress had to print more and more Continentals to pay for troops and supplies. However, when there is too much of something, it can lose its value. To make up for this loss of value, people began to ask for more money in exchange for goods. This led to **inflation,** or an increase in prices. Also, as supplies decreased and prices increased, people began to hoard goods. To **hoard** is to gather for one's own future use. Hoarding made goods even harder to get and drove prices up further. To make matters worse, profiteers took advantage of the situation. A **profiteer** is a person who charges unfairly high prices for goods. Congress passed laws against profiteers, but such actions continued.

2. How did the drop in value of the Continental affect the American economy? *Cause and Effect*

Trouble Among the Troops

Inflation also caused great suffering for soldiers in the Continental Army. As prices rose, the government could afford less food and supplies for the soldiers. Also, Congress often did not have enough money to pay the soldiers. Many troops went a long time without pay or enough food. As a result, some of them participated in mutinies. A **mutiny** is an open rebellion against authority, usually by sailors or soldiers. George Washington and other leaders were able to restore order, but the Continental Army struggled to stay together throughout the war.

3. Why did mutinies occur during the war? *Cause and Effect*

Families at War

The Revolution caused many problems within American families too. Many families had both Loyalist and Patriot members. Benjamin Franklin's son William was a Loyalist. He was the royal governor of New Jersey. During the war, William Franklin was put in jail for his views and lost his property. His father never forgave him for remaining loyal to Britain. Families also suffered personal hardship through the loss of loved ones in battle.

4. Underline the main idea in this section. Number the sentences that contain details supporting the main idea. *Main Idea and Details*

Benjamin Franklin's Loyalist son William was arrested in 1776. His father later wrote, "Nothing has ever hurt me so much as to find myself deserted . . . by my only son, and . . . to find him taking up arms against me."

Summary

The Revolutionary War had major personal and economic impacts on the lives of many Americans. How did the Revolution cause hardships for American families and soldiers?

Skill

Cost-Benefit Analysis

Learn More Before you make an important decision, it is helpful to consider the costs and benefits of that decision. This is called a cost-benefit analysis. Costs are the losses that may result from a decision. Benefits are the gains or improvements that may result from the decision. The chart below lists the costs and benefits that colonists may have considered before going to war with Britain. Study the chart and then answer the questions below.

Costs to Colonists	Benefits for Colonists
Loss of life and destruction to property	Freedom to make one's own decisions
Loss of an established system of government	Freedom to set up a new, representative government
Money to raise and maintain armed forces	Freedom to collect taxes and set spending
Loss of Britain as major trading partner	Freedom from British trade laws
Loss of established social roles	Freedom to create fairer social roles

Try It

1. **The colonies did not have a strong military. Put a star next to the cost of overcoming this.** *Identify*
2. **Many colonists felt that they did not have a voice in the British government. Place a check mark by the benefit that might have changed this.** *Interpret*
3. **Underline a benefit that might convince a colonial merchant to fight for independence.** *Apply*
4. **Which benefit would persuade you to support the Patriot cause? Why?** *Analyze*

____

____

Name:

H-SS 5.6.5 Explain how state constitutions that were established after 1776 embodied the ideals of the American Revolution and helped serve as models for the U.S. Constitution.

Lesson
5

How did the American Revolution affect the creation of state governments?

SET THE SCENE What kind of plans do you make when you face a new situation? Because of the American Revolution, the colonies became independent states that ruled themselves. How would they use the beliefs that led to the American Revolution to create their own state governments?

Preview the Lesson

Vocabulary

constitution *(n.)* a written plan of government

ideal *(n.)* an important belief or aim

ratify *(v.)* to approve officially

Vocabulary Activity Circle the vocabulary word above that describes what people would do if they voted to approve a constitution in their state.

People

George Mason

Reading: Sequence

Reading Skill

A *sequence* is the order in which events take place. Sometimes dates or signal words such as *first*, *then*, and *finally* can help you understand a sequence of events. As you read page 142, circle the signal words that show the sequence of events that led to the passing of the Massachusetts state constitution.

Colonies Become States

Even before the Declaration of Independence was written in 1776, some colonies had begun to write constitutions that would establish them as new and independent states. A **constitution** is a written plan of government.

The Continental Congress did not interfere with how states wrote their constitutions. Its leaders did not want the states to view the Congress as a controlling national government, like the British monarchy. Also, citizens' rights and self-government were among the **ideals,** or important beliefs or aims, that led the states to fight for independence. Congress did not want to take away ideals the states had fought so hard to achieve.

1. Sequence **When did some colonies begin writing constitutions?**

A Voice in Government

Many of the colonies had been established by royal charters from the king of Britain. However, when it came time to write state constitutions, citizens played an important role. For example, in 1778 Massachusetts tried to pass a new constitution. At first, it was rejected because many people did not think the state's citizens had been given a voice in its creation. The constitution was then rewritten by a convention of delegates elected by the citizens. Finally, in 1780 Massachusetts became the first state whose citizens ratified its constitution. To **ratify** means to approve officially. Other states began to give their citizens a voice in writing and ratifying new constitutions too.

2. Sequence **Number the events that led to the ratification of the Massachusetts state constitution.**

Before the Revolution, charters put royal governors, such as Alexander Spotswood of Virginia (left), in charge of the colonies. Later, citizens helped write new constitutions that called for elected governors, such as George Clinton of New York (right).

A Balance of Power

States used their constitutions to create governments that had a balance of powers among elected officials. Before the Revolution, the colonies had been ruled by royal governors who were appointed by the British king. These governors had the power to dismiss elected assemblies. New state constitutions called for elected governors with limited powers. Elected assemblies held powers not given to the governor. To make these assemblies fair, each member represented a certain number of people. This ensured that no individual or group would have more power than others.

3. How were colonial and state governments different? *Compare and Contrast*

State Constitutions as Models

Many of the ideals in state constitutions became models for the U.S. Constitution. For example, some state constitutions had a section called a bill of rights. This section guaranteed the basic rights of all citizens, such as freedom of speech. When George Mason wrote Virginia's bill of rights, he stated that citizens were a part of the government, not separate from it. Citizens had to obey all laws, but their rights could not be taken away from them by the government. These ideals became a model not only for the U.S. Constitution but for constitutions all over the world.

4. Underline the ideals that George Mason included in the Virginia bill of rights. *Main idea and Details*

THE VIRGINIA DECLARATION OF RIGHTS

George Mason wanted citizens in Virginia to have the same rights.

Summary

New state constitutions included the ideals of the American Revolution and helped serve as models for the U.S. Constitution. How did the ideals of self-government and citizens' rights affect the writing of state constitutions?

Citizenship

The Magna Carta

Learn More As new state constitutions began to be written, leaders used many ideas found in the Magna Carta. This document whose title means "Great Charter" in Latin, limited the power of the king of England. In 1215 King John was raising the taxes of powerful people called barons and sending them to prison if they did not pay. So the barons wrote the Magna Carta and forced the king to sign it. The Magna Carta guaranteed fairer taxes for the barons, as well as their right to be consulted on important matters. It also created a fairer legal system. More than 500 years later, the Magna Carta's limits on the power of government and guarantees of citizens' rights became important ideals for the American states as they wrote their new constitutions.

Answer the questions below.

1. **Underline the sentence that describes how the Magna Carta and state constitutions were similar.** *Identify*
2. **Why do you think that only the English barons gained rights and privileges in the Magna Carta?** *Analyze*

____

____

____

____

____

Name:

H-SS 5.6.6 Demonstrate knowledge of the significance of land policies developed under the Continental Congress (e.g., sale of western lands, the Northwest Ordinance of 1787) and those policies' impact on American Indians' land.

Lesson 6

How did the United States move into western lands?

SET THE SCENE If you received a large piece of new land, what would you do with it? After gaining new lands in the west following the Revolution, the United States government had to find ways to manage them. What plans did Congress put in place as people moved west?

Preview the Lesson

Vocabulary

territory *(n.)* land owned or controlled by a particular country

policy *(n.)* a plan for doing or managing something

Vocabulary Activity Many words have Latin root words. The Latin word *terra* means "land" or "earth." Circle the word above that comes from the Latin word *terra*. Explain below how its meaning relates to its root word.

Reading: Sequence

Reading Skill

As you have learned, looking for dates can be useful in helping you understand a sequence of events. As you read page 146, circle years that help you understand the sequence of events that led to the settlement of western lands.

1763 The Proclamation of 1763 bans settlements west of the Appalachians.

Settling Western Lands

The 1783 Treaty of Paris that ended the American Revolution gave the United States control of a large new territory between the Appalachian Mountains and the Mississippi River. A **territory** is land owned or controlled by a particular country. Some settlers had moved into this area before the war, even though the British government had banned settlements west of the Appalachians in the Proclamation of 1763. After the British were defeated, even more settlers wanted to move west.

Congress soon realized that it needed to create a new policy for settling western lands. A **policy** is a plan for doing or managing something. So Congress passed the Land Ordinance of 1785. This ordinance sent surveyors, or people who measure land, to map and divide the territory into sections of land to be sold to settlers. It also set prices for the land. This policy was very successful, and over time many people bought and moved to western lands.

1. Sequence **In the text, number in order the policies and events that affected western settlement.**

George Washington *(center)* worked as a surveyor before the American Revolution. After Congress passed the Land Ordinance of 1785, surveyors measured the new western territory.

The Northwest Ordinance of 1787

Land sales led many people to move west. But how could the United States govern settlers who lived so far from the eastern states? The Northwest Ordinance of 1787 set up rules for governing new lands. It divided the area north of the Ohio River into territories that were run by appointed officials. Each territory had at least 5,000 free adult males. People in a territory could elect their own assembly and send a nonvoting representative to Congress. When the population reached 60,000, a territory could write its own constitution and apply for statehood.

2. Sequence **How could territories become states under the Northwest Ordinance of 1787?**

1780 | 1790 | 1800

1783

1787 The Northwest Ordinance sets up rules for governing western lands.

1785 The Land Ordinance of 1785 allows for the sale of western lands.

Eventually, five states were created in the Northwest Territory. The Northwest Ordinance placed these new states "on an equal footing with the original states." This meant that new states could participate in national elections and assemblies. Citizens of these states had the same rights as all other Americans. The ordinance also banned slavery in the Northwest Territory.

The Northwest Territory, 1787

CANADA (BRITISH)
Legend
Northwest Territory
Present-day borders and names of states are shown.
Boundaries Indefinite
Lake Superior
Lake Huron
Lake Michigan
Lake Ontario
Lake Erie
Mississippi River
Ohio River
WISCONSIN
MICHIGAN
NEW YORK
PENNSYLVANIA
OHIO
ILLINOIS
INDIANA
WEST VIRGINIA
VIRGINIA
KENTUCKY
ATLANTIC OCEAN
N
0 100 200 Miles
0 100 200 Kilometers

Circle the names of states created in the Northwest Territory.

The Rights of American Indians

The Northwest Ordinance also had a policy for American Indians in the territories. It said that American Indians' ". . . property, rights, and liberty, . . . shall never be invaded or disturbed, . . ." However, settlers moved onto American Indian lands anyway. When American Indian groups resisted the settlers, the U.S. government sent soldiers to put down the resistance. Over time, many of these groups were defeated and forced to sell their land to the United States. Many American Indians began to move south or west as large numbers of settlers moved onto their land.

3. Underline how the actions of the U.S. government toward American Indians differed from the policy of the Northwest Ordinance. Compare and Contrast

Settlers increasingly moved into the Northwest Territory in the late 1700s.

Summary

The U.S. government developed western land policies that affected settlers, states, and American Indians. How did the Northwest Ordinance of 1787 affect the United States and many American Indian groups?

Primary Source

Interviews: Big Eagle

Learn More An interview is a primary source because it can provide an eyewitness account from someone who was part of a historical event. As you have learned, many American Indians were forced to give up their land as settlers moved west. They reacted to the settlers in different ways. Often efforts were made on both sides to live peacefully. However, disputes over land sometimes led to conflict. One such conflict took place in 1862 between the Dakota and the U.S. Army in present-day Minnesota. In an interview in 1894, a Dakota chief named Big Eagle described some of the problems that occurred before the conflict. Read the excerpt from his interview below, then answer the questions.

"Then many of the white men often abused the Indians and treated them unkindly. . . . [A] little while before the outbreak there was trouble among the Indians themselves. Some of the Indians . . . began to live like white men. The government built them houses, furnished them tools, seed, etc., and taught them to farm. . . . Others stayed in their tepees. . . . The "farmers" were favored by the government. . . . The other Indians did not like this. They . . . disliked [the farmers] because they had gone back on the customs of the tribe and because they were favored."

1. **Underline the reasons Big Eagle gave to explain why some of the Dakota were upset with other members of their group.** Identify
2. **How do you think these events led to fighting between the Dakotas and the settlers?** Interpret

____

____

____

____

____

____

Name:

H-SS 5.6.7 Understand how the ideals set forth in the Declaration of Independence changed the way people viewed slavery.

Lesson 7

How did people's views on slavery change after independence?

SET THE SCENE The Declaration of Independence says that all people have the right to "life, liberty, and the pursuit of happiness." Yet many African Americans remained enslaved after its signing. How did African Americans and others work to fulfill the ideal of freedom?

Preview the Lesson

Vocabulary

abolish *(v.)* to end

Vocabulary Activity *Synonyms* are words that have similar meanings. In the sentence below, circle a synonym for *abolish*.

Students wanted to end the rule that did not let them play tag at recess.

People

Harriet Tubman
Frederick Douglass

Reading: Cause and Effect

Remember that a *cause* is what makes something occur. An *effect* is the result of that event or action. A signal word such as *because* can help you identify cause-and-effect relationships. As you read, circle the clue word in the last paragraph on page 150.

The Call for Freedom

The ideal of freedom announced in the Declaration of Independence did not really apply to everybody in the United States. Slavery was widespread, especially in the Southern states. However, after independence more and more people began to argue that enslaved African Americans should be freed.

People called abolitionists wanted to **abolish,** or end, slavery. The Religious Society of Friends, also known as Quakers, included many abolitionists. They believed everyone should be treated fairly.

Prince Hall was one of many former enslaved people who spoke out against slavery. After being freed by his owner after many years of service, he became an important leader among African Americans in Boston. In 1777 Hall and others sent a petition to the government of Massachusetts asking it to abolish slavery. The petition was denied.

Mum Bett, who was born into slavery, believed that the ideals in the Declaration of Independence should apply to her too. In 1781 she took her owners to court in Massachusetts. In deciding the case, the court noted that the state's new constitution said all people were "born free and equal." The court also decided that no state law had ever made slavery legal. Because of the court's decision, Bett was freed from slavery. She then changed her name and became known as Elizabeth Freeman.

1. What was the result of Mum Bett taking her owners to court?
Cause and Effect

Prince Hall and Elizabeth Freeman believed that the ideal of freedom in the Declaration of Independence should apply to all Americans.

Many people helped enslaved African Americans escape to freedom. This picture shows a schoolteacher helping an enslaved African escape from slavery.

The Debate over Slavery

After gaining independence, the states began a debate about slavery that would continue for many years. Which states would allow slavery and which would not? Most Northern states had banned slavery by 1790. The Northwest Ordinance of 1787 banned slavery in new western states. Yet slavery was still an important part of Southern states' economies, which relied on enslaved people to work on large plantations. People in Southern states worried that if Congress had more members from "free states" than from "slave states," the free states could vote to ban slavery everywhere. Proponents of slavery worked hard to make sure that there was always an equal number of free states and slave states.

2. What did slave states think would happen if many free states were added to the country? *Cause and Effect*

The Struggle for Freedom

In the 1800s, many abolitionists continued to fight against slavery. Harriet Tubman was a former enslaved person who helped others escape to freedom along the Underground Railroad. This was a secret system of travel from Southern states to the Northern states and Canada. After he gained his freedom, Frederick Douglass lectured and wrote about his life as an enslaved person. He also helped recruit African Americans to fight for the North during the Civil War, which was a war between the Northern free states and Southern slave states. During that war, in 1863 President Abraham Lincoln declared that enslaved people in the states fighting against the North were free. In 1865 an addition to the U.S. Constitution freed all enslaved people.

3. Circle the names of two people who fought against slavery in the 1800s. *Main Idea and Details*

In 1863 President Abraham Lincoln issued the Emancipation Proclamation, which declared all enslaved people in states fighting against the North to be free.

The ideals in the Declaration of Independence changed the way some people viewed slavery. How did the Declaration of Independence influence abolitionists?

Primary Source

Documents: Drafts of the Declaration of Independence

Learn More As you have learned, documents are primary sources because they are official statements written by people or government. When we read documents like the Declaration of Independence, we should remember that they are the final product of a long process. Sometimes a writer will include an idea in an early draft of a document but leave it out of the final draft.

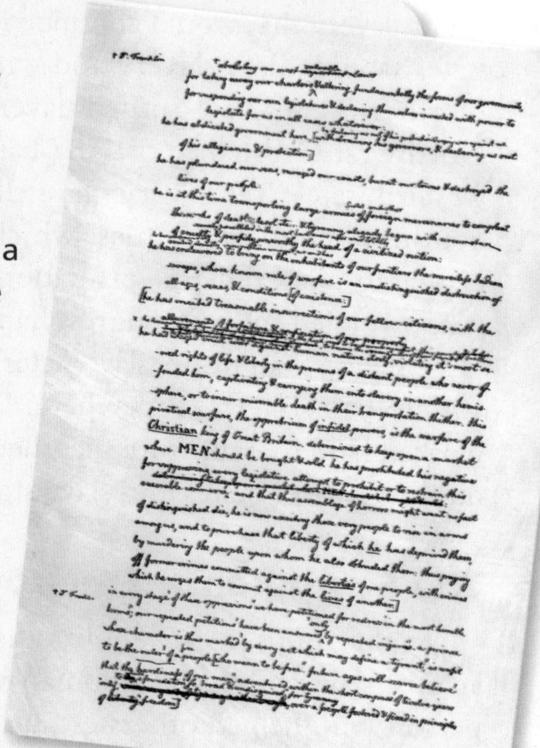

One of Thomas Jefferson's early drafts of the Declaration of Independence contained a passage that blamed the colonies' slave trade on Britain's king, George III. Jefferson suggested that slavery was one way the king tried to control the colonies. Yet the passage never made it into the final draft of the Declaration of Independence. Even though Jefferson did most of the writing, a large group of delegates to the Continental Congress had to approve the final draft. Many colonists, including Jefferson and several other delegates, were landowners who profited from the work of enslaved Africans. The passage about slavery was removed after two Southern states objected to it. Read the passage below and then answer the questions.

1. **Circle the "sacred rights" that Jefferson accuses George III of denying to enslaved Africans.** Identify
2. **Underline a phrase in Jefferson's statement that describes how he viewed the king's role in the slave trade.** Analyze

"He [George III] has waged cruel war against human nature itself, violating its most sacred rights of life and liberty in the persons of a distant people who never offended him, captivating [capturing] and carrying them into slavery in another hemisphere, or to incur miserable death in their transportation thither [here]. This piratical [illegal] warfare . . . is the warfare of the . . . King of Great Britain, determined to keep open a market where MEN should be bought & sold. . . ."

Name:

Study Journal

In this unit you will learn about the people and events that have shaped the U.S. Constitution, our state and national governments, and our rights and responsibilities as citizens. Complete the activities on these pages as you read the unit.

What I know about . . .

our federal government:

The Three Branches of Government

Classify information about our government in the chart below.

	Legislative Branch	Executive Branch	Judicial Branch
Purpose			
Who			
Checks on its power by . . .	Executive Branch Judicial Branch	Legislative Branch Judicial Branch	Executive Branch Legislative Branch

Complete these sections as you read the unit.

Write three details for the main idea below.

Main Idea: The Articles of Confederation placed limits on the federal government.

Detail 1:

____

____

Detail 2:

____

____

Detail 3:

____

____

Choose one of the Constitutional debates from the list and then explain the different viewpoints and compromise that was made.

- **Great Compromise**
- **Three-Fifths Compromise**
- **Federalists and Antifederalists**

Viewpoint 1: ______________________

____

Viewpoint 2: ______________________

____

Compromise: ______________________

____

____

____

Fill in the chart below with three rights and responsibilities of citizens.

Rights of Citizens	Responsibilities of Citizens
1.	1.
2.	2.
3.	3.

I have learned . . .

____

Name:

H-SS 5.7.1 List the shortcomings of the Articles of Confederation as set forth by their critics.

What problems did the new United States government face?

SET THE SCENE If you had to write a set of rules for your school, what would those rules be? Would some rules be for just your class, while others were for the entire school? As American leaders set up a government for our new country, they faced similar questions.

Preview the Lesson

Vocabulary

confederation *(n.)* a group of states that unites to form a larger state with a central government

federal *(adj.)* of or relating to the central government of a confederation

Vocabulary Activity The root word *foederis* means "treaty or league." Find and circle the root word in both vocabulary words above.

People

Alexander Hamilton

Reading: Draw Conclusions

Reading Skill

When you *draw conclusions,* you use facts from the text to form an opinion, or conclusion. Writers sometimes present their own conclusions. Signal words such as *therefore* can tell you when a writer is drawing a conclusion. As you read, circle signal words that tell you the writer is drawing a conclusion.

A New Government Is Created

After declaring independence, the United States needed to form a new central government. However, leaders were afraid of giving this government too much power. They feared that a strong central government would abuse its power, as Britain's King George III and Parliament had done. Therefore, leaders decided to create a central government with limited powers.

The Continental Congress wrote a document called the Articles of Confederation to plan this government. A **confederation** is a group of states that unites to form a larger state with a central government. The Articles were ratified in 1781, and they created a central government with few powers. For example, Congress needed approval from the states in order to pass new laws. Leaders would soon see that such limits on the central government created problems for the new nation.

1. Draw Conclusions **Underline a sentence in the text that draws a conclusion based on the fact that American leaders felt the British government had abused its power.**

ARTICLES
OF
Confederation
AND
Perpetual Union
BETWEEN THE
STATES
OF
NEW-HAMPSHIRE, MASSACHUSETTS-BAY, RHODE-ISLAND AND PROVIDENCE PLANTATIONS, CONNECTICUT, NEW-YORK, NEW-JERSEY, PENNSYLVANIA, DELAWARE, MARYLAND, VIRGINIA, NORTH-CAROLINA, SOUTH-CAROLINA AND GEORGIA.

LANCASTER:
PRINTED BY FRANCIS BAILEY.
M,DCC,LXXVII.

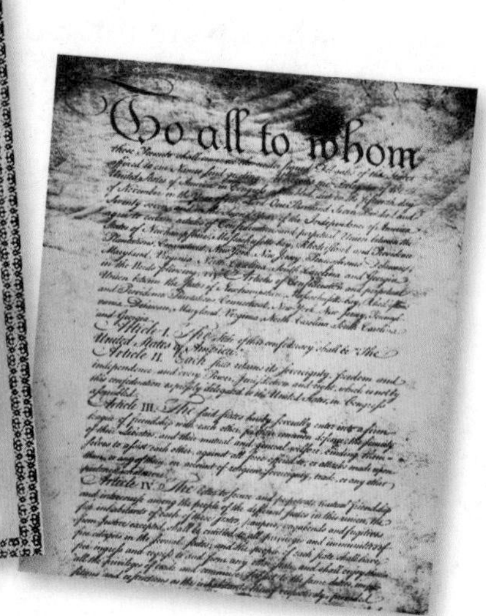
To all to whom

The Articles of Confederation were legally in use from 1781 to 1789.

Short of Money

One way the Articles of Confederation limited the power of the central government was by not allowing Congress to tax the states. Instead, Congress could only ask the states to give money to support the government. This created a problem because after the Revolution, the United States had millions of dollars of debt. The United States had needed to borrow this money from France and other countries in order to defeat Britain. Without the ability to tax the states, Congress had no way to pay back the money the country owed.

2. What limit in the Articles of Confederation made Congress unable to pay back the debts the United States owed?
Main Idea and Details

Problems with Trade

The Articles of Confederation also limited the central government's ability to control foreign trade. After the war, the British government forced American merchants to pay high taxes on items exported to Britain. Yet British merchants were able to export goods freely and cheaply into most of the United States. Why? Congress did not have the power to pass laws that taxed goods coming into the country.

Congress did not have the power to control trade between the states either. Most states had their own laws about trade and taxes. States could print their own currency, or paper money, too. These currencies often had different values. With different laws and money among the states, merchants in the United States had a difficult time doing business with one another.

3. Why was trade between the states so difficult?
Main Idea and Details

Congress and the states printed paper money during and after the Revolution.

Leaders Call for a New Government

Alexander Hamilton and other leaders began to worry about the future of the United States. They believed that the government created by the Articles of Confederation would lose the respect of its own citizens and of other countries. Therefore, the new nation might fail. Hamilton supported creating a stronger federal government. **Federal** means of or relating to the central government of a confederation. Hamilton's ideas, and those of other leaders, would become part of a new plan of government—the United States Constitution.

4. Draw Conclusions **Underline a sentence in the text that draws a conclusion about the future of the United States under the Articles of Confederation.**

Summary

The limits on the central government created by the Articles of Confederation led to problems for the new United States. What problems did the Articles cause for the new nation?

Primary Source

Documents: The Albany Plan

Learn More Sometimes documents and other primary sources can help us understand the history of an idea. The Albany Plan was a document written by Benjamin Franklin and Thomas Hutchinson at the Albany Congress in 1754. It proposed to unite the colonies under a "general," or central, government. This government would protect the colonies in case war broke out between Britain and France.

Neither the colonies nor Britain accepted the Albany plan, but the idea of a central government did not go away. In 1781 the Articles of Confederation created a central government for the new United States. However, this government had only limited powers. Finally, in 1787 the U.S. Constitution united the nation under a strong central government. Read the excerpts from the Albany Plan below and then answer the questions.

Thomas Hutchinson

Benjamin Franklin

1. **Underline some powers that the government would be given under the Albany Plan.** *Identify*

2. **Why do you think the colonies rejected the Albany Plan?** *Analyze*

____

____

____

____

____

____

"It is proposed that humble application be made . . . of which one general government may be formed in America, including all the said colonies, within and under which government each colony may retain [keep] its present constitution. . . .

1. *That the said general government be administered by a President-General, to be appointed and supported by the crown; and a Grand Council, to be chosen by the representatives of the people. . . .*

15. *That they raise and pay soldiers and build forts for the defence of any of the Colonies . . .*

16. *That for these purposes they have power to make laws, and lay and levy [collect] . . . taxes, as to them shall appear most equal and just . . ."*

Name:

H-SS 5.7.2 Explain the significance of the new Constitution of 1787, including the struggles over its ratification and the reasons for the addition of the Bill of Rights.

How did the United States create a constitution?

SET THE SCENE Have you ever started to work on something and then realized that you needed to start over? As you have learned, the Articles of Confederation created a weak government that did not have the respect of its people or the rest of the world. How did leaders work to solve this problem?

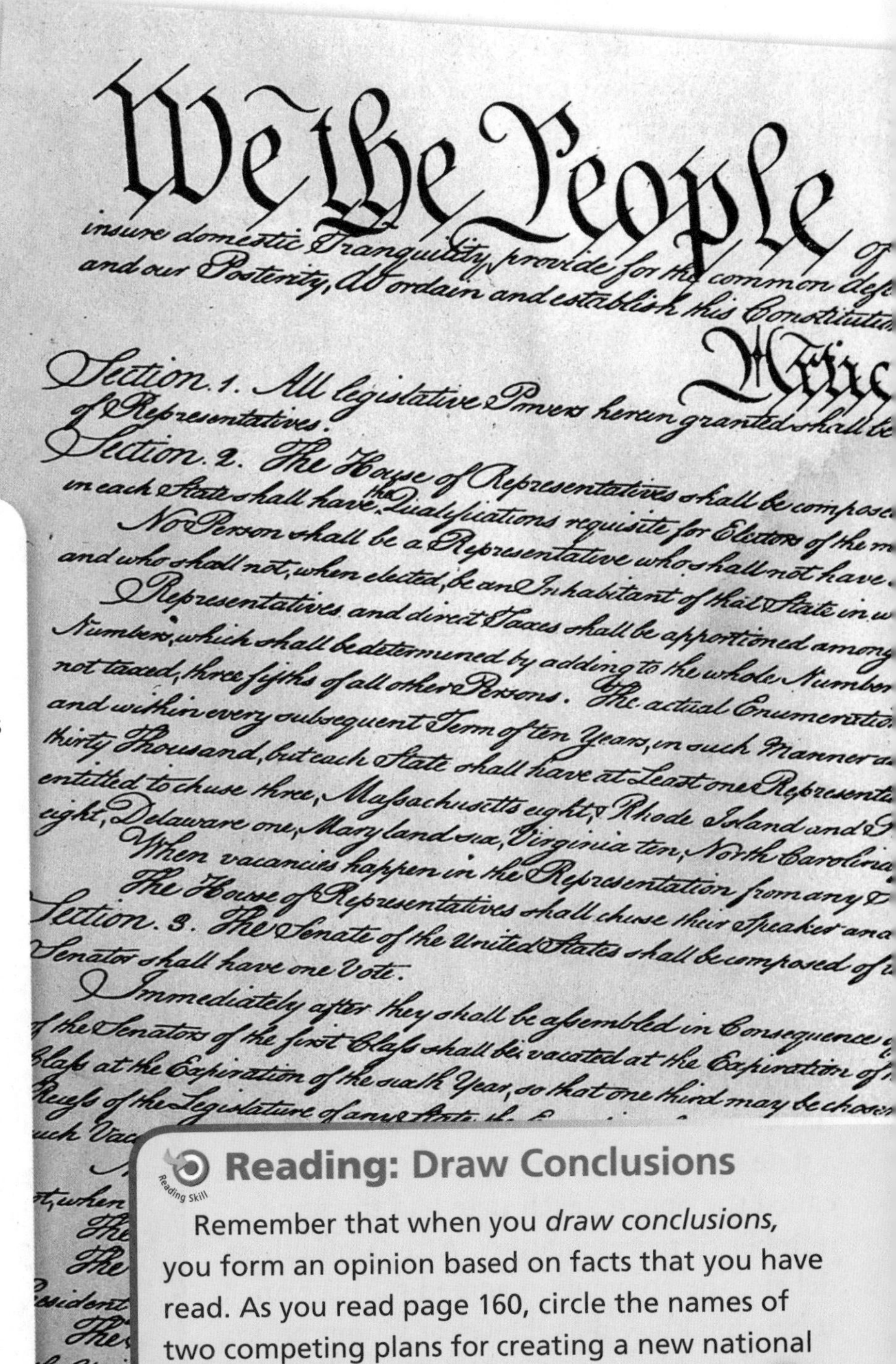

Preview the Lesson

Vocabulary

compromise *(n.)* a settlement of a disagreement in which each side agrees to give up part of its demands

Federalist *(n.)* a person who supported a strong national government and was in favor of adopting the Constitution

Antifederalist *(n.)* a person who opposed a strong national government

amendment *(n.)* a change or addition

Vocabulary Activity The prefix *anti-* means "against." When you use this prefix, you usually create an antonym, or a word that means the opposite of another. Circle the two words in the list above that are antonyms.

People

James Madison

Reading: Draw Conclusions

Reading Skill

Remember that when you *draw conclusions*, you form an opinion based on facts that you have read. As you read page 160, circle the names of two competing plans for creating a new national government.

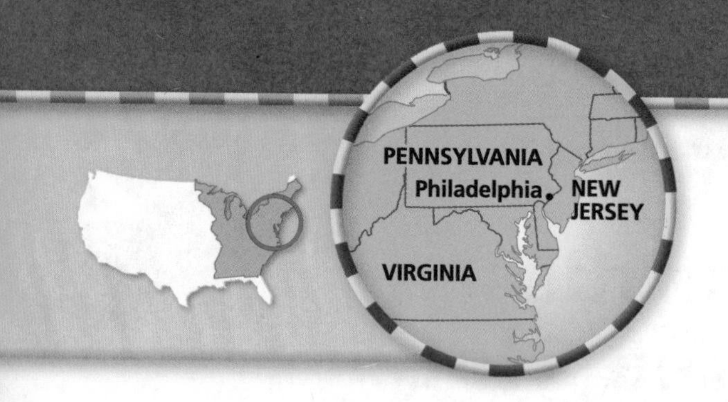

New Plans for a National Government

In May 1787, fifty-five delegates from throughout the United States met in Philadelphia, Pennsylvania. Their goal was to revise, or change, the Articles of Confederation. This meeting became known as the Constitutional Convention.

Most of the convention delegates wanted to create a stronger national government. However, they soon realized that to do so they would have to replace the Articles of Confederation rather than simply revise them. Delegates from Virginia suggested the Virginia Plan as a replacement for the Articles. This plan gave Congress greater power over the states. It also split Congress into two houses, or assemblies. The number of representatives a state had in each house of Congress would be based on its population.

Some delegates thought the Virginia Plan was unfair. They felt it gave states with many people more power because those states would have more representatives. These delegates proposed the New Jersey Plan. This plan created only one house in Congress in which each state had the same number of representatives.

To solve this disagreement, delegates came up with a compromise. A **compromise** is the settlement of a disagreement in which each side agrees to give up part of its demands. This new plan created a Congress with two houses. In one house, called the House of Representatives, the number of representatives was based on a state's population. In the other house, called the Senate, each state had the same number of representatives. After a month of debate, the convention agreed to this plan. It became known as the Great Compromise.

1. Draw Conclusions **Why did supporters of both the Virginia Plan and the New Jersey Plan agree to the Great Compromise?**

Delegates to the Constitutional Convention met behind closed doors and boarded windows so they could speak freely.

Debate over Enslaved People

Delegates also debated whether enslaved people should be counted as part of a state's population. States with many enslaved people wanted them counted. This would give these states more representatives in Congress. States with fewer enslaved people disagreed. Finally, delegates reached another compromise. Only three out of five enslaved people would be counted as part of a state's population. This solution became known as the Three-Fifths Compromise.

Ratifying the Constitution

After the convention, the new plan of government, called the Constitution, had to be ratified by the states before it could go into effect. **Federalists** supported a strong national government and wanted to ratify the Constitution. **Antifederalists** opposed a strong national government. They believed that it gave the government too much power and did not protect people's rights. Antifederalists wanted **amendments,** or changes and additions, made to the Constitution to list the rights of all citizens. The Federalists agreed to add this list at a later time, and in 1788 the Constitution was ratified. In 1791 Congress passed ten amendments that became known as the Bill of Rights.

Beginning in 1787, Federalists wrote a series of essays for New York newspapers in support of the Constitution. The essays were collected in a book called *The Federalist* in 1788.

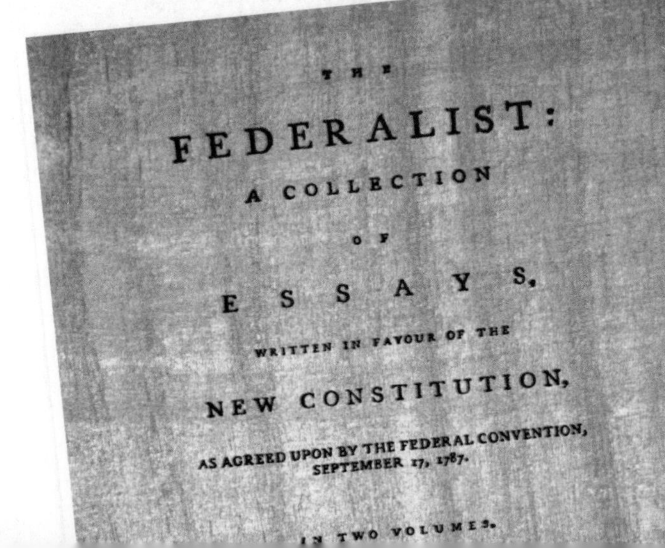
THE

FEDERALIST:

A COLLECTION

OF

ESSAYS,

WRITTEN IN FAVOUR OF THE

NEW CONSTITUTION,

AS AGREED UPON BY THE FEDERAL CONVENTION, SEPTEMBER 17, 1787.

IN TWO VOLUMES.

2. Why did some states want to count enslaved people as part of their population?
Main idea and Details

3. Underline the Antifederalists' concerns about the Constitution.
Main idea and Details

"If men were angels, no government would be necessary. If angels were to govern men, [no] . . . controls on government would be necessary."
— James Madison,
The Federalist: No. 51, 1788

Summary

At the Constitutional Convention, there were many debates about how to create a new central government. What compromises led to the creation and ratification of the U.S. Constitution?

Biography

James Madison, 1751–1836

Learn More James Madison was a small, soft-spoken man with big ideas and strong beliefs. Throughout his career in politics, he held many offices, including Secretary of State and President. However, he also made important contributions to our country by helping to write, ratify, and amend the Constitution.

During the 1787 Constitutional Convention, Madison kept a detailed daily journal of what the delegates said and did. Because the delegates met behind closed doors, Madison's journal helps us understand what actually happened at the convention. In 1787 and 1788, Madison wrote some of *The Federalist Papers*, along with Alexander Hamilton and John Jay. These essays helped convince the states to ratify the new Constitution. In 1789 Madison proposed twelve amendments to the Constitution. Ten of these amendments were ratified by 1791. They are known today as the Bill of Rights.

Read the quotation and then answer the questions below.

1. **Circle two offices that Madison held during his long career in politics.** *Identify*
2. **How do Madison's accomplishments still contribute to our country today?** *Analyze*

____

____

____

____

____

____

". . . the Union of so many States is, in the eyes of the world, a wonder; the harmonious establishment of a common Government over them all, a miracle."

— James Madison,
in a speech to the Virginia
state convention, 1829

Name:

H-SS 5.7.3 Understand the fundamental principles of American constitutional democracy, including how the government derives its power from the people and the primacy of individual liberty.

Lesson 3

What are the rights of U.S. citizens?

SET THE SCENE The writers of the Constitution created rules to guide the relationship between our country's citizens and their government. They made certain that the new government would protect citizens' freedoms and encourage them to become involved. What rights do U.S. citizens have? How are those rights protected?

Preview the Lesson

Vocabulary

Preamble *(n.)* the introduction of the U.S. Constitution

liberty *(n.)* the condition of being free

republic *(n.)* a form of government in which citizens elect representatives to make laws and run the government

principle *(n.)* a rule or idea

Vocabulary Activity Words that sound alike but do not have the same meaning are called homophones. A *principal* is the head of a school. Circle a homophone for *principal* in the list above.

Reading: Draw Conclusions

Reading Skill

When you *draw conclusions*, you use information in the text to help you make statements not directly stated in the text. As you read the first section on page 164, underline information that will help you state ideas about the importance of the introduction of the U.S. Constitution.

The Power of the People

The Constitution explains the rights of all U.S. citizens. These rights begin with the very first words in the Preamble. The **Preamble** is the introduction of the Constitution. It states that "We the People"—rather than a king, a queen, or any other kind of ruler—form the government. The Preamble also explains the purposes of the Constitution: to establish justice, to ensure peace, to defend the nation, and to protect the people's well-being and liberty. **Liberty** is the condition of being free.

1. Draw Conclusions **What is the importance of the Preamble to the Constitution?**

We the People of the United States, in Order to form a more perfect Union, establish Justice, insure domestic Tranquility, provide for the common defense, promote the general Welfare, and secure the Blessings of Liberty to ourselves and our Posterity, do ordain and establish this Constitution for the United States of America.

The Preamble to the Constitution states the role that people have in our government.

The Right to Vote

The Constitution says that citizens will form a government by electing representatives. This means that the United States is a republic. A **republic** is a form of government in which citizens elect representatives to make laws and run the government. The right to vote is one of the most important **principles,** or rules or ideas, in a republic. When citizens vote, they choose the person they feel will best represent them. If citizens feel that their representatives are not serving them well, they may vote for somebody else. Citizens vote to elect the President and members of both houses of Congress in the federal government.

2. **In a republic, how do citizens participate in government?** *Main Idea and Details*

The Bill of Rights

As you have learned, after the Constitutional Convention, the Federalists agreed to add a list of amendments to the Constitution. The Bill of Rights is the first ten amendments to the Constitution. It lists the rights that are guaranteed to all U.S. citizens.

The writers of the Bill of Rights believed in the importance of fairness. They remembered how the British government had treated the colonists in the years before the American Revolution. The British passed laws and collected taxes that attempted to control what the colonists could do, but they did not give the colonists a voice in the government. When the colonists protested, Britain sent soldiers rather than listen to the colonists' complaints.

The amendments in the Bill of Rights make sure that the government respects the liberty of individual people. The First Amendment guarantees the freedom of religion, speech, and the press. It also says that people may gather peacefully to discuss issues. Citizens may petition, or formally ask, the government to correct something that is wrong. This means that people can express their ideas freely, even if they do not agree with the government. Other amendments give people who are accused of a crime the right to a "speedy and public trial" by jury. A jury is a group of citizens who decide the outcome of a trial. People and their belongings are also protected against "unreasonable searches and seizures" by the government. This means that officials must have a good reason for looking through or taking away a citizen's property. The freedoms listed in the Bill of Rights and in other amendments apply to all U.S. citizens.

3. Draw Conclusions **Underline details in the second paragraph that help you draw the conclusion that Britain treated the colonists unfairly.**

The Bill of Rights secures citizens' right to practice religion, to speak and write freely, and to have a fair trial.

Summary

The Constitution protects the rights of all U.S. citizens. Describe some ways in which the Bill of Rights affects the lives of citizens of the United States.

Citizenship

Amending the Constitution

Learn More The U.S. Constitution has been called a "living document" because it can be changed to reflect new ideas about individual rights and the role of government. However, amendments to the Constitution are added only after a long process. That is why thousands of amendments have been suggested, but only twenty-seven have been officially approved.

So far, every amendment has passed in the same way: two-thirds of the members of both houses of Congress must vote to propose, or suggest, the amendment. After that, an amendment must be ratified by three-fourths of the state legislatures. The chart below lists some important amendments about citizens' rights that have been added over time. Look at the chart and then answer the questions.

Key Amendments to the U.S. Constitution

Amendment	Purpose	Ratified
Thirteen	Outlawed slavery	1865
Fourteen	Guaranteed equal rights for all U.S. citizens	1868
Fifteen	Gave all men the right to vote	1870
Nineteen	Gave women the right to vote	1920
Twenty-six	Lowered the voting age to eighteen	1971

1. **Three amendments have a similar purpose. Circle the word in each that shows the similarity.** *Analyze*
2. **Why do you think so few suggested amendments have been ratified?** *Evaluate*

____

____

____

____

____

____

Name:

H-SS 5.7.4 Understand how the Constitution is designed to secure our liberty by both empowering and limiting central government and compare the powers granted to citizens, Congress, the president, and the Supreme Court with those reserved to the states.

Lesson 4

What is the role of government?

SET THE SCENE What kind of rules do you have at home? How are decisions made? The U.S. Constitution defines the rules and roles for each part of our nation's government. How do the different parts and levels of government work together?

Preview the Lesson

Vocabulary

legislative branch *(n.)* the part of government that writes and passes laws

Congress *(n.)* the Senate and the House of Representatives

executive branch *(n.)* the part of government that carries out laws

veto *(v.)* to reject a bill or law

judicial branch *(n.)* the part of government that interprets and applies laws

federalism *(n.)* a system in which the national government and the states share power

Vocabulary Activity The root word *legis* means "law." Circle the vocabulary word above that has this word as its root. How does knowing the meaning of *legis* help you understand the word's meaning?

____

____

Reading: Main Idea and Details

The *main idea* is the most important idea of a paragraph. Writers often state the main idea in a topic sentence. As you read the first section on page 168, underline the topic sentence, which gives you the main idea about the powers of the federal government.

A Balanced Government

The framers of the Constitution did not want the federal government to become too powerful. So they created three branches, or parts, of government, no one of which can have complete control. How does this work? Each branch of government has different powers and responsibilities. This is called the "separation of powers." However, the branches also work together by means of a system of "checks and balances." This system gives each branch the power to check, or block, some of the decisions made by other branches.

1. Why did the framers create a federal government with three different branches?

Main Idea and Details

Three Branches of Government

The Constitution explains the powers held by each of the three branches of government. The **legislative branch** writes and passes laws. This branch is called **Congress,** and it is made up of the Senate and the House of Representatives. The **executive branch** carries out laws passed by Congress. The President is the head of the executive branch. The President cannot make laws but he can **veto,** or reject, laws passed by Congress. Congress can overrule the President's veto if two-thirds of Congress agrees. The **judicial branch** interprets and applies the laws. The Supreme Court heads this branch. If the justices, or judges, on the Supreme Court decide that a law is against the Constitution, they can overturn it. This means that the law no longer has to be followed.

2. What check does Congress have on the powers of the President?

Main Idea and Details

The Federal Government

Executive Branch

President

Elected to serve no more than two 4-year terms

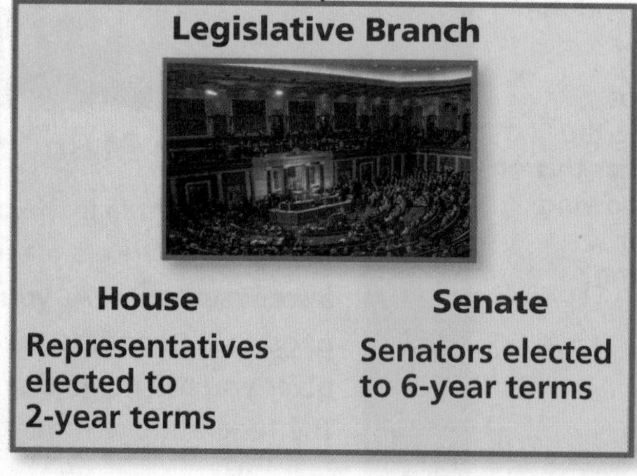

Legislative Branch

House

Representatives elected to 2-year terms

Senate

Senators elected to 6-year terms

Judicial Branch

Supreme Court

Justices appointed by President to serve life terms

State and Federal Government

The United States has a form of government called federalism. **Federalism** is a system in which the national government and the states share power. The federal, or national, government has powers that the state governments do not have. For example, only the federal government can declare war, print money, and control foreign trade. But state governments have powers too. They run public schools and control business within the state. Both federal and state governments share some powers, such as collecting taxes. The Tenth Amendment to the Constitution states that any powers not specifically given to the federal government belong to the states and to the people.

3. Draw Conclusions **How are the powers of the states preserved in the Constitution?**

The Role of Citizens in Government

What powers do U.S. citizens have in our government? It could be said that citizens provide the final check over all three branches of government. This is because citizens have the power to decide who will represent them in the government. They use this power when they vote for the candidates who run for elected positions in the government. When citizens vote, they choose the candidate they feel will best represent their views. That is why voting is an important responsibility of being a citizen.

4. **Underline the sentence that explains how U.S. citizens provide the final check over our government.** *Main Idea and Details*

Citizens play an important role in our state and federal governments by registering, or signing up, to vote.

Summary

The separation of powers keeps any one branch or level of government from becoming too powerful through a system of checks and balances. How do the different branches and levels of government work together?

Skill

Flow Charts

Learn More The Constitution limits the powers of the three branches of government with a system of checks and balances. The flow chart below shows how this system works. Arrows that point away from a branch represent checks that it has on the other branches. Arrows pointing toward a branch represent checks on its power from the other branches. Notice that the powers of each branch are checked in some way by the other branches. Use the flow chart to answer the questions below.

Try It

1. **Circle the branch that has the power to appoint Supreme Court judges.** *Identify*
2. **Place a check mark next to the branch with the power to refuse appointments to the Supreme Court.** *Identify*
3. **Place stars next to the checks the Judicial Branch has on the other branches' powers to write and carry out laws.** *Apply*
4. **Explain what might happen if the Supreme Court did not have the power to check the other two branches.** *Explain*

____

____

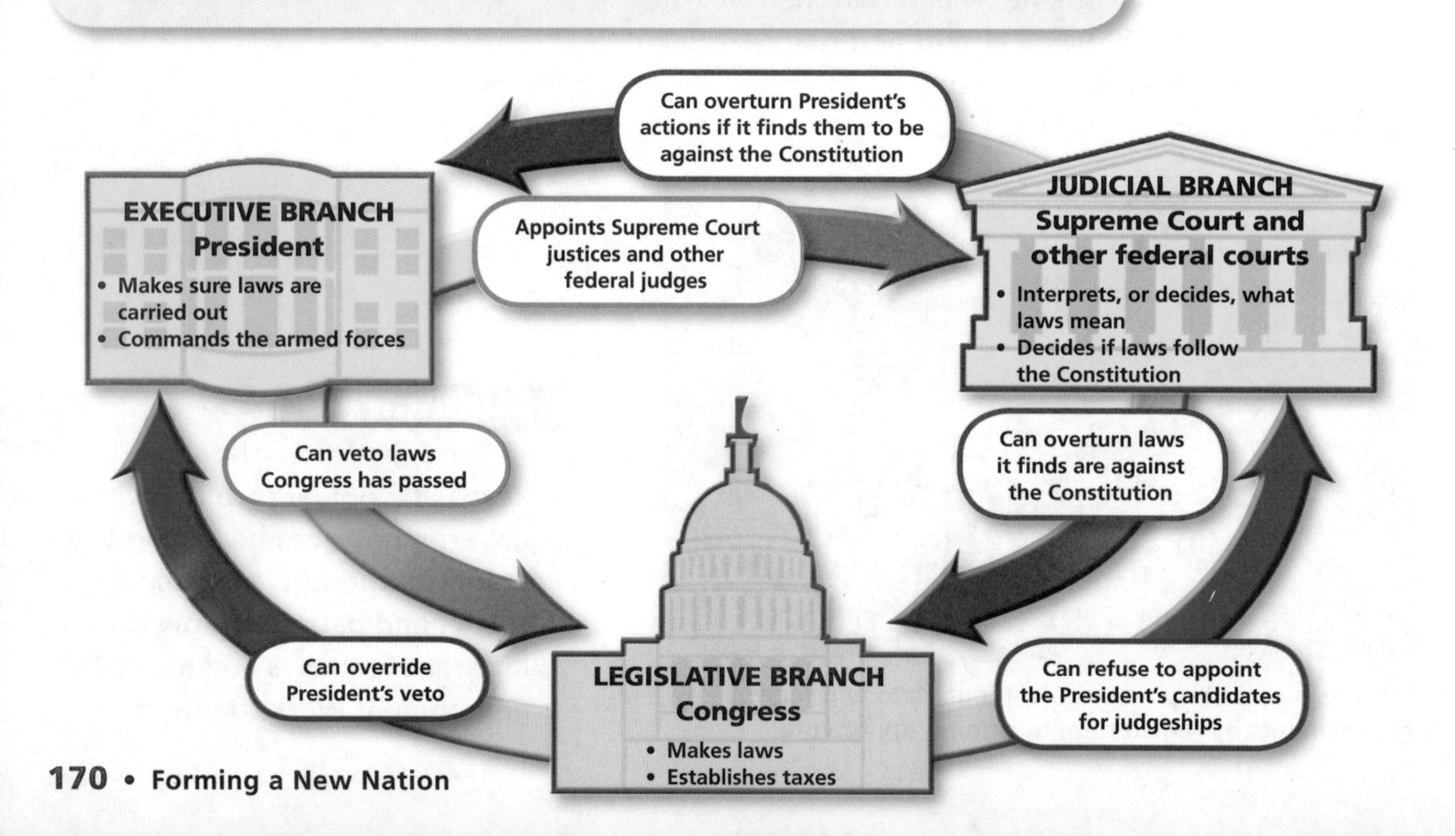

Name:

H-SS 5.7.5 Discuss the meaning of the American creed that calls on citizens to safeguard the liberty of individual Americans within a unified nation, to respect the rule of law, and to preserve the Constitution.

Lesson 5

How do citizens help protect liberty?

Preview the Lesson

Vocabulary

suffrage *(n.)* the right to vote

safeguard *(v.)* to protect

Vocabulary Activity A *compound word* is a word created by combining two or more words. Draw a vertical line between the two word parts that make up the word *safeguard*. How does knowing the meanings of those two word parts help you understand the meaning of *safeguard*?

People

Susan B. Anthony
Elizabeth Cady Stanton
Martin Luther King, Jr.

SET THE SCENE You have learned that the federal government receives its power from the Constitution and the citizens of the United States. This means that citizens have rights. However, they also have responsibilities. How can we, as citizens, help preserve liberty and promote justice for all?

Reading: Draw Conclusions

Reading Skill

Remember that when you *draw conclusions*, you form an opinion based on information you have read. As you read the first section on page 172, underline details that help you draw a conclusion about the responsibilities of citizens.

The Responsibilities of Citizens

All U.S. citizens have important responsibilities to their country. The right to vote gives citizens a voice in our country's government. At age eighteen, citizens can register to vote. In order to be an educated voter, it is important to learn about the candidates and discuss the issues. Citizens also have the responsibility to pay taxes. The government raises the money it needs from taxes. By carrying out their responsibilities, citizens help preserve their individual rights and the system of government set up by the Constitution.

1. Draw Conclusions **Why is it important for people to carry out their responsibilities as U.S. citizens?**

Citizens and Laws

Laws provide for the safety and protection of every citizen. Citizens have the responsibility to uphold, or support, these laws for the well-being of all. For example, each citizen must serve on juries when called to do so. However, people also have the right to protest laws they think are unfair. Sometimes people hold demonstrations, or gatherings, to show they disagree with a law. Citizens can also contact elected officials to express their views. One way to do this is by writing or signing petitions.

2. How can citizens protest against laws they think are unfair?
Main Idea and Details

Citizens help enforce laws by serving on juries (*left*). Signing petitions is one way citizens can work to create new laws or change laws they think are unfair (*below*).

Elizabeth Cady Stanton (*left*) and Susan B. Anthony (*right*) worked to gain the right to vote for women.

Citizens Work for Reform

The power of citizens to call for reform, or change, can been seen throughout our nation's history. In the 1830s, a spirit of reform swept the United States. Some reformers focused on improving public education. Others worked to end slavery. Susan B. Anthony and Elizabeth Cady Stanton led the women's suffrage movement. **Suffrage** is the right to vote. These reforms often required many years of effort. Women finally won the right to vote in all elections when the Nineteenth Amendment to the Constitution was passed in 1920.

In the 1950s and 1960s, the Civil Rights movement helped bring equal rights to African Americans. Even though slavery ended by law in 1865, many African Americans were not treated equally. Certain laws, especially in the South, made it difficult for them to vote. Laws also established separate schools for African Americans and unfair rules for using public services.

Dr. Martin Luther King, Jr., was an important leader of the Civil Rights movement. In 1956, after a year-long boycott, Dr. King forced Montgomery, Alabama, to offer the same public services to all people. In 1963 Dr. King helped organize a huge gathering in Washington, D.C. Its purpose was to push for equal rights for all people, as guaranteed by the Constitution. Congress finally passed the Civil Rights Act of 1964, which made it illegal to treat people differently based on race, color, religion, or national origin. The actions of Dr. King and other reformers show how individual citizens can help **safeguard**, or protect, the liberty of all Americans.

3. Underline two things Dr. Martin Luther King, Jr., did to win equal rights for all Americans.
Main Idea and Details

In 1965 Dr. Martin Luther King, Jr., *(center)* led a march to call for voting reforms for African Americans.

Summary

U.S. citizens have important responsibilities to their country. What are some ways in which citizens can help preserve the Constitution, respect the rule of law, and safeguard liberty?

Citizenship

The Seneca Falls Convention

Learn More Good citizens work to safeguard the rights of all Americans. One way we can do this is to express our thoughts and feelings when we think laws are unfair. Suffrage is one of the most important rights of any citizen, yet women did not always have the right to vote. In July 1848, a group of women and men gathered in Seneca Falls, New York, at the first women's rights convention in the United States. Elizabeth Cady Stanton, one of the organizers, presented her "Declaration of Sentiments." The declaration was modeled after the Declaration of Independence. In it she stated that women should work to obtain the right to vote. Sixty-eight women and thirty-two men signed the Declaration of Sentiments. They were citizens who were willing to take action to protect the rights of all people.

Read the excerpts and answer the questions below.

1. **Circle the two words in the Declaration of Sentiments that do not appear in the Declaration of Independence.** *Identify*

2. **Why do you think Stanton modeled her document after the Declaration of Independence?** *Analyze*

____

____

____

____

____

____

"We hold these truths to be self-evident, that all men are created equal, that they are endowed by their Creator with certain unalienable rights, that among these are Life, Liberty and the pursuit of Happiness."

— Declaration of Independence, 1776

"We hold these truths to be self-evident: that all men and women are created equal; that they are endowed by their Creator with certain inalienable rights; that among these are life, liberty, and the pursuit of happiness. . . ."

— Declaration of Sentiments, 1848

Name:

H-SS 5.7.6 Know the songs that express American ideals (e.g., "America the Beautiful," "The Star Spangled Banner").

Lesson 6

How does music express American ideals?

SET THE SCENE As you have learned, the United States stands for freedom and equal rights for all. One way to demonstrate these ideals is through music. Today, Americans enjoy many songs that reflect their love for their country and its ideals.

Preview the Lesson

Vocabulary

patriotic *(adj.)* showing support for one's country

national anthem *(n.)* the official song of a nation

Vocabulary Activity The suffix *-ic* means "having the character of." Circle the suffix *-ic* in a word above. Then underline the root word.

People

Francis Scott Key

Reading: Main Idea and Details

Remember, writers often use a topic sentence to express the main idea in a paragraph. As you read the first section on page 176, underline the topic sentence in each paragraph.

Songs That Show National Pride

Americans are **patriotic,** or show support for their country, in many ways. One way Americans show that they are patriotic is through music. Patriotic songs allow us to show our support and love for the United States. In some songs, we sing about the ideals on which our country was founded, such as liberty, justice, and equal rights. In others, we sing about our country's history and natural beauty.

The United States has a rich collection of patriotic songs, many of which you may know. "Hail to the Chief" honors our President. Do you know the song that begins, "My country, 'tis of thee/Sweet land of liberty"? It is Samuel Francis Smith's "America," which praises the freedoms of the United States.

One popular patriotic song describes the natural beauty of our country. In 1893 a teacher named Katharine Lee Bates visited Colorado. Near the top of a mountain peak, she looked around at "the wonder of America" and was inspired to write the poem "America the Beautiful." Her poem was later set to music.

1. What are two ways patriotic songs allow us to show our love of our country?
Main Idea and Details

America the Beautiful

O beautiful for spacious skies,
For amber waves of grain.
For purple mountain majesties
Above the fruited plain!
America! America!
God shed his grace on thee
And crown thy good with brotherhood
From sea to shining sea!

Americans sing patriotic songs to express their love and support for our country.

1875	1900	1925	1950

1893

____

____

1931 "The Star Spangled Banner" becomes the national anthem of the United States.

"The Star Spangled Banner"

Times of struggle have also inspired patriotic songs. Francis Scott Key wrote the words to "The Star Spangled Banner" during the War of 1812. One night, Key witnessed a British attack on Fort McHenry, near Baltimore, Maryland. During the attack, the sky was filled with British "bombs bursting in air." Yet, the next morning, Key saw the American flag still flying above the fort. He wrote a poem to describe what he had seen. This poem was later set to music. In 1931 Congress made "The Star Spangled Banner" our **national anthem,** or official song of the nation.

The Star Spangled Banner

Oh, say can you see by the dawn's early light
What so proudly we hail'd at the twilight's last gleaming?
Whose broad stripes and bright stars through the perilous fight
O'er the ramparts we watch'd were so gallantly streaming!
And the rockets' red glare, the bombs bursting in air,
Gave proof through the night that our flag was still there.
Oh, say does that star spangled banner yet wave
O'er the land of the free and the home of the brave?

2. Draw Conclusions **In what ways does "The Star Spangled Banner" express American ideals?**

____

____

____

____

Francis Scott Key wrote the poem "The Star Spangled Banner" after he saw the American flag still flying after a fierce battle.

Summary

Patriotic songs express many American ideals. What are some of the ideals we can sing about?

The New Colossus

Learn More In 1875 the building of the Statue of Liberty, a gift to the United States, began in France. The statue symbolized the two countries' friendship and belief in liberty. In 1883 poet Emma Lazarus wrote "The New Colossus" to help raise money to build the statue's pedestal, or base, on an island in New York City's harbor. The poem is a sonnet, or a rhyming poem of fourteen lines. The *colossus* in the title refers to a large statue that stood in the harbor of an ancient Greek island.

In 1903 a plaque with "The New Colossus" was added to the statue's pedestal. This poem gave new meaning to the Statue of Liberty. It described the United States as a place where people from around the world could come to start a new life of freedom. Because of Lazarus's poem, the statue gained new meaning as a symbol for the many immigrants who entered the United States through New York City.

Read the poem's last lines and then answer the questions.

1. **Circle the words in the poem that describe the hopes of people who come to America.** Identify
2. **Why do you think Lazarus wrote the poem from the point of view of the Statue of Liberty, using words such as *I* and *me*?** Interpret

____

____

____

____

____

____

". . . Give me your tired, your poor,
Your huddled masses yearning to breathe free,
The wretched refuse of your teeming shore,
Send these, the homeless, tempest-tossed to me,
I lift my lamp beside the golden door!"

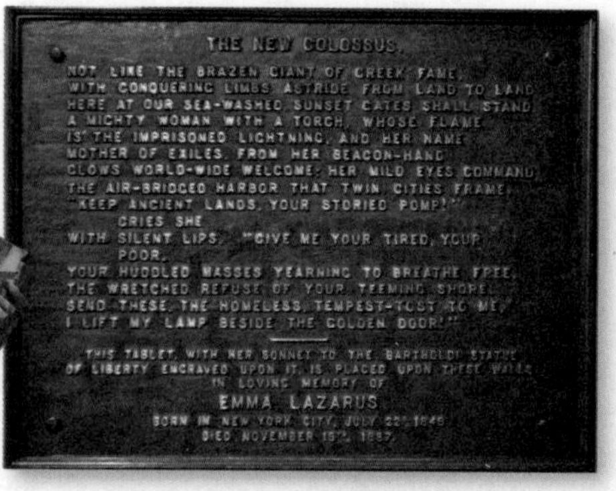

Name:

Unit 8

Study Journal

In this unit you will learn about the western expansion of the United States from 1789 to 1850. You will understand how geography, transportation systems, and economics affected how and why people traveled west. Complete the activities on these pages as you read the unit.

What I know about . . .

western expansion of the United States:

Western Expansion, 1800s

Enter information for each event below:

Lewis and Clark Expedition—Years:

People:

Effect:

Texas Revolution—Years:

People:

Effect:

Mexican-American War—Years:

People:

Effect:

Complete these sections as you read the unit.

Write a paragraph about westward expansion using the following vocabulary words:

- overland
- pioneer
- resourceful
- terrain

Choose a trail from the list below and then answer the questions.

- California Trail
- Mormon Trail
- Oregon Trail
- Old Spanish Trail

Trail:

Who traveled on the trail?

What factors pulled people west?

Fill the time line below with the correct events.

I have learned . . .

Name:

H-SS 5.8.1 Discuss the waves of immigrants from Europe between 1789 and 1850 and their modes of transportation into the Ohio and Mississippi Valleys and through the Cumberland Gap (e.g., overland wagons, canals, flatboats, steamboats).

Lesson 1

How did people reach lands west of the Appalachians?

SET THE SCENE Would you cross tall mountains in a horse-drawn wagon? Would you travel down long rivers in a small boat? Between 1789 and 1850, many people made choices such as these as they traveled into western lands. Why would they take such risks?

Preview the Lesson

Vocabulary

immigrant *(n.)* a person who comes to a country from another country

overland *(adj.)* a route across land

terrain *(n.)* the physical characteristics of an area of land

pioneer *(n.)* an early settler of a region

steamboat *(n.)* a boat that moves by the power of a steam engine

canal *(n.)* a human-made waterway

flatboat *(n.)* a boat with a flat bottom for transporting heavy loads on canals

Vocabulary Activity A *compound word* is a word made up of two or more words. Knowing the meanings of each word in a compound word can help you predict its meaning. Draw a line separating the word parts in three compound words above.

People

Daniel Boone

Reading: Compare and Contrast

Reading Skill

To *compare* is to show how two or more things are similar. To *contrast* is to show how they are different. In the first section on page 182, underline the sentences that compare and contrast the reasons Americans moved west.

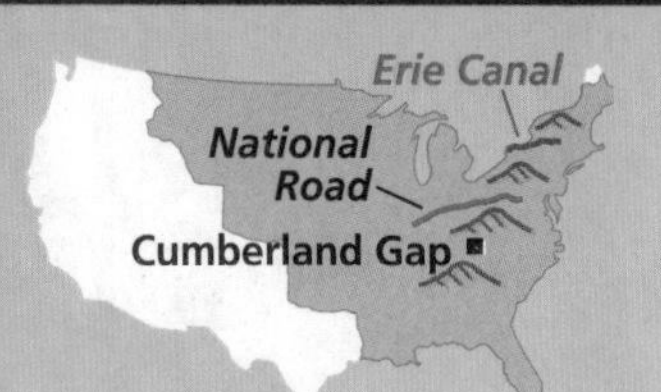

1775 Pioneers begin moving west through the Cumberland Gap.

1783 The Treaty of Paris is signed.

The Nation Grows

As you have learned, the 1783 Treaty of Paris ended the American Revolution and added new land to the United States. This land stretched west from the Appalachian Mountains to the Mississippi River. Americans had been eager to move into this land for some time. Now they could finally do so.

Many Americans moved west in the 1800s. They did so for reasons called push factors and pull factors. Push factors drive people away from a place. Poverty, disease, and crowded cities in the East pushed people to leave their homes. Pull factors draw people to new areas. Cheap land that was good for farming and other natural resources pulled many settlers west.

1. Compare and Contrast **How were push factors and pull factors in the 1800s similar? How were they different?**

Immigrants Move West

Meanwhile, waves of European immigrants began arriving in the United States. An **immigrant** is a person who comes to a country from another country. Immigrants from Europe also wanted a better life. People from Britain came here looking for jobs and religious freedom. Irish immigrants came after a crop failure caused the Irish Potato Famine, which left many people in Ireland hungry. Political problems caused many Germans to leave their country for the United States. Between 1800 and 1850, nearly 3 million European immigrants came to the United States.

2. Compare and Contrast **In the text, underline a reason for coming to the United States that immigrants shared. Place check marks next to reasons that were different.**

In the 1700s, an army officer called the Ohio River Valley "the most healthy, the most pleasant . . . spot of earth. . . ."

1800 | 1815 | 1830

1811

1825 The Erie Canal is completed.

New Routes to the West

At first, routes leading west into the Ohio and Mississippi River Valleys along **overland** paths, or routes across land, were poor. The **terrain,** or physical characteristics of the land, included thick forests and tall mountains. This made travel by wagon difficult. Most people had to travel by foot or on horses, which was slow and tiring.

Pioneers began building roads to make travel easier. A **pioneer** is an early settler of a region. Roads let people in wagons travel faster and in larger groups. As early as 1775, Daniel Boone and other pioneers began creating a trail that would become known as the Wilderness Road. It ran on a stretch of flat land between the Appalachians called the Cumberland Gap, in Kentucky. In 1811 the U.S. government began building the National Road. Eventually this road ran from Maryland to Illinois.

Travel on roads still was not easy, so people looked for new ways to travel. Improvements in technology made travel by water faster and easier. **Steamboats,** or boats moved by the power of a steam engine, could carry more people and supplies than earlier boats. **Canals,** or human-made waterways, such as the Erie Canal in New York, allowed many settlers to travel west. Travel also improved with the invention of **flatboats,** or boats with flat bottoms for transporting heavy loads on canals.

3. In the text, circle the names of the land and water routes that improved westward travel.

Cause and Effect

The 363-mile Erie Canal in New York connected the Hudson River and Lake Erie.

Summary

More land, push and pull factors in the United States and Europe, and improvements in technology caused many people to migrate west. Use details to describe why and how people moved west during the 1800s.

Skill

Bar Graphs

Learn More A bar graph can be used to compare amounts and show change over time. The bar graph below shows the number of people born in other parts of the world who lived in the United States in 1900 and 2000. This kind of graph makes it possible for you to see, at a glance, that the number of immigrants from different parts of the world changed during the century. The growing diversity of immigrants coming to the United States has contributed to the increase in ethnic groups, languages, customs, and religions found in the country today. Use the graph to answer the questions about changes in the foreign-born population of the United States during the last century.

Try It

1. On the graph, circle the number closest to the amount of foreign-born people from Asia in 2000. *Identify*
2. Underline the name of the region where most foreign-born people came from in 2000. *Apply*
3. Place a check mark by the region that had fewer of its people living here in 2000 than in 1900. *Apply*
4. About how many foreign-born people were living in the United States in 2000? *Analyze*

____

____

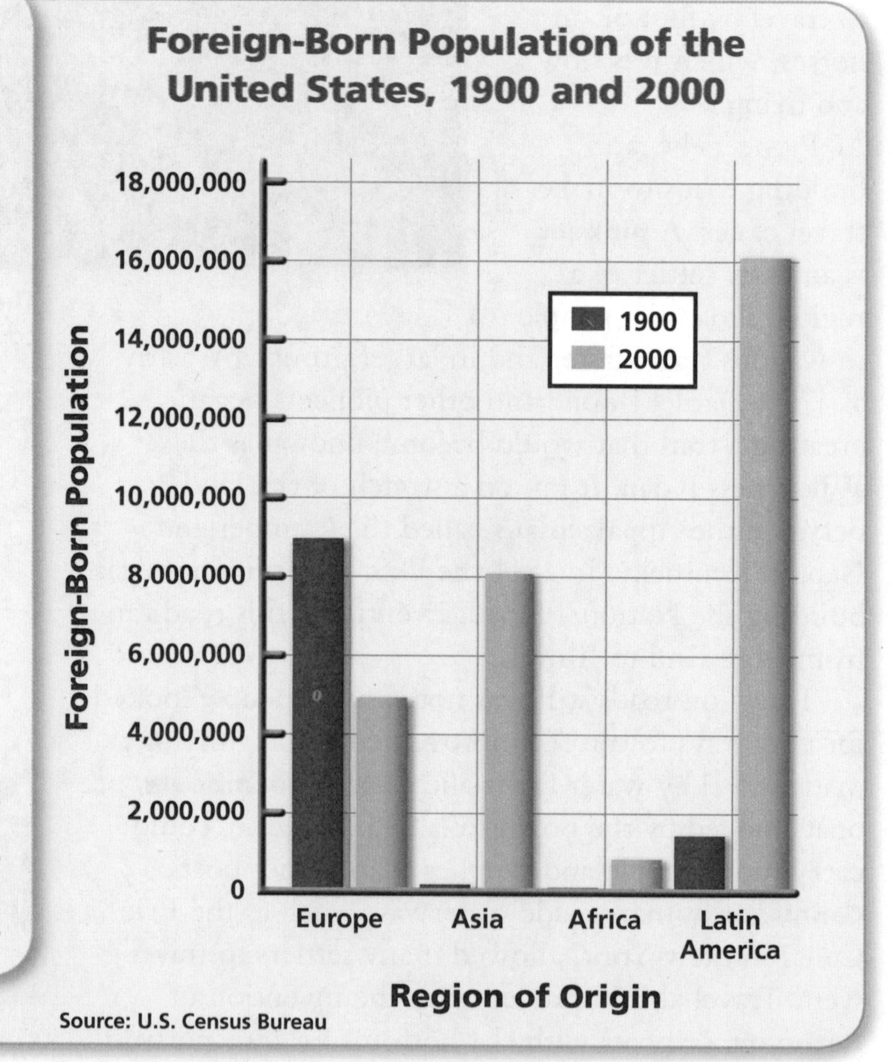

Name:

H-SS 5.8.2 Name the states and territories that existed in 1850 and identify their locations and major geographical features (e.g., mountain ranges, principal rivers, dominant plant regions).

Lesson 2

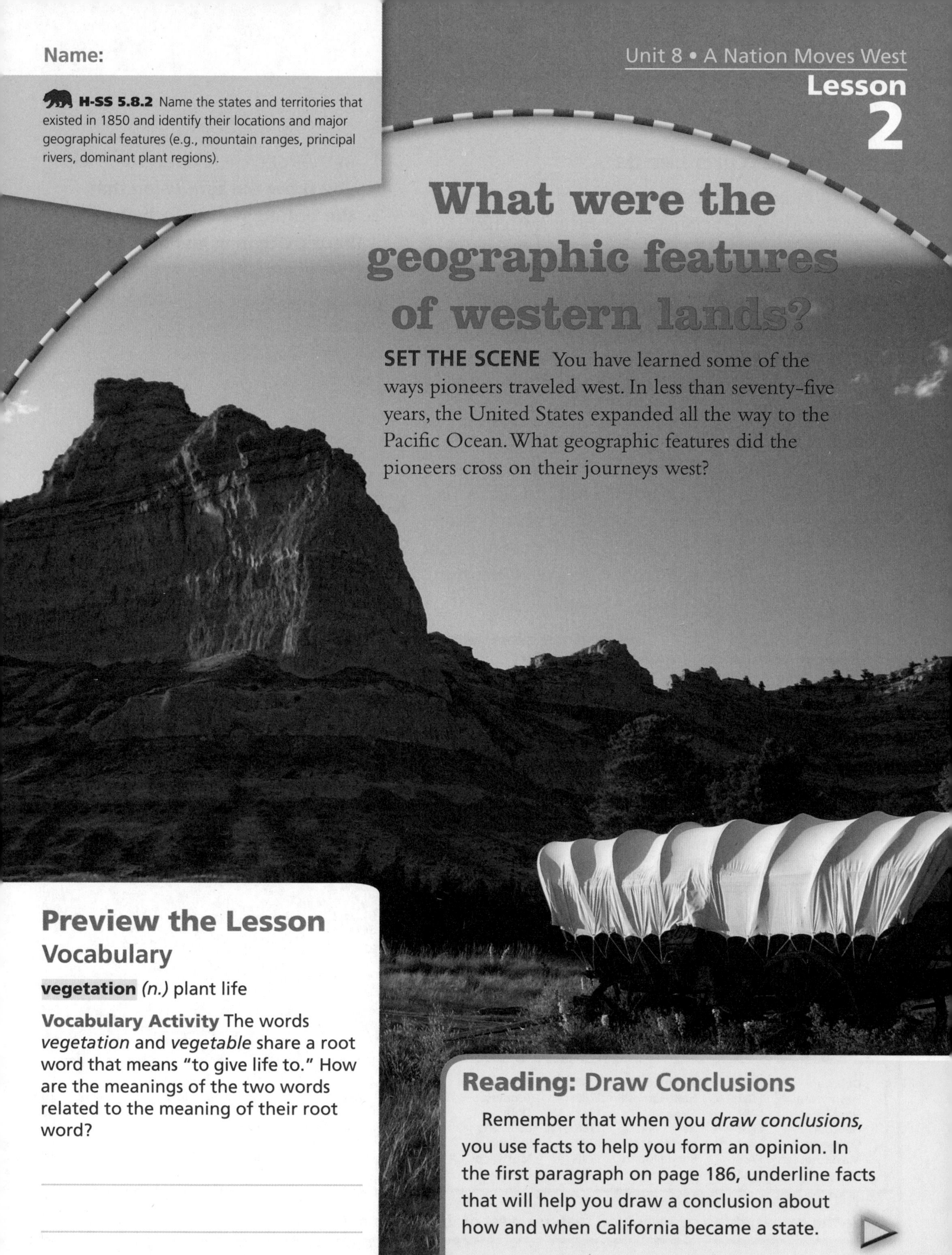

What were the geographic features of western lands?

SET THE SCENE You have learned some of the ways pioneers traveled west. In less than seventy-five years, the United States expanded all the way to the Pacific Ocean. What geographic features did the pioneers cross on their journeys west?

Preview the Lesson

Vocabulary

vegetation *(n.)* plant life

Vocabulary Activity The words *vegetation* and *vegetable* share a root word that means "to give life to." How are the meanings of the two words related to the meaning of their root word?

____

____

Reading: Draw Conclusions

Remember that when you *draw conclusions,* you use facts to help you form an opinion. In the first paragraph on page 186, underline facts that will help you draw a conclusion about how and when California became a state.

Gaining Western Lands

The United States expanded into the far West in the 1800s. These new lands were either purchased, won in wars, or gained in treaties with other countries. For example, in 1803 the U.S. government bought a large area of land west of the Mississippi River from France. The Louisiana Purchase, as it was called, doubled the size of the United States. A treaty with Britain in 1846 added the Oregon Territory, which was the first land that the United States controlled along the Pacific Ocean. In 1848 the United States defeated Mexico in a war and gained most of the Southwest, including land in California. Some parts of these territories quickly became states. In 1850 California became the thirty-first state, only two years after it was won from Mexico. It was the first state to border the Pacific Ocean.

1. In the text, circle dates that help you draw the conclusion that the United States reached to the Pacific Ocean in less than seventy-five years. *Draw Conclusions*

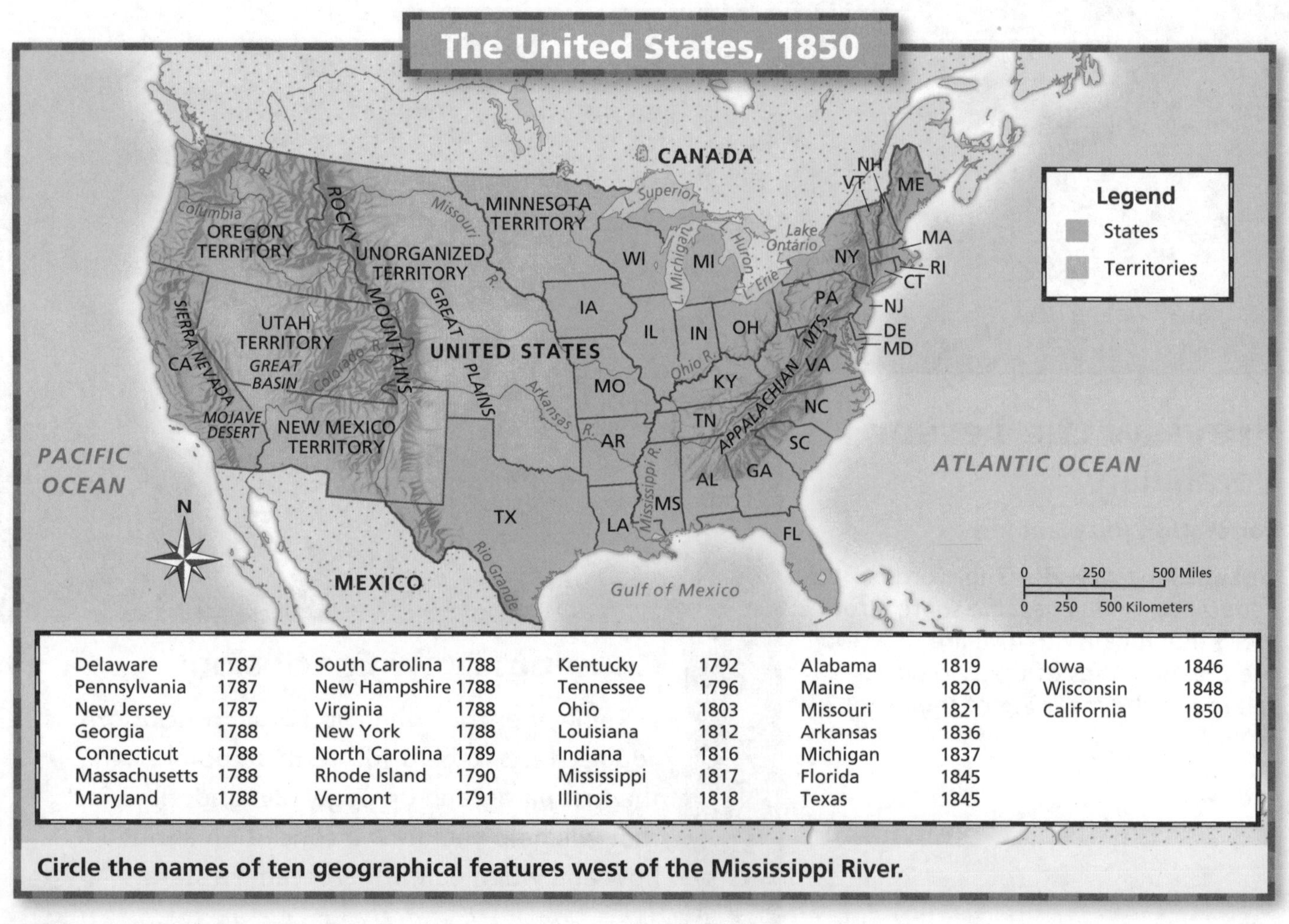

Delaware	1787	South Carolina	1788	Kentucky	1792	Alabama	1819	Iowa	1846
Pennsylvania	1787	New Hampshire	1788	Tennessee	1796	Maine	1820	Wisconsin	1848
New Jersey	1787	Virginia	1788	Ohio	1803	Missouri	1821	California	1850
Georgia	1788	New York	1788	Louisiana	1812	Arkansas	1836		
Connecticut	1788	North Carolina	1789	Indiana	1816	Michigan	1837		
Massachusetts	1788	Rhode Island	1790	Mississippi	1817	Florida	1845		
Maryland	1788	Vermont	1791	Illinois	1818	Texas	1845		

Circle the names of ten geographical features west of the Mississippi River.

Pioneers on their way to the Oregon Territory faced many challenges, including crossing rivers.

A Variety of Landscapes

As pioneers made their way west, they came across a wide variety of geographic features and **vegetation,** or plant life. The first region that pioneers came to after crossing the Mississippi River is called the Great Plains. This region is a large, generally flat grassland that stretches north from Texas to Canada. To the west of the Great Plains, the Rocky Mountains rise high above the landscape. Pioneers could cross the Rockies through passes, or relatively flat areas between mountains. Beyond the Rockies, the rich forests of the Oregon Territory lay to the north. Farther south there is a dry, flat area with little vegetation called the Great Basin. Pioneers who continued west to California had two choices. They could cross the Sierra Nevada in the north and central part of the area, or they could cross the Mojave Desert.

Because western terrain made travel difficult, many settlers traveled on or near rivers. The Missouri and Colorado Rivers supplied water for cooking, cleaning, and drinking. Also, settlers could transport cargo more easily on water than over land.

2. Circle the names of two mountain ranges that pioneers may have crossed on their way to California.
Main Idea and Details

Summary

By the 1850s, the United States reached to the Pacific Ocean. However, the geography of the West could make travel difficult. Describe the geography and vegetation that pioneers encountered as they made their way west.

Skill

Physical Maps

Learn More A physical map shows geographical features such as mountains and rivers. Color is used to show vegetation. The map below is a physical map of the western United States. In the 1800s, thousands of pioneers began traveling across the continent to settle in the West. Use the map to answer the questions below.

Try It

1. **Circle the first mountain range pioneers faced after crossing the Great Plains.** *Identify*

2. **Circle the part of the legend that describes vegetation in the Mojave Desert.** *Interpret*

3. **Locate where the Missouri and Mississippi Rivers meet. Draw a straight line west from that point to the Pacific Ocean. What geographical features does this line go through?** *Analyze*

____

____

____

4. **Draw an arrow along connecting rivers that pioneers might have followed from the Rocky Mountains to the Pacific Ocean.** *Apply*

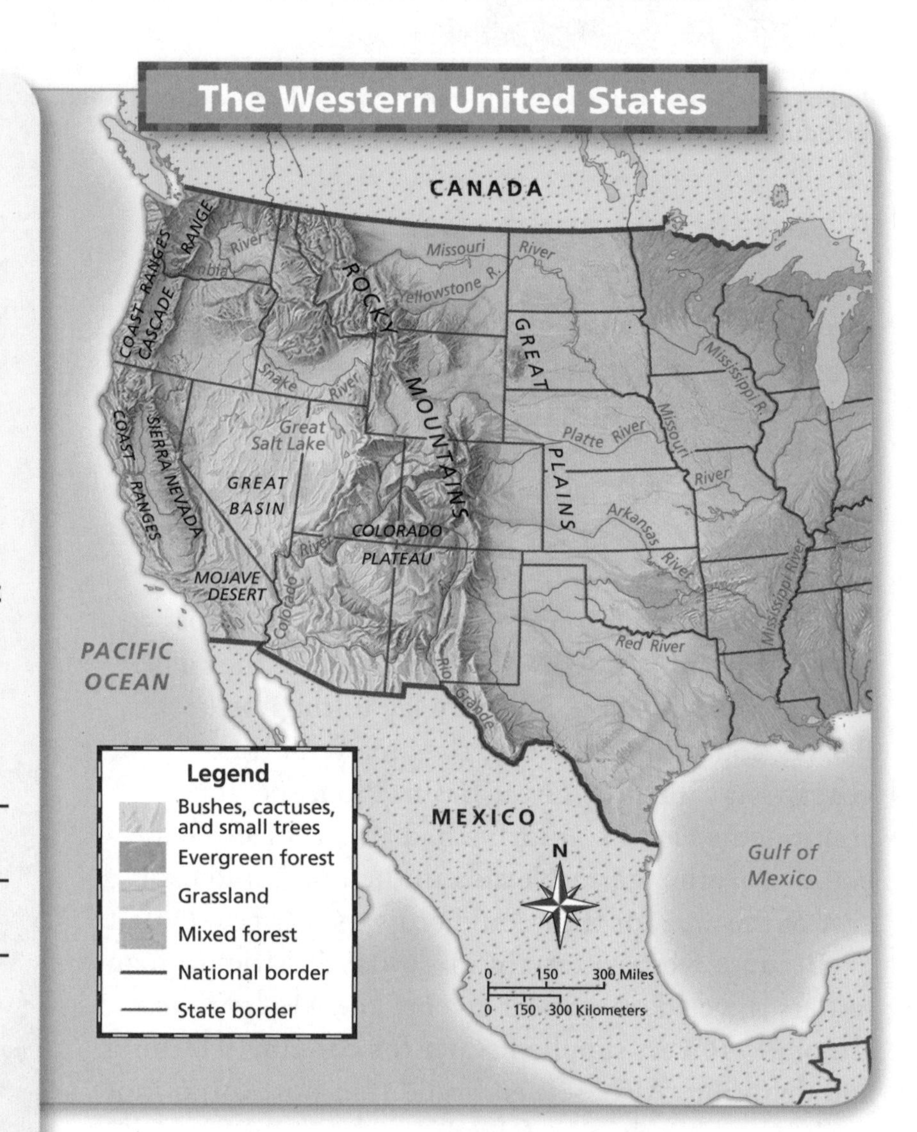

Name:

H-SS 5.8.3 Demonstrate knowledge of the exploration of the trans-Mississippi West following the Louisiana Purchase (e.g., Meriwether Lewis and William Clark, Zebulon Pike, John Fremont).

Lesson 3

What were the major explorations of western lands?

SET THE SCENE If you bought a piece of land, would you want to explore it to see what was on the land? In 1803 the U.S. government knew little about a huge territory it had bought from France. The next year, an expedition set out to learn about what lay between the Mississippi River and the Pacific Ocean.

Preview the Lesson

Vocabulary

topography *(n.)* the surface features of a place or region

Vocabulary Activity The root word *topos* is Greek for "place." Circle the root word in the vocabulary word above.

People

Meriwether Lewis
William Clark
York
Sacagawea
Zebulon Pike
Robert Stuart
John Frémont

Reading: Make Generalizations

Generalizations are statements that are thought to be true for most people, places, or events. As you read page 191, underline a sentence that makes a generalization about the success of the Lewis and Clark expedition.

1804

1806

LOUISIANA TERRITORY

1804 The Lewis and Clark expedition begins.

1805

The Louisiana Purchase

Under President Thomas Jefferson, the United States purchased the Louisiana Territory from France in 1803. Napoleon, the ruler of France, needed money to fight wars in Europe, so he sold the land at a very low price. This sale, called the Louisiana Purchase, was a good deal for the United States. The huge new territory stretched from the Mississippi River to the Rocky Mountains. However, not much was known about its people or resources. Jefferson wanted to learn more.

1. What was known about western lands at the time of the Louisiana Purchase? *Make Generalizations*

Lewis and Clark Explore the West

President Jefferson asked Congress to pay for an expedition to explore the new territory and the lands beyond. When Congress approved the idea, Jefferson chose a former soldier named Meriwether Lewis to lead a group into the new territory. Lewis chose another former soldier named William Clark to help him lead the expedition. Jefferson wanted Lewis and Clark to search for a water route to the Pacific Ocean, study the area's resources, and meet with the territory's American Indians.

2. What were Jefferson's goals for the Lewis and Clark expedition? *Main Idea and Details*

During their expedition, Lewis and Clark kept journals to record the new kinds of animals they saw. They also noted how American Indians used plants as medicines.

1808 | 1810 | 1812

1812 Robert Stuart finds a pass through the Rocky Mountains.

In May 1804, the Lewis and Clark expedition set out west from a camp near St. Louis. There were thirty-three permanent members of the group. These people had different roles. An African American named York hunted food and sometimes cared for the sick. A Shoshone woman named Sacagawea (sah KAH gah WAY ah) later served as a guide and translator.

The expedition met many of its goals. The group reached the Pacific coast of present-day Oregon in 1805. They did not find a continuous water route, but Lewis and Clark mapped the mountains, plains, and lakes they had crossed. They also met the Mandan, Nez Percé, and other American Indian groups. When the expedition returned in 1806, President Jefferson was pleased with what they had accomplished.

Lewis and Clark Expedition

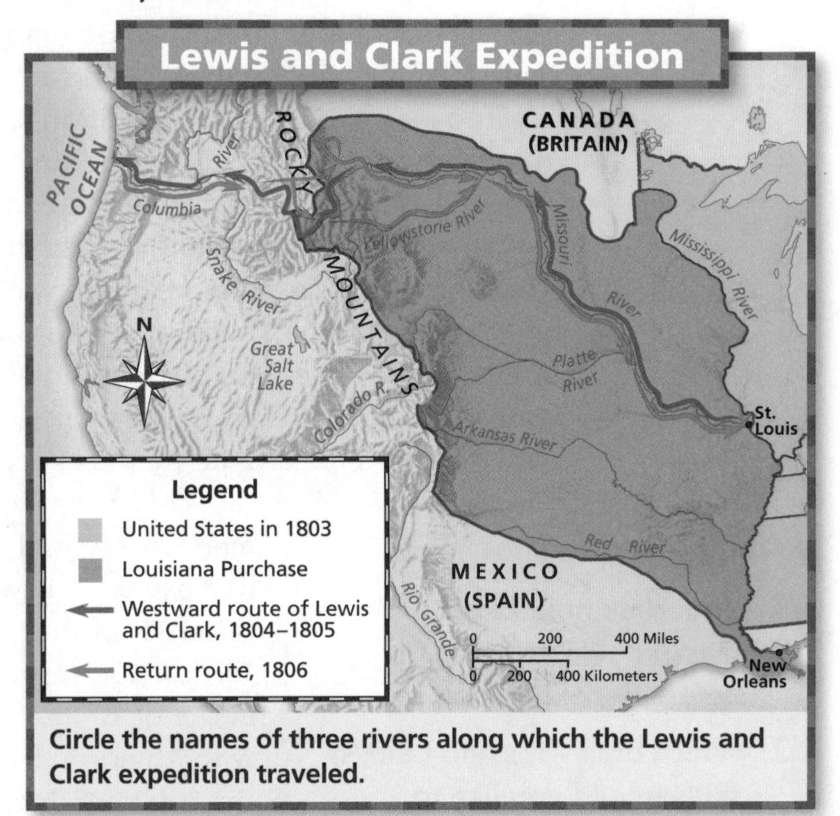

Circle the names of three rivers along which the Lewis and Clark expedition traveled.

Opening Up the West

After Lewis and Clark's expedition, other explorers helped open up the rest of the West for settlement. Zebulon Pike explored present-day Colorado and New Mexico starting in 1806. In 1812 Robert Stuart found a pass that allowed wagons to cross through the Rocky Mountains. Later, John Frémont led an expedition that mapped areas of the Great Basin and Pacific Coast. As more and more areas of the West were explored and mapped, pioneers began moving there in increasing numbers.

3. Circle the name of each explorer who came after Lewis and Clark. Underline their accomplishments.
Main Idea and Details

Summary

The U.S. government gained land through the Louisiana Purchase and sent Lewis and Clark to explore it. How did their expedition help open the West for settlement?

Biography

Meriwether Lewis, 1774–1809
William Clark, 1770–1838

Learn More Meriwether Lewis and William Clark served together in the U.S. Army before their expedition. Each man had a variety of skills that helped make the expedition a success.

Lewis was always interested in the outdoors. As a boy, he had a formal education but also learned many frontier skills. Later, in 1801 Lewis took a job as President Jefferson's secretary. When Jefferson asked Lewis to lead a westward expedition, Lewis accepted and then trained in subjects such as geography and botany, or the study of plants. He also studied medicine and navigation.

Lewis

Clark also had many skills. He had little formal schooling, but his experience in the Army taught him about wilderness survival and **topography,** or the surface features of a place or region. This knowledge helped Clark create maps and interact with American Indians during the expedition.

After the expedition, both men worked in the lands they had explored. Lewis became governor of the Louisiana Territory. Jefferson put Clark in charge of interactions with American Indians in the Louisiana Territory. Clark later became the first governor of the Missouri Territory.

Clark

Answer the questions below.

1. **Underline how Lewis and Clark knew each other before the expedition.** *Identify*

2. **Which of Lewis's and Clark's skills would you like to have performed for the expedition? Why?** *Apply*

Name:

Lesson
4

H-SS 5.8.4 Discuss the experiences of settlers on the overland trails to the West (e.g., location of the routes; purpose of the journeys; the influence of the terrain, rivers, vegetation, and climate; life in the territories at the end of these trails).

What was life like on the overland trails?

SET THE SCENE Powerful river currents, illness, bad weather, and water shortages were some of the dangers faced by people who migrated west. You have learned about how explorers helped open up the West for settlement. Who settled the West and why did they go?

Preview the Lesson

Vocabulary

resourceful *(adj.)* good at finding solutions to problems

Vocabulary Activity Circle the context clues in the sentence below that help you determine the meaning of the word *resourceful*.

Joanne is very resourceful because she used a map to find a shorter way home from school.

People

Marcus Whitman
Narcissa Whitman
Joseph Smith
Brigham Young

Reading: Compare and Contrast

Reading Skill

You have learned that to *compare* and *contrast* information as you read means to look for similarities and differences. Underline a similarity on page 194 that explains why people moved west.

1830

1835

OREGON COUNTRY
ROCKY MTS.
Independence

1836 The Whitmans build a mission in Oregon Country.

Reasons for Heading West

Settlers had many reasons for moving west. Some moved for the economic opportunities offered by the West's rich farmland, mineral wealth, and harbors for shipping. Others wanted religious freedom. The one thing most settlers had in common was the hope for a better life at the end of difficult overland trails.

Settlers began moving west in the 1830s. In 1836 Marcus and Narcissa Whitman built a mission for American Indians in Oregon Country. Narcissa Whitman was one of the first American women to cross the Rocky Mountains. By the 1840s, thousands of settlers were moving to the area along the 2,000-mile-long Oregon Trail. Many of these settlers were farmers headed for the rich soil of the Willamette Valley.

The Mormons were a religious group founded by Joseph Smith in New York in 1830. To avoid persecution, the Mormons moved to Illinois. After Smith was killed by an anti-Mormon crowd in 1844, the group followed their new leader, Brigham Young, to present-day Utah. In 1847 the Mormons founded Salt Lake City. The route they followed became known as the Mormon Trail.

Two trails brought traders and settlers to present-day California. The Old Spanish Trail connected routes that had been used by American Indians and Spanish explorers. In 1849 more than 80,000 gold-seekers and farmers traveled the California Trail to the Sacramento area.

1. Compare and Contrast **List the different opportunities that awaited settlers at the end of the major western trails.**

Trace the route of the Oregon Trail on the map. Circle the names of the communities at the end of each trail.

1840

1845

1850

1847

1849 Thousands of settlers move to California during the Gold Rush.

Severe weather on the Great Plains sometimes made travel to the West difficult.

Life on the Overland Trails

Geography and climate played an important role in the routes chosen for moving west. However, they also caused many hardships for settlers. To complete their journey west, settlers had to be **resourceful,** or good at finding solutions to problems.

Most people walked the entire 2,000 or more miles to California and Oregon. Horses pulled wagons of supplies. The travelers could not set out on the trails until spring, when grass to feed the horses and other animals began to grow on the prairies. Even then, thunderstorms and hail pounded travelers as they made their way west. Trails often followed major rivers, but crossing those rivers was dangerous. Swift currents could carry away entire wagons full of supplies. Lack of water in deserts could be deadly. Some trails ran through tall mountains, where sudden snowstorms could trap settlers. Other trails, such as the California Trail, had shortcuts, but these often ran through even more difficult terrain.

Settlers faced many other dangers too. Illness killed more settlers on the Oregon Trail than anything else. Sometimes encounters with American Indians led to conflicts. Yet despite all these difficulties, thousands of families followed the trails to a new life in the West.

2. Circle the biggest danger faced by settlers on the Oregon Trail.
Main Idea and Details

Summary

In the 1800s many settlers hoping for a better life moved west along overland trails. List some of the trails and describe some of the hardships settlers faced on their way west.

Primary Source

Diaries: Lucia Eugenia Lamb Everett

Learn More Diaries are primary sources because they contain a particular person's writings about his or her thoughts and feelings. Lucia Eugenia Lamb Everett was born in Illinois in 1840. In 1862 she and her husband set out west to make a new home in Nevada and later in California. Everett kept a diary of the journey. The passages below were written as Everett passed through the Great Plains. Read them and answer the questions below.

June 9, 1862
"Two miles from here we found a ranche and store, and one mile farther; was the Platte Vally House, here we stopped for dinner. We never lack for company now, on the road many we find have passed on before us and many are still following after . . . miles farther we came to Shell Creek, we camped for the night. It is a very pretty little creek . . . . "

June 18, 1862
"[Leaving] our camping place which was on the banks of Elm Creek, in very good time, as the creek, was dry. [W]e had much trouble in getting water sufficient to do the necessary cooking[.] What we succeeded in procuring [getting], had to be dipped up by the cup-full, from some shallow holes nearby . . . ."

1. **Circle a geographical feature that is mentioned in both passages.** Identify
2. **How does the diary entry for June 18 show the Everetts to be resourceful pioneers?** Analyze

____

____

____

____

____

Immigrants crossing the Great Plains

Name:

H-SS 5.8.5 Describe the continued migration of Mexican settlers into Mexican territories of the West and Southwest.

Lesson 5

Why have Mexican settlers migrated into the West and Southwest?

SET THE SCENE What evidence of Mexican culture do you see around you? Many events in the history of Mexico and the United States, such as the Mexican War, have affected the history of our own state. How has the migration of Mexican settlers influenced culture in the United States?

Preview the Lesson

Vocabulary

equality *(n.)* having the same conditions and opportunities as everyone else

Vocabulary Activity The suffix *-ity* means "the state of being." For example, *diversity* means "the state of being diverse." Use the meaning of *-ity* to write a new definition for *equality* below.

___

___

Reading: Main Idea and Details

Remember that writers often state a main idea at the start of a paragraph to tell you what the paragraph is about. Writers include other sentences to provide details that support the main idea. As you read the first paragraph on page 198, underline the main idea and place check marks next to the details that support it.

1600 1650 1700

1610 Spanish settlers establish Santa Fe.

Land in the Southwest Changes Hands

Spain's influence in the West and Southwest dates back hundreds of years. Spanish explorers first came to present-day New Mexico as early as the mid-1500s. The city of Santa Fe was established in 1610. New Spain won independence from Spain in 1821 and changed its name to Mexico. With that victory, Mexico included the present-day states of California, Nevada, New Mexico, Texas, and Arizona as well as parts of Colorado and Utah.

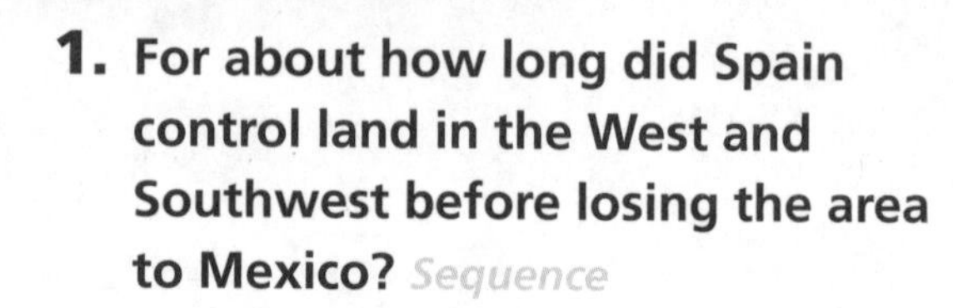

1. For about how long did Spain control land in the West and Southwest before losing the area to Mexico? *Sequence*

Mexicans Migrate North

After gaining independence, many Mexican settlers made their way north to search for new opportunities. Some settlers came to mine gold and silver. Many others wanted land for farms and ranches. However, the Mexican government wanted to send even more people to the northern territory. To do this, they gave some people large areas of land. Under this system, called the rancho system, landowners were given special rights. Many of these owners used their land grants as cattle ranches.

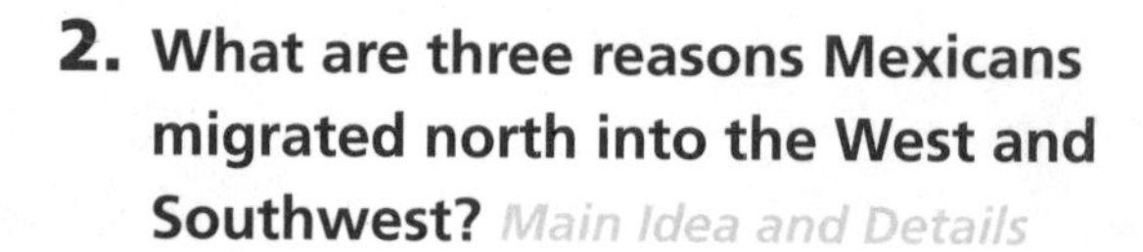

2. What are three reasons Mexicans migrated north into the West and Southwest? *Main Idea and Details*

In 1848, after two years of war with the United States, Mexico gave most of its northern territory to the United States. Many Mexicans who lived in the area decided to stay. As the United States expanded west, more Mexicans migrated north to take jobs that filled the growing nation's labor needs. Since then, large numbers of Mexicans have immigrated to the United States to find new opportunities or to join family members who are already here.

Under the rancho system of the 1800s, many people in the Southwest worked on horse and cattle ranches.

1750 1800 1850

1821

Mexican American Culture

The culture of the modern West and Southwest has been influenced by the American Indians of the Desert Southwest and the area's early Spanish settlers. The adobe style of architecture, which is still popular today, originated with the Anasazi. American Indian farming techniques, such as irrigation, are also still important. In addition, many skills used by modern cowboys, such as roping and herding cattle, were first developed by Spanish cowboys, called *vaqueros*.

The influence of Mexican American culture in the United States has grown over time. In the 1900s, millions of Mexican immigrants came to this country. In 2000 Mexicans made up 30 percent of all immigrants to the United States, more than any other country. Each new wave of Mexican immigrants has brought with them new ideas that have influenced life in the West and Southwest and throughout the United States.

3. Underline two details in the text that show American Indian influences on Mexican-American culture. *Main Idea and Details*

The unique colors and designs of Mexican art can be seen in pottery (*below*) and in blankets called *serapes* (*left*). Author Sandra Cisneros (*right*) has written award-winning stories about the lives of Mexican Americans.

Summary

Mexicans have migrated to the West and Southwest and influenced this area's culture for many years. What factors encouraged Mexican settlement in the West and Southwest?

Biography

César Chávez, 1927–1993

Learn More César Chávez was born into a Mexican American family in 1927. Growing up, Chávez's family moved to different places in the Southwest to pick crops. He learned firsthand about farm workers' low pay, poor housing, and long, hot hours in the fields.

As an adult, Chávez began organizing farm workers to fight for **equality**, better pay, and working conditions. He founded the National Farm Workers Association in 1962. Three years later, Chávez led California's grape pickers in a strike. Other workers soon joined the strike. They refused to go back to work unless farm owners met their demands. One of their demands was the right to form a labor union. A union is a group that represents the workers' interests in discussions with business owners.

Under Chávez's leadership, in 1971 the workers formed a labor union called the United Farm Workers of America. He had succeeded in giving farm workers a voice that could help protect their rights. In 1994 Chávez was awarded the Presidential Medal of Freedom for his support of nonviolence in achieving change.

Answer the questions below.

1. **Circle the conditions that migrant workers faced.** *Identify*

2. **Why do you think Chávez was successful in his efforts to help farm workers?** *Analyze*

____

____

____

____

____

____

Name:

H-SS 5.8.6 Relate how and when California, Texas, Oregon, and other western lands became part of the United States, including the significance of the Texas War for Independence and the Mexican-American War.

Lesson 6

How did the United States expand in the 1800s?

SET THE SCENE Today, the United States is a large country, but this was not always so. You have learned that the 1783 Treaty of Paris and the Louisiana Purchase of 1803 added important lands to our country. What other events helped the United States become a country that stretched "from sea to shining sea"?

Preview the Lesson

Vocabulary

annex *(v.)* to add or attach

Vocabulary Activity Circle the word in the following sentence that is a synonym for the vocabulary word *annex*.

The city had to add some nearby land before the park could expand.

People

Stephen F. Austin
Sam Houston
Antonio López de Santa Anna
James K. Polk

Reading: Sequence

It is important to follow the *sequence*, or order, of events when you read history. Dates can help you understand the sequence. As you read the lesson, circle important dates in the westward expansion of the United States.

1835

1840

1836 Texas defeats Mexico and becomes an independent republic.

The Texas Revolution

After winning independence in 1821, Mexico began asking settlers to move to a territory called Texas. Mexican settlers, later called Tejanos (tay HAH nohs), moved to the area. Stephen F. Austin started an early American settlement there. Before long, American settlers greatly outnumbered the Tejanos.

The Mexican government and the settlers had many conflicts about how the territory should be run. In 1835 Texans decided to fight for independence. Despite early losses, the settlers fought on. In 1836 a Texan army led by Sam Houston defeated General Antonio López de Santa Anna's Mexican forces. Later that year, Texas became an independent republic.

The Mexican-American War

In the 1840s, many Americans believed that the United States should control land from the Atlantic Ocean to the Pacific Ocean. This idea came to be known as "manifest destiny." President James K. Polk believed strongly in manifest destiny. To achieve it, Polk wanted to gain more western land from Mexico.

In 1845 Congress voted to **annex,** or add, Texas as a new state, even though Mexico strongly opposed the idea. Fighting broke out along the border between Texas and Mexico, and in 1846 Polk asked Congress to declare war. That same year, American settlers who were unhappy with Mexican rule declared independence in California. This event became known as the Bear Flag Revolt. Polk sent U.S. troops to drive the Mexican army out of California. By 1847 U.S. troops had pushed Mexican troops out of the West and Southwest and captured Mexico City.

1. Underline what happened after the settlers' early losses in the Texas Revolution. *Sequence*

The Mexican army defeated Texan troops at an old Spanish mission called the Alamo. Soon Texas fought back and became an independent republic.

2. What main issue led to the Mexican-American War?
Cause and Effect

1845

1850

1855

1846 The Mexican-American War begins.

1853

Manifest Destiny Is Achieved

Even as the Mexican-American War began in 1846, the United States peacefully gained land in the Northwest. The Oregon Treaty of 1846 settled a conflict about the border between the United States and land owned by Great Britain.

In 1848 the United States and Mexico signed the Treaty of Guadalupe Hidalgo, which officially ended the Mexican-American War. The United States received a large area of land from the treaty, including parts of what later became seven western states.

In 1853 the United States bought more southwestern land from Mexico in the Gadsden Purchase. This purchase gave the United States control of the rest of the land that would become the first forty-eight states. Our nation finally reached "from sea to shining sea."

3. In the text, underline the name of the country that signed the Oregon Treaty of 1846 with the United States. *Main Idea and Details*

Expansion of the United States

Circle the area the United States gained by signing the Oregon Treaty.

Summary

In the 1800s, many Americans wanted the United States to expand all the way to the Pacific Ocean. How did the United States achieve this goal?

Skill

Chronology on Maps

Learn More Maps can be used to show chronology, or the order in which events happen. The map below shows the development of new routes and transportation technologies from 1775 to 1869. As travel became faster and easier, more people moved west. Today, California has the biggest population of any state. Use the map to answer the questions below.

Try It

1. **Draw a star next to the event that made it easier for settlers to cross the Appalachians in the 1700s.** *Identify*

2. **Circle the bodies of water connected by the Erie Canal in 1825.** *Identify*

3. **About how long did it take to complete the Transcontinental Railroad?** *Analyze*

____

4. **What routes and transportation technologies of today might you add to the map? Why?** *Apply*

____

____

____

____

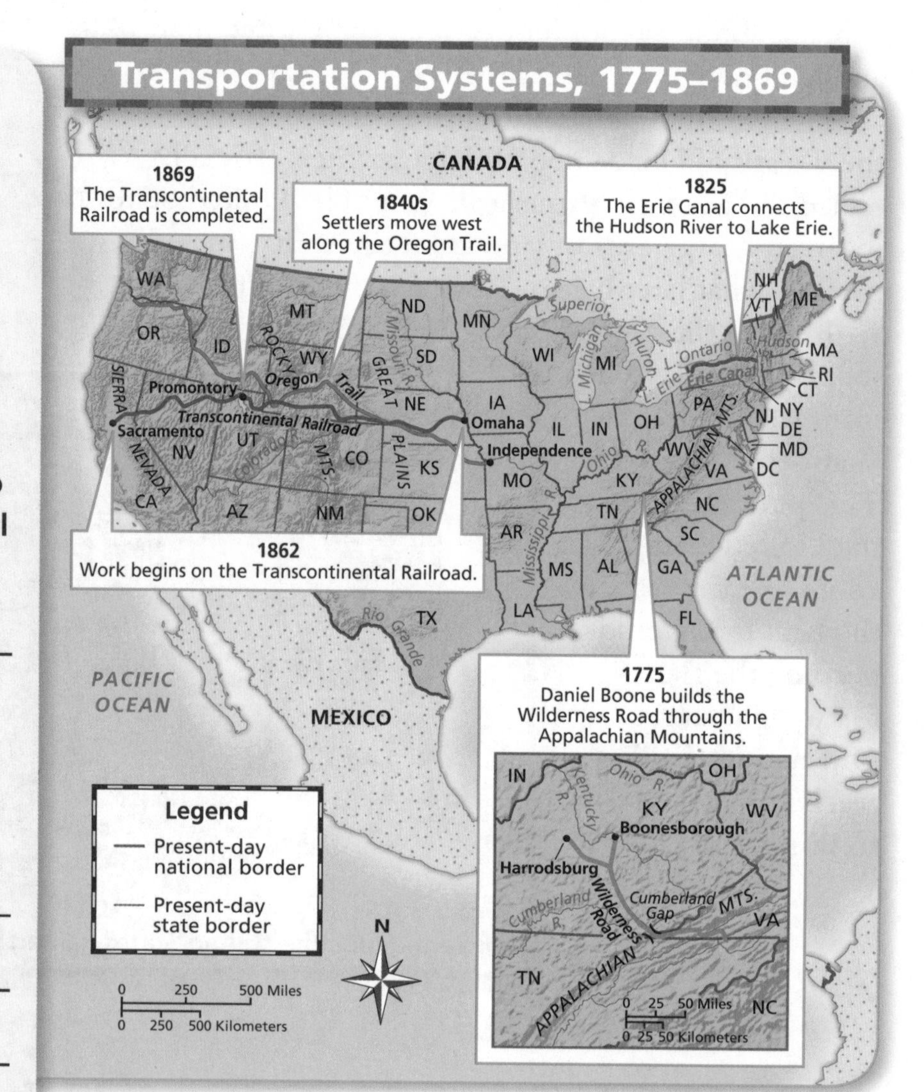

Name:

Study Journal

In this unit you will learn about the locations of the fifty states and the names of their capitals. Complete the activities on these pages as you read the unit.

What I know about . . .

state capitals:

____

Capitals of Western States

Identify the states and capitals shown in the map below.

1. ______________________________
2. ______________________________
3. ______________________________
4. ______________________________
5. ______________________________
6. ______________________________
7. ______________________________
8. ______________________________
9. ______________________________
10. ______________________________
11. ______________________________

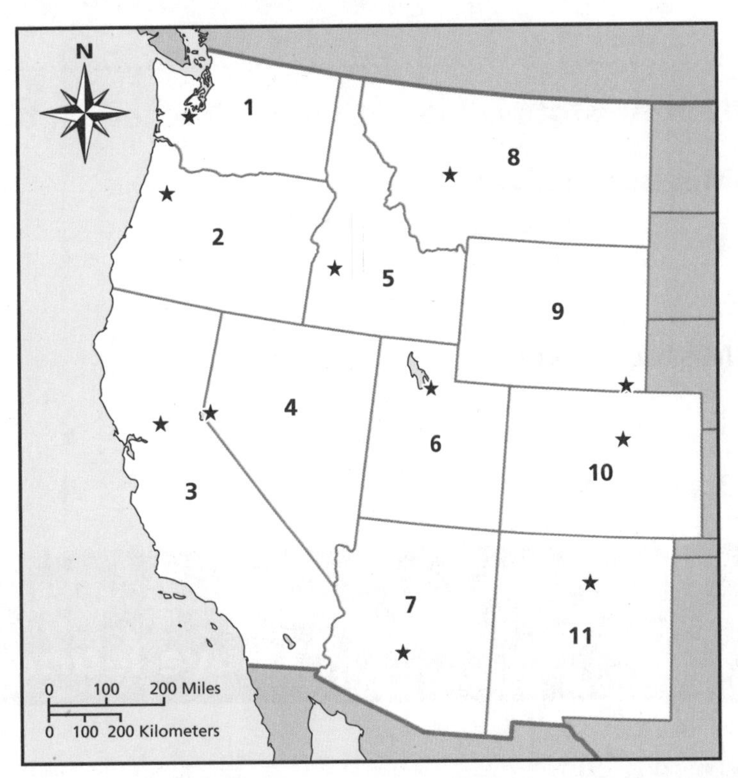

Complete these sections as you read the unit.

Write a paragraph that includes the following words:

- capital
- capitol
- Sacramento
- Washington, D.C.

Which states have capitals named for the following people?

Christopher Columbus (2)

James Madison

Andrew Jackson

Stephen F. Austin

Abraham Lincoln

List the state capitals that are located on these rivers:

Mississippi River

1.

2.

Missouri River

1.

2.

3.

4.

I have learned . . .

Name:

H-SS 5.9 Students know the location of the current 50 states and the names of their capitals.

Lesson 1

What are the fifty states and capitals?

CONNECT TO YOU The governor of California works in a city where many important decisions are made about our state. Lawmakers also work in this city to serve the people of our state. What is the name of this city and where is it located?

Preview the Lesson

Vocabulary

capitol *(n.)* the building in which a state or national legislature meets

Vocabulary Activity A *homophone* is a word that has the same sound as another word but a different spelling and meaning. For example, *two* and *too* are homophones. *Capital* and *capitol* are also homophones. How are the definitions of these two words different?

Reading: Main Idea and Details

Reading Skill

A *main idea* is the most important idea of a paragraph. *Details* are facts that support the main idea. Read the first paragraph on page 208. Underline the main idea. Then number two details that support that main idea.

The United States and State Capitals

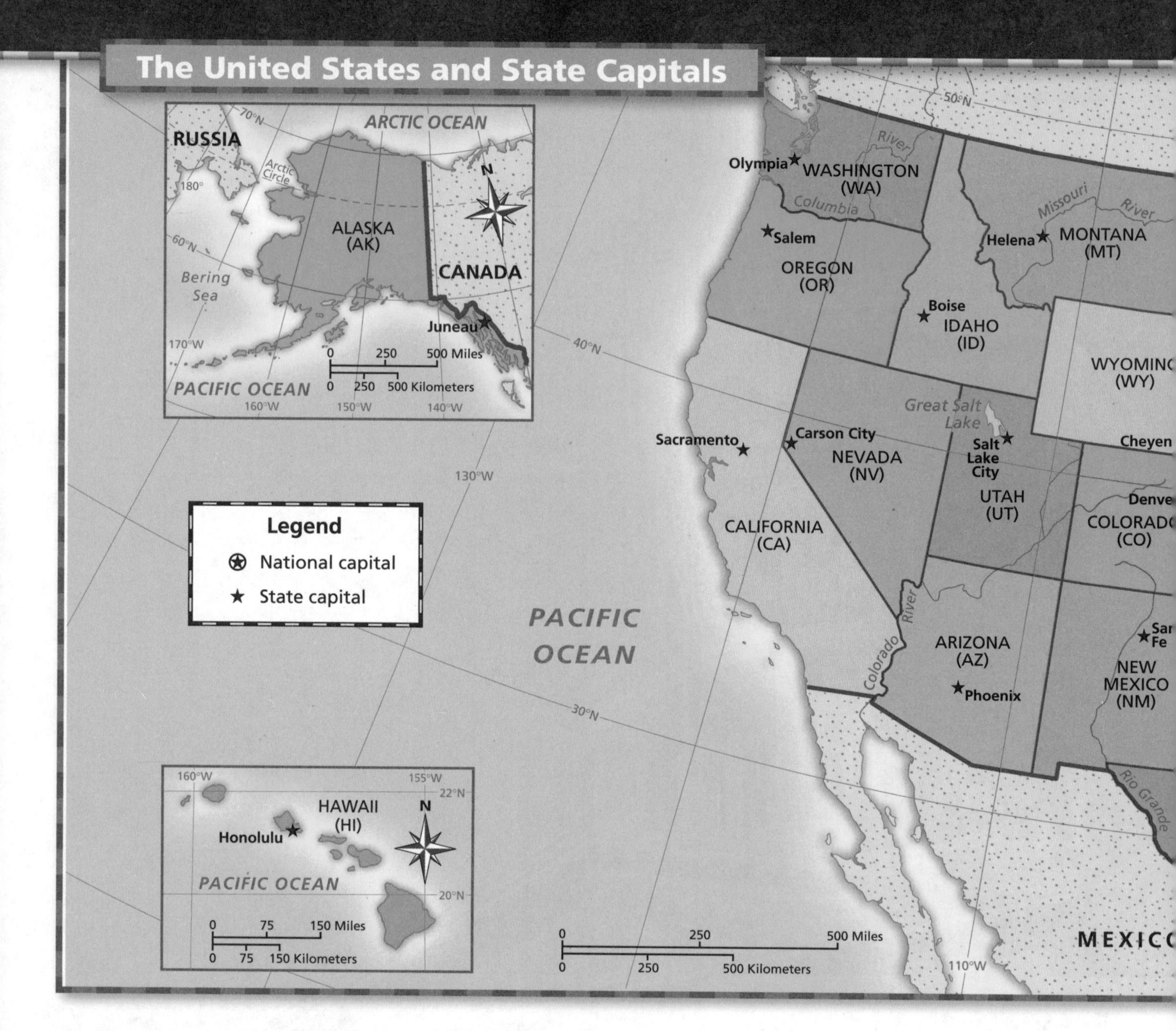

The Role of Capitals

The United States and all fifty states each have a capital. A capital is the city where a national or state government is centered. Washington, D.C., is the capital of the United States. Sacramento is the capital of California.

California's state leaders perform many of their duties in Sacramento. These include making decisions about which laws to pass and how to spend the state's money. Many of these decisions are made in a building called the capitol. A **capitol** is the building in which a state or national legislature meets.

1. Main Idea and Details **Where in Sacramento do California's state leaders carry out many of their duties?**

Locations of State Capitals

State capitals are usually located in areas that are accessible, or easy to reach. Why? Lawmakers from many parts of a state have to travel to its capital for meetings. Many capitals are located near water. This is because in the past, traveling by water was easier than traveling on land. Early cities often developed along water routes, and many of them later became capitals. As our country grew westward and land routes such as roads and railroads developed, capitals grew along these routes too.

2. Underline the sentence in the text that explains why state capitals are usually located in accessible areas. *Cause and Effect*

Summary

Capitals are centers for government. What factors have been important in deciding where to locate state capitals?

Citizenship

State and Federal Government

Learn More Our state and federal governments serve citizens in many ways. State and federal governments are both made up of three branches—executive, legislative, and judicial. In the federal government, in Washington, D.C., the legislative branch is made up of the Senate and the House of Representatives. These groups meet in the U.S. Capitol. In California's state government, the legislative branch is made up of the state senate and the state assembly. They meet in the capitol building in Sacramento.

Look at the diagrams to the right and then answer the questions below.

1. **Fill in the chart to show the two parts of the state and federal legislatures.** *Identify*
2. **Write one sentence that compares the branches of our state and federal governments and one that contrasts them.** *Analyze*

____

____

____

____

____

____

____

____

____

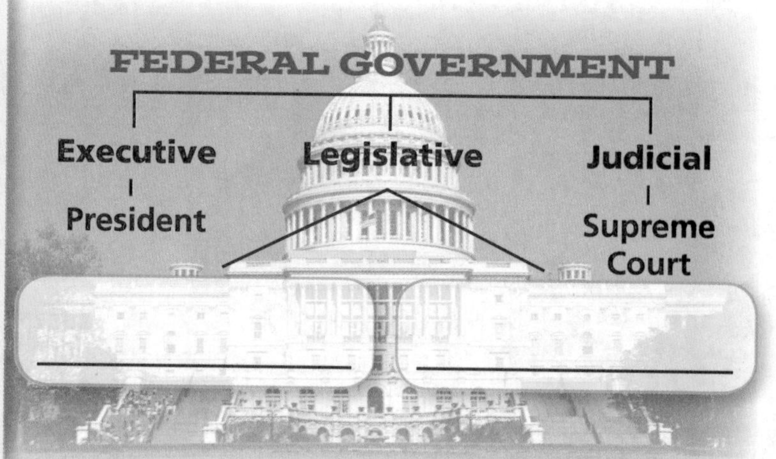

FEDERAL GOVERNMENT

Executive
President

Legislative
_______________ _______________

Judicial
Supreme Court

STATE GOVERNMENT

Executive
governor

Legislative
_______________ _______________

Judicial
state supreme court

Table of Contents

Map of California History to 1850

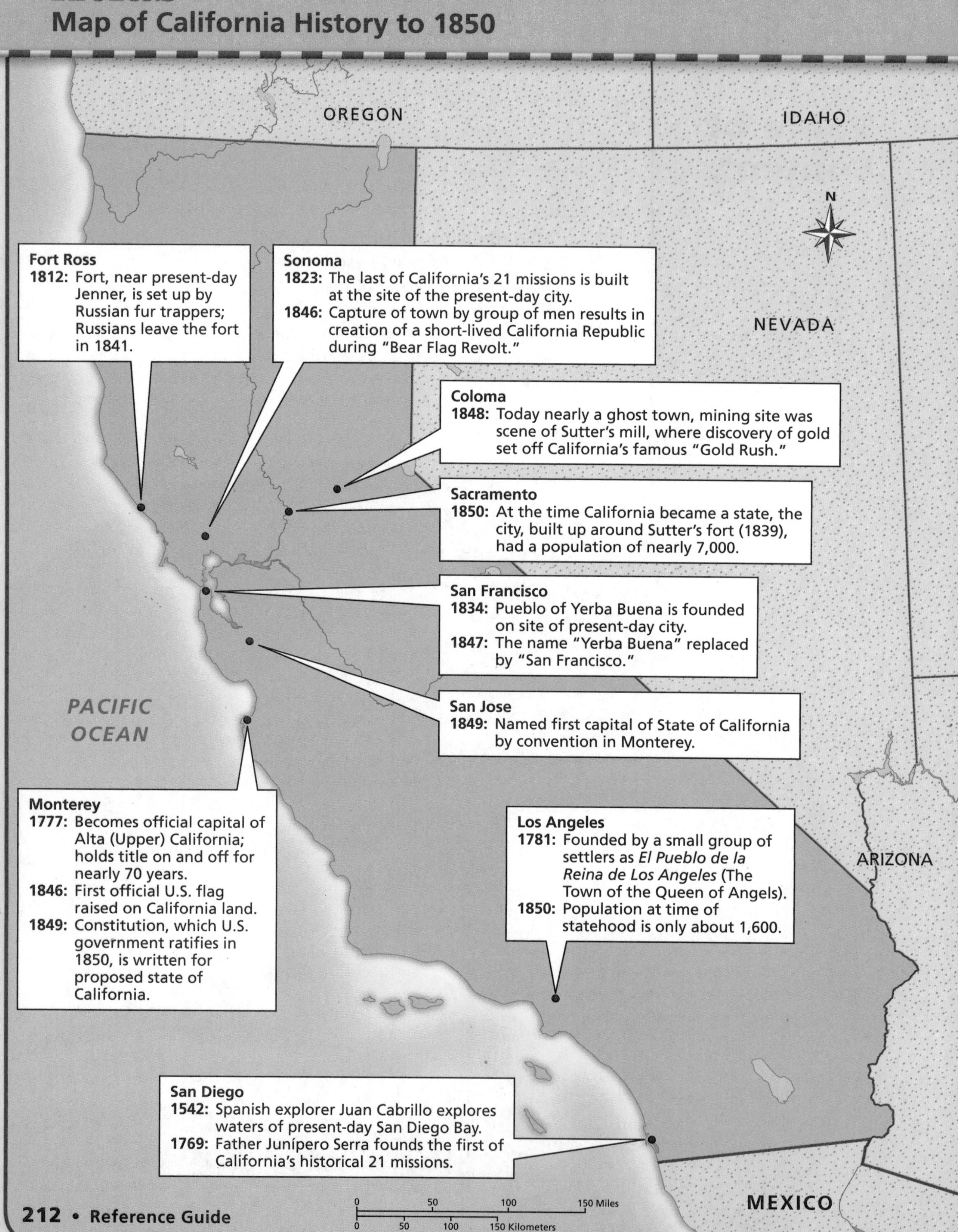

Map of California: Physical

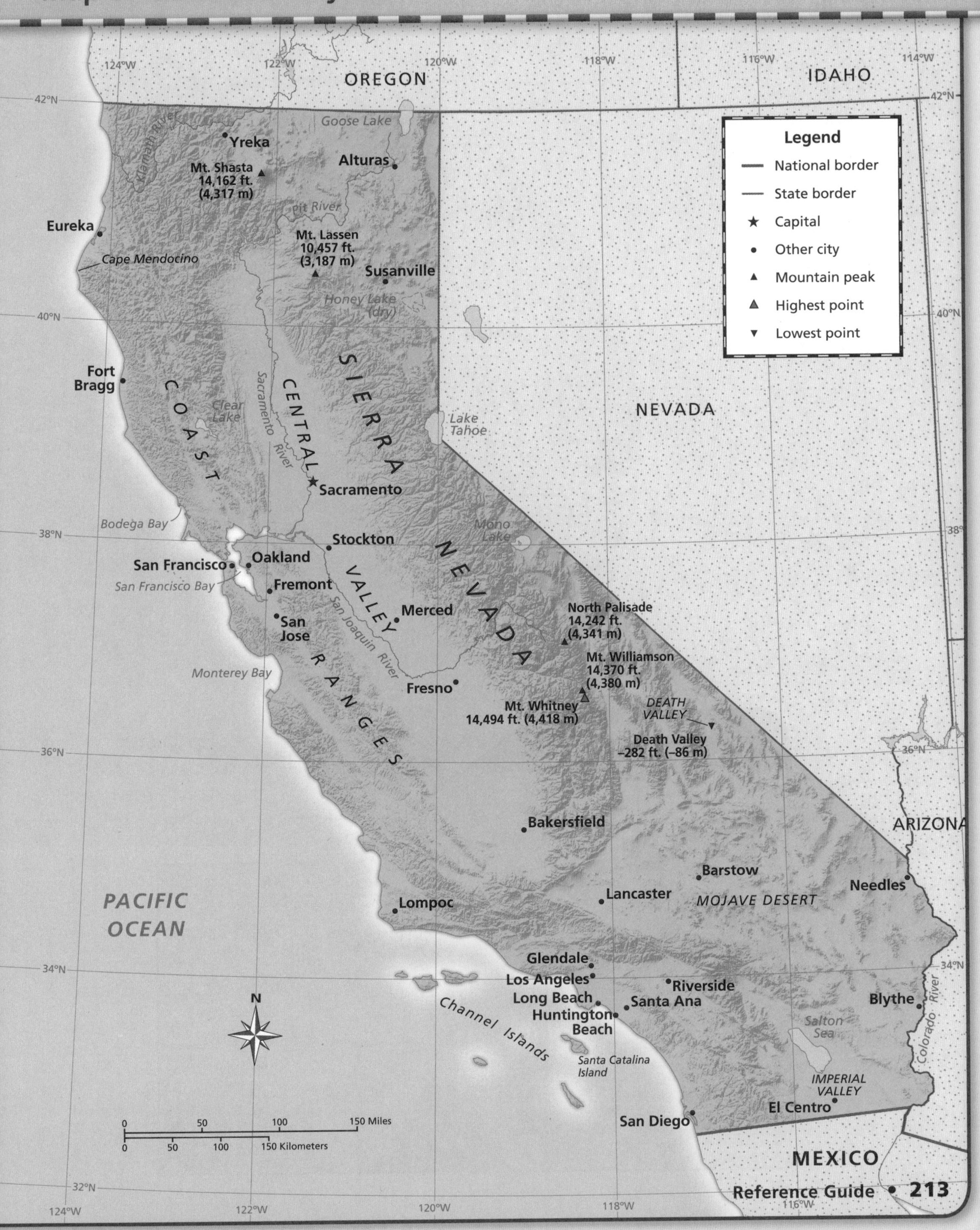

Map of the World: Political

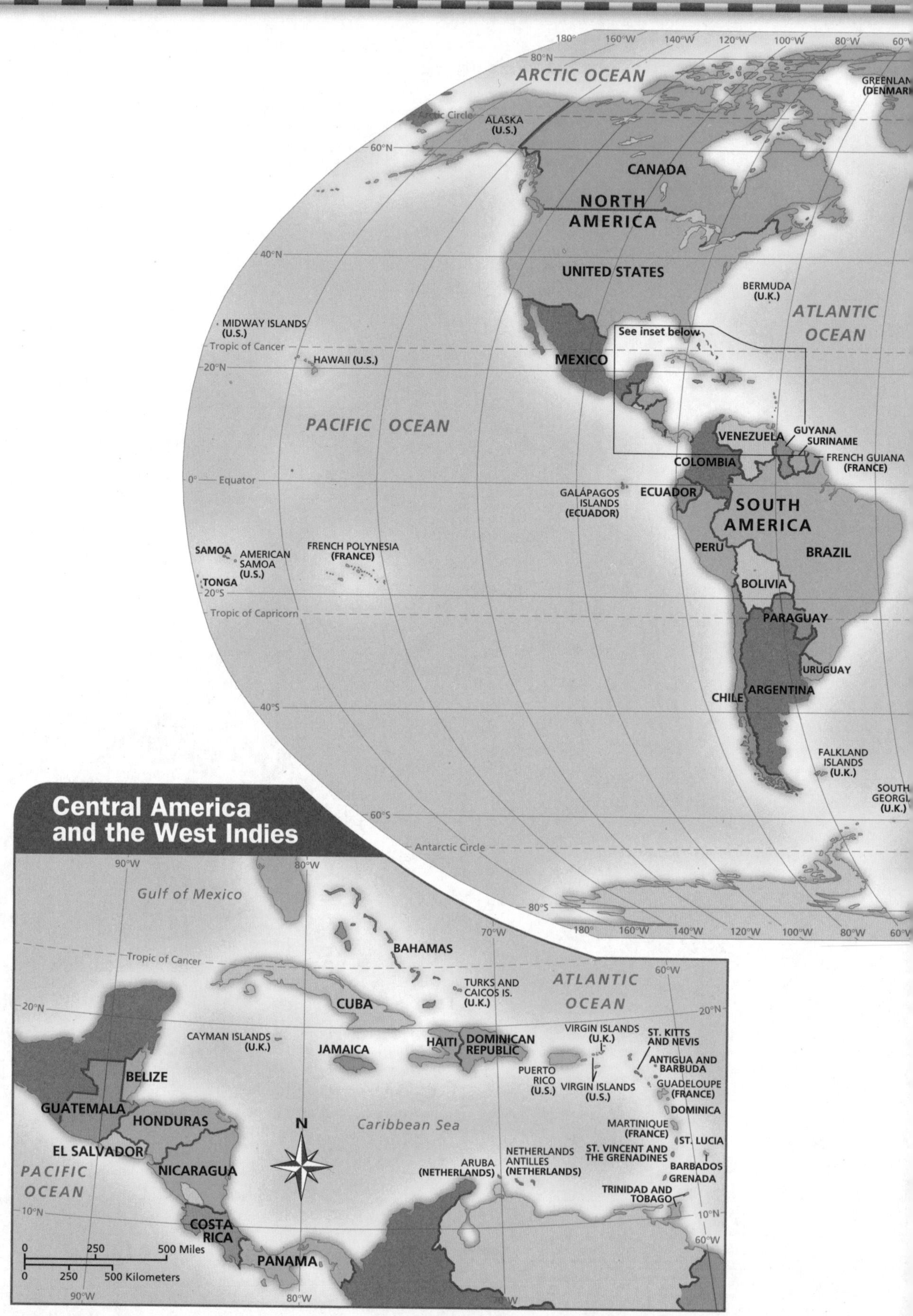

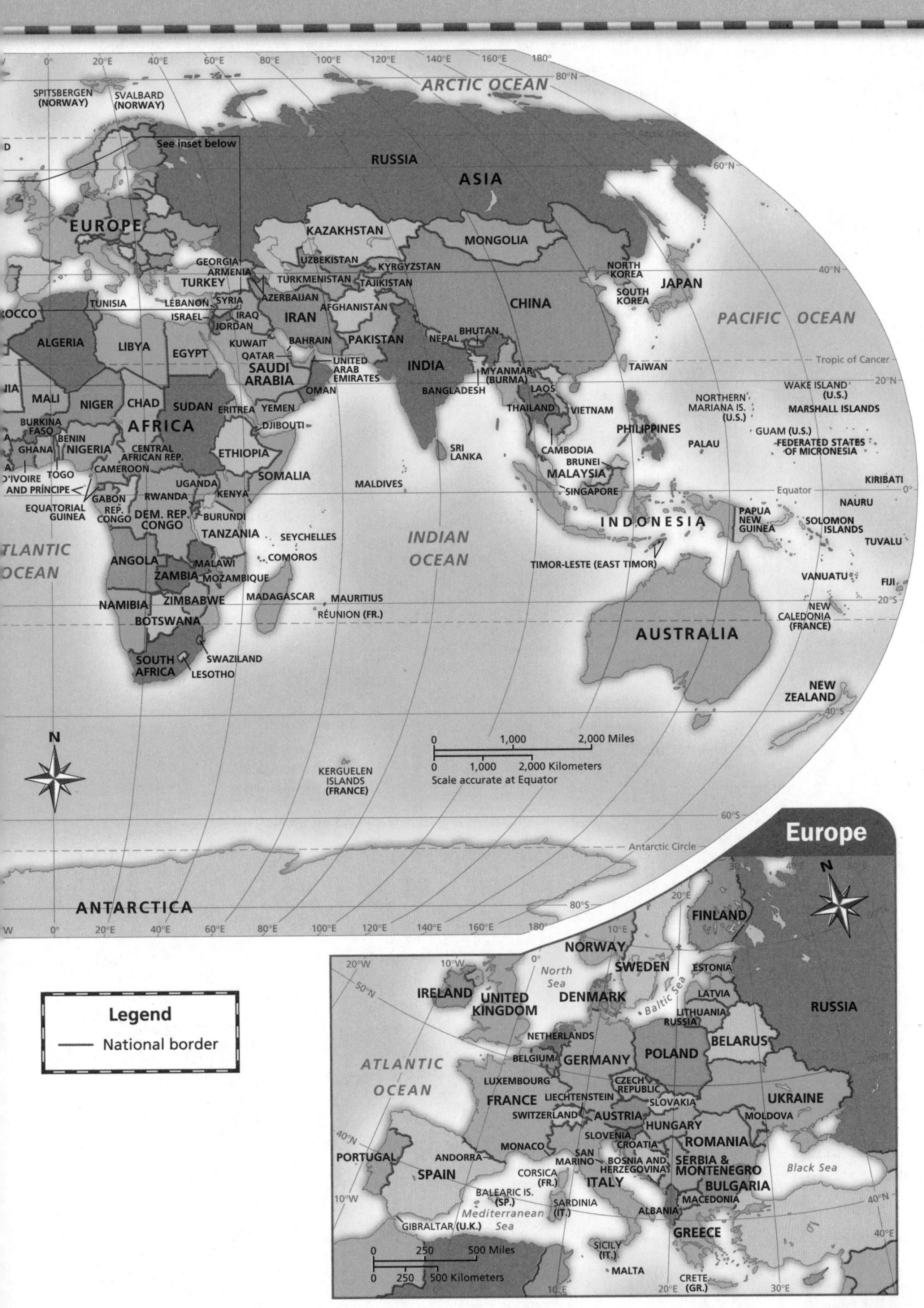
ARCTIC OCEAN
SPITSBERGEN (NORWAY)
SVALBARD (NORWAY)
See inset below
RUSSIA
ASIA
EUROPE
KAZAKHSTAN
MONGOLIA
GEORGIA
ARMENIA
UZBEKISTAN
KYRGYZSTAN
TURKEY
TURKMENISTAN
TAJIKISTAN
AZERBAIJAN
NORTH KOREA
SOUTH KOREA
JAPAN
TUNISIA
LEBANON
SYRIA
ISRAEL
IRAQ
JORDAN
IRAN
AFGHANISTAN
CHINA
PACIFIC OCEAN
ALGERIA
LIBYA
EGYPT
KUWAIT
BAHRAIN
QATAR
SAUDI ARABIA
UNITED ARAB EMIRATES
OMAN
PAKISTAN
NEPAL
BHUTAN
INDIA
BANGLADESH
MYANMAR (BURMA)
LAOS
TAIWAN
Tropic of Cancer
MALI
NIGER
CHAD
SUDAN
ERITREA
YEMEN
DJIBOUTI
AFRICA
BURKINA FASO
BENIN
GHANA
NIGERIA
CENTRAL AFRICAN REP.
CAMEROON
TOGO
ETHIOPIA
SOMALIA
THAILAND
VIETNAM
CAMBODIA
PHILIPPINES
BRUNEI
MALAYSIA
SINGAPORE
SRI LANKA
MALDIVES
WAKE ISLAND (U.S.)
NORTHERN MARIANA IS. (U.S.)
MARSHALL ISLANDS
GUAM (U.S.)
PALAU
FEDERATED STATES OF MICRONESIA
KIRIBATI
NAURU
Equator
AND PRÍNCIPE
GABON
EQUATORIAL GUINEA
REP. CONGO
DEM. REP. CONGO
UGANDA
KENYA
RWANDA
BURUNDI
TANZANIA
SEYCHELLES
COMOROS
INDIAN OCEAN
INDONESIA
PAPUA NEW GUINEA
SOLOMON ISLANDS
TUVALU
ATLANTIC OCEAN
ANGOLA
ZAMBIA
MALAWI
MOZAMBIQUE
TIMOR-LESTE (EAST TIMOR)
VANUATU
FIJI
NAMIBIA
ZIMBABWE
MADAGASCAR
MAURITIUS
RÉUNION (FR.)
BOTSWANA
NEW CALEDONIA (FRANCE)
AUSTRALIA
SOUTH AFRICA
SWAZILAND
LESOTHO
NEW ZEALAND
0 1,000 2,000 Miles
0 1,000 2,000 Kilometers
Scale accurate at Equator
KERGUELEN ISLANDS (FRANCE)
Antarctic Circle
ANTARCTICA
N
Legend
National border
Europe
FINLAND
NORWAY
SWEDEN
ESTONIA
North Sea
Baltic Sea
IRELAND
UNITED KINGDOM
DENMARK
LATVIA
LITHUANIA
RUSSIA
NETHERLANDS
BELARUS
BELGIUM
GERMANY
POLAND
ATLANTIC OCEAN
LUXEMBOURG
CZECH REPUBLIC
SLOVAKIA
UKRAINE
FRANCE
LIECHTENSTEIN
SWITZERLAND
AUSTRIA
MOLDOVA
HUNGARY
SLOVENIA
CROATIA
ROMANIA
MONACO
SAN MARINO
BOSNIA AND HERZEGOVINA
SERBIA & MONTENEGRO
PORTUGAL
ANDORRA
SPAIN
CORSICA (FR.)
ITALY
BULGARIA
Black Sea
BALEARIC IS. (SP.)
SARDINIA (IT.)
MACEDONIA
ALBANIA
GIBRALTAR (U.K.)
Mediterranean Sea
GREECE
SICILY (IT.)
MALTA
CRETE (GR.)
0 250 500 Miles
0 250 500 Kilometers

Map of North America: Political

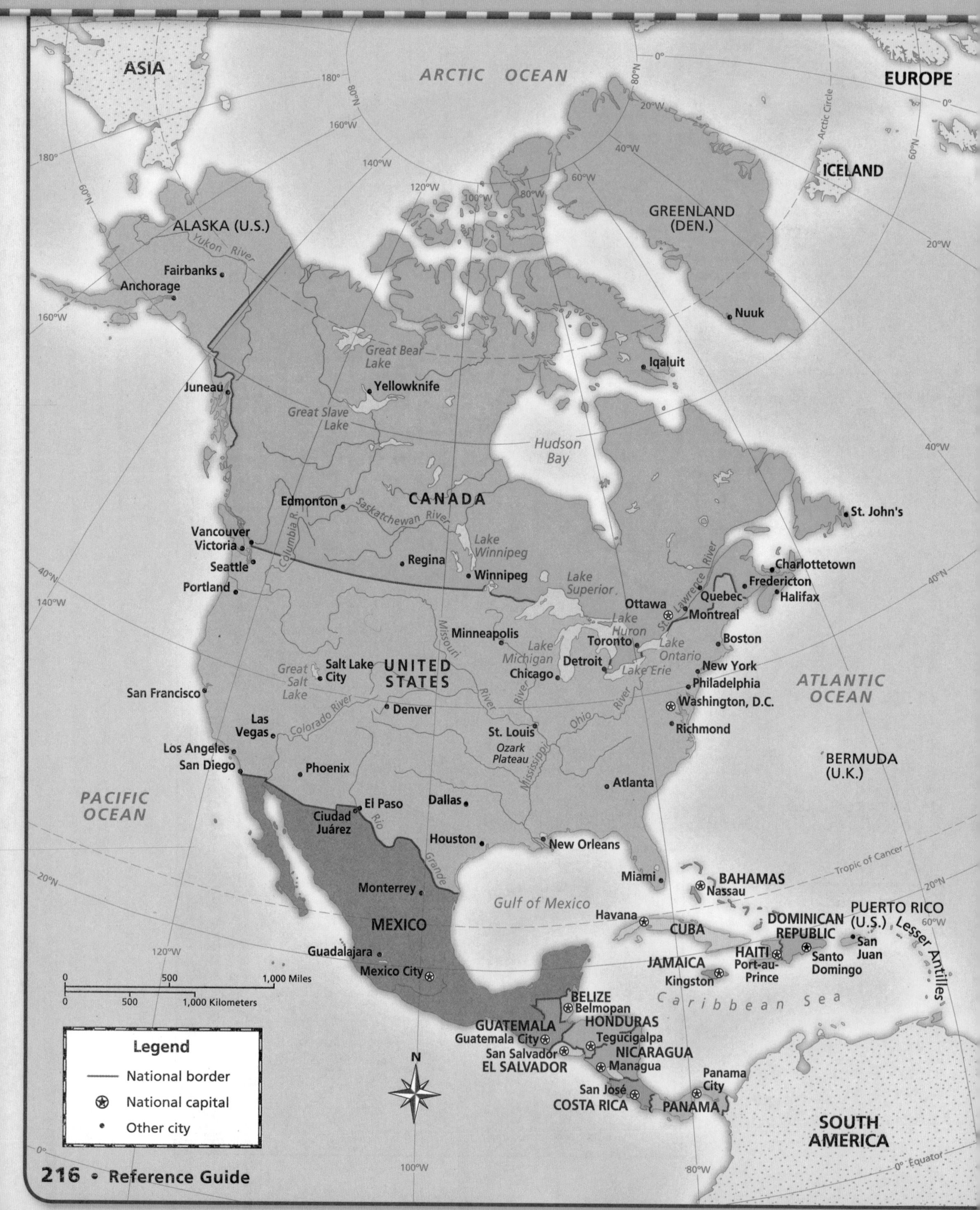

Atlas
Map of North America: Physical

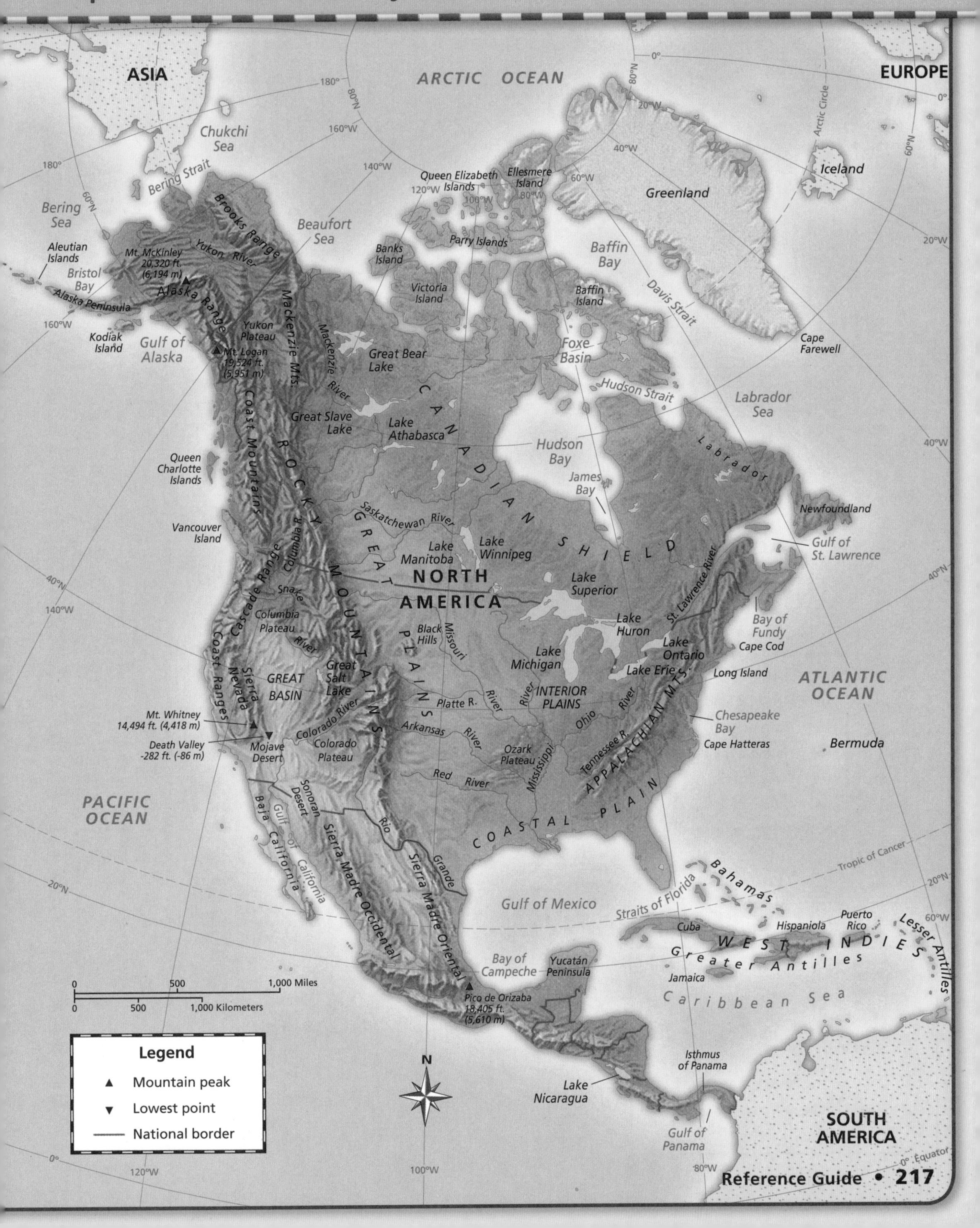

Map of Our Fifty States: Political

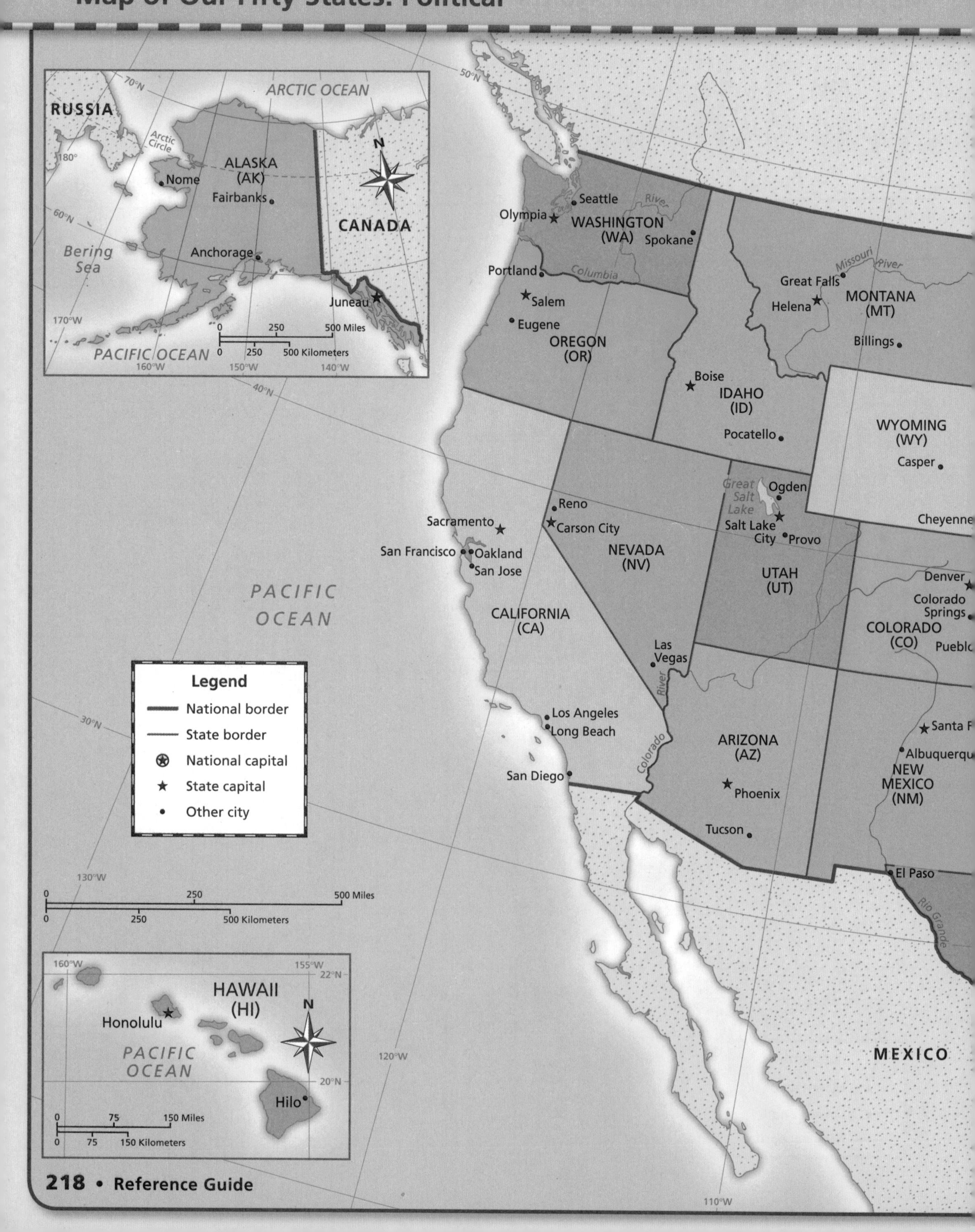

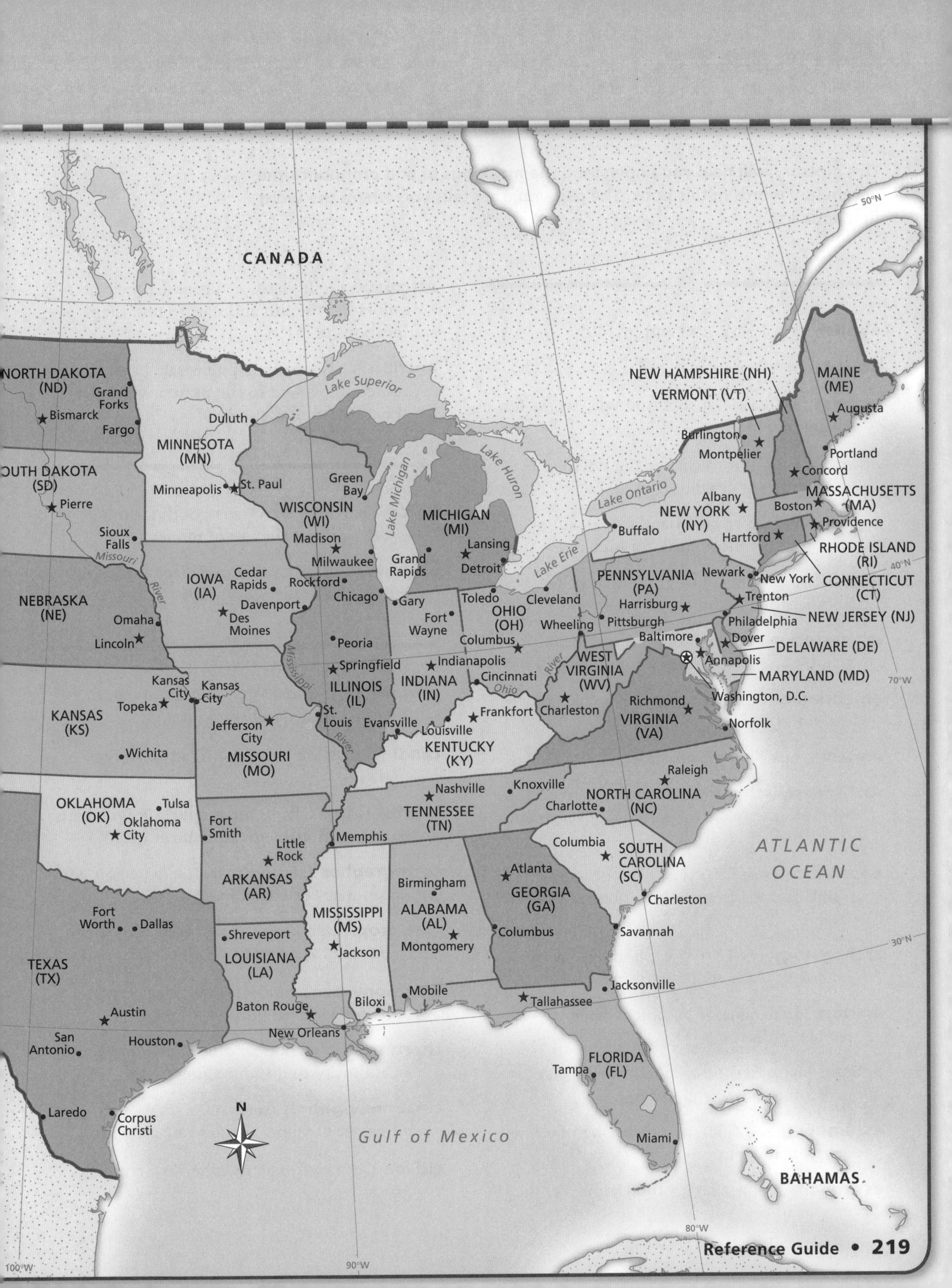
CANADA
NORTH DAKOTA (ND)
Grand Forks
Bismarck
Fargo
MINNESOTA (MN)
Duluth
Minneapolis
St. Paul
SOUTH DAKOTA (SD)
Pierre
Sioux Falls
Missouri River
NEBRASKA (NE)
Omaha
Lincoln
IOWA (IA)
Cedar Rapids
Davenport
Des Moines
WISCONSIN (WI)
Green Bay
Madison
Milwaukee
Lake Superior
Lake Michigan
Lake Huron
Lake Ontario
Lake Erie
MICHIGAN (MI)
Lansing
Grand Rapids
Detroit
ILLINOIS (IL)
Rockford
Chicago
Peoria
Springfield
Mississippi River
INDIANA (IN)
Gary
Fort Wayne
Indianapolis
Evansville
OHIO (OH)
Toledo
Cleveland
Columbus
Cincinnati
Ohio River
KANSAS (KS)
Kansas City
Topeka
Wichita
MISSOURI (MO)
Kansas City
Jefferson City
St. Louis
KENTUCKY (KY)
Louisville
Frankfort
WEST VIRGINIA (WV)
Wheeling
Charleston
PENNSYLVANIA (PA)
Pittsburgh
Harrisburg
Philadelphia
NEW YORK (NY)
Buffalo
Albany
New York
VERMONT (VT)
Burlington
Montpelier
NEW HAMPSHIRE (NH)
Concord
MAINE (ME)
Augusta
Portland
MASSACHUSETTS (MA)
Boston
RHODE ISLAND (RI)
Providence
CONNECTICUT (CT)
Hartford
NEW JERSEY (NJ)
Newark
Trenton
DELAWARE (DE)
Dover
MARYLAND (MD)
Baltimore
Annapolis
Washington, D.C.
VIRGINIA (VA)
Richmond
Norfolk
NORTH CAROLINA (NC)
Raleigh
Charlotte
TENNESSEE (TN)
Nashville
Knoxville
Memphis
OKLAHOMA (OK)
Tulsa
Oklahoma City
ARKANSAS (AR)
Fort Smith
Little Rock
SOUTH CAROLINA (SC)
Columbia
Charleston
GEORGIA (GA)
Atlanta
Columbus
Savannah
ALABAMA (AL)
Birmingham
Montgomery
Mobile
MISSISSIPPI (MS)
Jackson
Biloxi
LOUISIANA (LA)
Shreveport
Baton Rouge
New Orleans
TEXAS (TX)
Fort Worth
Dallas
Austin
San Antonio
Houston
Laredo
Corpus Christi
FLORIDA (FL)
Tallahassee
Jacksonville
Tampa
Miami
ATLANTIC OCEAN
Gulf of Mexico
BAHAMAS
N
50°N
40°N
30°N
70°W
80°W
90°W
100°W

Glossary

This glossary will help you understand the meanings of and pronounce the vocabulary words in this book. The page number tells you where the word first appears.

A

abolish (ə bol′ish), *v.* to end (p. 149)

act (akt), *n.* a law (p. 61)

activist (ak′tə vist), *n.* a person who works for change (p. 133)

adapt (ə dapt′), *v.* to change the way one lives to fit different conditions (p. 3)

agriculture (ag′rə kul′chər), *n.* the skill of raising plants and animals for human use (p. 3)

ally (al′ī), *n.* a person or group that helps another for a common purpose (p. 45)

ambassador (am bas′ə dər), *n.* a representative sent by one government to another (p. 129)

amendment (ə mend′mənt), *n.* a change or addition (p. 159)

annex (ə neks′), *v.* to add or attach (p. 201)

Antifederalist (an′ti fed′ər ə list), *n.* a person who opposed a strong national government (p. 159)

apprentice (ə pren′tis), *n.* a person who learns a skill or trade from an experienced worker (p. 85)

archaeology (är′kē ol′ə jē), *n.* the study of objects to learn about life in the past (p. 3)

artifact (är′tə fakt), *n.* an object made by people (p. 3)

artisan (är′tə zən), *n.* a skilled worker who makes things by hand (p. 85)

assembly (ə sem′blē), *n.* a gathering of elected representatives for a specific purpose (p. 93)

assimilate (ə sim′ə lāt), *v.* to become like the people around you (p. 53)

astrolabe (as′trə lāb), *n.* a tool that helped sailors use the sun and stars to find their location (p. 21)

auction (ȯk′shən), *n.* a public sale in which something is sold to the person who offers the most money (p. 89)

B

barter (bär′tər), *v.* to trade goods for other goods without the use of money (p. 15)

boycott (boi′kot), *n.* an organized refusal to buy goods or services (p. 99)

C

campaign (kam pān′), *n.* a series of battles to achieve a specific purpose (p. 121)

canal (kə nal′), *n.* a human-made waterway (p. 181)

capitol (kap′ə təl), *n.* the building in which a state or national legislature meet (p. 207)

cartographer (kär tog′rə fər), *n.* a person who makes maps or charts (p. 25)

cash crop (kash krop), *n.* a crop that is grown to be sold for profit (p. 67)

ceremony (ser′ə mō′nē), *n.* a set of activities done for a special purpose (p. 11)

charter (chär′tər), *n.* an official document from an authority to do something (p. 35)

circumnavigation (sėr′kəm nav ə gā′shən), *n.* the act of sailing around something (p. 25)

citizen (sit′ə zən), *n.* a member of a country (p. 93)

Glossary

colony (kol′ə nē), *n.* an area or place that is ruled by a distant country (p. 25)

committee (kə mit′ē), *n.* an organized group that meets to make decisions (p. 107)

compromise (kom′prə mīz), *n.* a settlement of a disagreement in which each side agrees to give up part of its demands (p. 159)

confederation (kən fed′ə rā′shən), *n.* a group of states that unites to form a larger state with a central government (p. 155)

conflict (kon′flikt), *n.* a struggle or disagreement (p. 41)

Congress (kong′gris), *n.* the Senate and the House of Representatives (p. 167)

constitution (kon′stə tü′shən), *n.* a written plan of government (p. 141)

convert (kən vėrt′), *v.* to change someone's or one's own beliefs (p. 25)

correspond (kôr′ə spond′), *v.* to communicate by writing letters (p. 107)

county seat (koun′tē sēt), *n.* a place where a county government is located (p. 93)

custom (kus′təm), *n.* an accepted way of doing something (p. 11)

D

delegate (del′ə git), *n.* a person chosen to represent others (p. 107)

democracy (di mok′rə sē), *n.* a government that is run by the people (p. 93)

dissenter (di sent′ər), *n.* a person whose views are different from those of his or her leaders (p. 71)

economy (i kon′ə mē), *n.* a system for organizing resources, such as money and goods (p. 15)

emperor (em′pər ər), *n.* the ruler of an empire (p. 25)

entrepreneur (än′trə prə nėr′ *or* än′trə prə nu̇r′), *n.* a person who starts a new business (p. 21)

equality (i kwol′ə tē), *n.* having the same conditions and opportunities as everyone else (p. 197)

executive branch (eg zek′yə tiv branch), *n.* the part of government that carries out laws (p. 167)

expedition (ek′spə dish′ən), *n.* a long and carefully organized trip (p. 21)

federal (fed′ər əl), *adj.* of or relating to the central government of a confederation (p. 155)

federalism (fed′ər ə liz′əm), *n.* a system in which the national government and the states share power (p. 167)

Pronunciation Key

a	in hat	ō	in open	sh	in she
ā	in age	ȯ	in all	th	in thin
â	in care	ô	in order	TH	in then
ä	in far	oi	in oil	zh	in measure
e	in let	ou	in out	ə	= a in about
ē	in equal	u	in cup	ə	= e in taken
ėr	in term	u̇	in put	ə	= i in pencil
i	in it	ü	in rule	ə	= o in lemon
ī	in ice	ch	in child	ə	= u in circus
o	in hot	ng	in long		

Glossary

Federalist (fed′ər ə list), *n.* a person who supported a strong national government and was in favor of adopting the Constitution (p. 159)

finance (fə nans′ *or* fī′nans), *v.* to provide money for (p. 129)

flatboat (flat′bōt′), *n.* a boat with a flat bottom for transporting heavy loads on canals (p. 181)

folklore (fōk′lôr′), *n.* a group's stories and customs (p. 11)

free-market economy (frē mär′kit i kon′ə mē), *n.* a system in which prices are not controlled by the government (p. 85)

government (guv′ərn mənt), *n.* a system of laws and the people who carry them out (p. 15)

grant (grant), *v.* to give something formally to someone (p. 67)

hoard (hôrd), *v.* to gather for one's own future use (p. 137)

ideal (ī dē′əl), *n.* an important belief or aim (p. 141)

immigrant (im′ə grənt), *n.* a person who comes to a country from another country (p. 181)

indentured servant (in den′chərd sėr′vənt), *n.* a person who agreed to work for an amount of time in exchange for the cost of housing, food, and the voyage to North America (p. 67)

inflation (in flā′shən), *n.* an increase in prices (p. 137)

interact (in′tər akt′), *v.* to talk to and work with others (p. 15)

intolerant (in tol′ər ənt), *adj.* to be not accepting of ideas or behaviors different from one's own (p. 77)

judicial branch (jü dish′əl branch), *n.* the part of government that interprets and applies laws (p. 167)

latitude (lat′ə tüd), *n.* a distance north or south of the equator, usually measured in degrees (p. 21)

legislative branch (lej′ə slā′tiv branch), *n.* the part of government that writes and passes laws (p. 167)

liberty (lib′ər tē), *n.* the condition of being free (p. 163)

longitude (lon′jə tüd), *n.* a distance east or west of the prime meridian, usually measured in degrees (p. 21)

Loyalist (loi′ə list), *n.* someone who felt the colonies should remain loyal to Britain (p. 111)

magnetic compass (mag net′ik kum′pəs), *n.* a tool that shows which direction is north (p. 21)

massacre (mas′ə kər), *n.* the cruel killing of many people (p. 49)

Glossary

mercenary (mėr′sə ner′ē), *n.* a soldier from one country who is paid to fight for another country (p. 121)

migration (mī grā′shən), *n.* movement from one place to another (p. 3)

militia (mə lish′ə), *n.* a civilian army that is used only in emergencies (p. 107)

mission (mish′ən), *n.* a place set up by a religious group to teach religion and other ways of life to native people (p. 31)

mutiny (myüt′n ē), *n.* an open rebellion against authority, especially by sailors or soldiers (p. 137)

N

national anthem (nash′ə nəl an′thəm), *n.* the official song of a nation (p. 175)

navigation (nav′ə gā′shən), *n.* a science used by sailors to find their place and plan their route (p. 21)

negotiate (ni gō′shē āt), *v.* to talk about something in order to reach an agreement (p. 129)

nomad (nō′mad), *n.* a person with no permanent home who travels from place to place (p. 3)

O

orator (ôr′ə tər), *n.* someone who gives speeches (p. 115)

overland (ō′vər land′), *adj.* a route across land (p. 181)

P

Parliament (pär′lə mənt), *n.* Great Britain's lawmaking assembly (p. 99)

Patriot (pā′trē ət), *n.* someone who felt the colonies should separate from Britain (p. 111)

patriotic (pā′trē ot′ik), *adj.* showing support for one's country (p. 175)

persecution (pėr′sə kyü′ shən), *n.* unjust treatment (p. 71)

petition (pə tish′ən), *n.* a document that people sign that formally asks leaders to do or change something (p. 99)

pilgrim (pil′grəm), *n.* a person who travels to a place for religious reasons (p. 71)

pioneer (pī′ə nir′), *n.* an early settler of a region (p. 181)

plantation (plan tā′shən), *n.* a large farm with many workers who lived on the land they worked (p. 67)

policy (pol′ə sē), *n.* a plan for doing or managing something (p. 145)

preacher (prē′chər), *n.* a person who gives speeches about religious subjects (p. 81)

Preamble (prē′am′bəl), *n.* the introduction of the U.S. Constitution (p. 163)

principle (prin′sə pəl), *n.* a rule or idea (p. 163)

profiteer (prof′ə tir′), *n.* a person who charges unfairly high prices for goods (p. 137)

propaganda (prop′ə gan′də), *n.* information written to persuade others to change their way of thinking (p. 111)

Pronunciation Key

a	in hat	ō	in open	sh	in she
ā	in age	ȯ	in all	th	in thin
â	in care	ô	in order	ᴛʜ	in then
ä	in far	oi	in oil	zh	in measure
e	in let	ou	in out	ə	= a in about
ē	in equal	u	in cup	ə	= e in taken
ėr	in term	u̇	in put	ə	= i in pencil
i	in it	ü	in rule	ə	= o in lemon
ī	in ice	ch	in child	ə	= u in circus
o	in hot	ng	in long		

Glossary

proponent (prə pō′nənt), *n.* a person who supports something (p. 89)

proprietor (prə prī′ə tər), *n.* an owner (p. 67)

protest (prə test′), *v.* to speak out against something (p. 99)

Puritan (pyůr′ə tən), *n.* a person from England who wanted to improve the Church of England (p. 71)

ratify (rat′ə fī), *v.* to approve officially (p. 141)

raw material (rȯ mə tir′ē əl), *n.* something from the Earth, such as wood or metal, that is changed so that people can use it (p. 41)

rebel (ri bel′), *v.* to resist or fight against authority (p. 89)

reform (ri fôrm′), *v.* to change (p. 25)

religion *n.* a system of faith or worship (p. 11)

repeal (ri pēl′), *v.* to do away with (p. 99)

representative (rep′ri zen′tə tiv), *n.* a person who is chosen to act for others (p. 93)

republic (ri pub′lik), *n.* a form of government in which citizens elect representatives to make laws and run the government (p. 163)

resourceful (ri sôrs′fəl), *adj.* good at finding solutions to problems (p. 193)

retreat (ri trēt′), *v.* to stop fighting and move away from the enemy (p. 121)

rivalry (rī′vəl rē), *n.* a relationship in which people or groups compete for the same thing (p. 57)

safeguard (sāf′gärd′), *v.* to protect (p. 171)

self-sufficient (self′ sə fish′ənt), *adj.* having the ability to produce most everything that one needs (p. 67)

Separatists (sep′ər ə tists), *n.* a group of people from England who wanted to separate themselves from the Church of England (p. 71)

settlement (set′l mənt), *n.* a place to live that is set up in a new area (p. 35)

siege (sēj), *n.* the surrounding of a place by an army in order to capture it (p. 121)

slavery (slā′vər ē), *n.* the practice of owning people and forcing them to work without pay (p. 31)

specialize (spesh′ə līz), *v.* to focus on one kind of product or activity (p. 15)

steamboat (stēm′bōt′), *n.* a boat that moves by the power of a steam engine (p. 181)

suffrage (suf′rij), *n.* the right to vote (p. 171)

surplus (sėr′pləs), *n.* more than is needed (p. 15)

T

tariff (tar′if), *n.* a tax on imported goods (p. 99)

technology (tek nol′ə jē), *n.* the use of scientific knowledge to solve problems (p. 3)

terrain (tə rān′), *n.* the physical characteristics of an area of land (p. 181)

territory (ter′ə tôr′ē), *n.* land owned or controlled by a particular country (p. 145)

topography (tə pog′rə fē), *n.* the surface features of a place or region (p. 189)

town common (toun kom′ən), *n.* an open space in the center of a town where cattle and sheep could graze (p. 85)

Glossary

town meeting (toun mē′ting), *n.* a gathering of people who live in a town to discuss issues (p. 93)

trading post (trād′ing pōst), *n.* a place where people meet to trade goods (p. 31)

tradition (trə dish′ən), *n.* a set of customs that people create over time (p. 11)

treaty (trē′tē), *n.* a written political agreement between two or more groups (p. 45)

tributary (trib′yə ter′ē), *n.* a river that flows into a larger river or lake (p. 31)

turning point (tėrn′ing point), *n.* a time when important changes occur (p. 121)

unify (yü′nə fī), *v.* to come together or unite (p. 107)

vegetation (vej′ə tā′shən), *n.* plant life (p. 185)

veto (vē′tō), *v.* to reject a bill or law (p. 167)

Pronunciation Key

a	in hat	ō	in open	sh	in she
ā	in age	ȯ	in all	th	in thin
â	in care	ô	in order	ᴛʜ	in then
ä	in far	oi	in oil	zh	in measure
e	in let	ou	in out	ə	= a in about
ē	in equal	u	in cup	ə	= e in taken
ėr	in term	u̇	in put	ə	= i in pencil
i	in it	ü	in rule	ə	= o in lemon
ī	in ice	ch	in child	ə	= u in circus
o	in hot	ng	in long		

Index

This Index lists the pages on which topics appear in this book. Page numbers after an *m* refer to a map. The terms *See* and *See also* will direct you to alternative entries.

Index

Index

Index

Index

Credits

Text

Excerpt from "Boston Massacre" from Encyclopedia Britannica Online, http://www.britannica.com/EBchecked/topic/74914/Boston-Massacre. Copyright © Encyclopedia Britannica Inc. p. 106.

Excerpt from "The Adams Papers: Adams Family Correspondence, Volume 1: December 1761-May 1776," edited by L.H. Butterfield, Cambridge, Mass.: The Belknap Press of Harvard University Press, Copyright © 1963 by the Massachusetts Historical Society. p. 136.

Illustrations

4, 5, 6, 8, 16, 21, 22, 24, 26, 28, 32, 33, 37, 42, 44, 50, 51, 54, 55, 59, 62, 68, 70, 72, 74, 82, 86, 90, 94, 105, 110, 112, 116, 122, 124, 128, 130, 131, 138, 146, 147, 156, 160, 172, 176, 182, 186, 188, 190, 191, 194, 195, 198, 202, 203, 204, 208, 212, 214, 216, 217, 218, Mapquest, Inc.; **10** Dan Bridy; **11** Albert Lorenz; **19** Mark Stephens; **54** Laurie Harden; **150** Troy Howell.

Photographs

Photo locators denoted as follows: Top (T), Center (C), Bottom (B), Left (L), Right (R), Background (Bkgd)

Front Matter: **i** SuperStock; **iii** ©Wendell Metzen/Getty Images, Alamy Images; **iv** (T) ©Peter Gridley/Getty Images, (TR) Corbis Bridge/Alamy Images; **v** (T) ©Bluestone Productions/SuperStock, (C) ©Van Bucher/Photo Researchers, Inc., (B) Charles Phelps Cushing/ClassicStock/Alamy Stock Photo; **vi** (Bkgd) Lissandra Melo/Shutterstock, Tracy Whiteside/Shutterstock.

Unit 1: **3** (C) Antiqua Print Gallery/Alamy Stock Photo; **4** (TR) NGS Image Collection; **6** Carbonbrain/Fotolia, (CR) The Image Works, Inc.; **7** (CR) John Elk/Lonely Planet Images/Getty Images, (B) SuperStock; **8** (B) North Wind Picture Archives, (CR) Prisma/SuperStock; **9** (T) Smithsonian American Art Museum/Art Resource, NY; **12** (BC) Bill Gozansky/Alamy Stock Photo; **13** (TR, C) ©Geoffrey Clements/Corbis; **14** (TR) 010617.000/Janine Sarna Jones/National Museum of the American Indian, Smithsonian Institution; **15** (CR) ©Smithsonian American Art Museum, Washington, DC, U.S.A./Art Resource, NY; **17** (TL) ©R. Hutchings/PhotoEdit, (BL) blickwinkel/Alamy Images, (BL) SuperStock; **18** (CR) ©Michael Newman/PhotoEdit, (BR) ©Syracuse Newspapers/Suzanne Dunn/The Image Works, Inc., (BR) AP/Wide World Photos, (BL) Blend Images/Jupiter Images, (CL) Chris Cheadle/Getty Images; **20** (CR) ©Arthur Schatz/Time Life Pictures/Getty Images, (TR) ©Underwood & Underwood/Corbis, (CL) AP/Wide World Photos; **21** MUSEO NAVAL/ MINISTERIO DE MARINA, MADRID, SPAIN /NewsCom;

Unit 2: **23** Garry Gay/Getty Images; **25** (Bkgd) SuperStock; **26** (BC) Lebrecht Music and Arts Photo Library/Alamy Stock Photo; **27** (BR) Corbis; **28** (BR) ©Randy Faris/Corbis, (BL) Art Heritage/Alamy Stock Photo; **29** (CR) ©Archiv/Photo Researchers, Inc., (TC) The Granger Collection, NY; **30** (B) ©Bildarchiv Preussischer Kulturbesitz/Art Resource, NY; **31** (C) Bridgeman Art Library; **32** (B) Call number 1963.002.1327/©Courtesy of the Bancroft Library, University of California, Berkeley; **33** (TL) ©Stock Montage/SuperStock; **35** (Bkgd) MPI/Hulton Archive/Getty Images; **36** (BR) ©"Charter for the Virginia Company of London, 1606." 1606. Virginia Records Time Line, 1553-1743, Jefferson Papers, American Memory collections/Library of Congress; **38** (BR) ©Mary Ellen Bartley/Jupiter Images, (CR) Marvin E. Newman/Getty Images;

Unit 3: **41** (C) The Granger Collection, NY; **42** (CR) The Granger Collection, NY; **43** (CR) The Granger Collection, NY; **45** (C) The Granger Collection, NY; **46** (BR) The Granger Collection, NY; **47** (TR) Heritage/AGE Fotostock, (C) North Wind Picture Archives; **48** (CR) SuperStock; **49** (C) The Granger Collection, NY; **50** (BR) The Granger Collection, NY; **51** (TL) North Wind Picture Archives; **52** (CR) North Wind Picture Archives/Alamy Stock Photo, (BR) The Granger Collection, New York; **53** (C) SuperStock; **56** (CL) ©MPI/Getty Images; **57** (C) North Wind Picture Archives; **58** (BR) Chronicle/Alamy Stock Photo; **60** (TR) ©Ed Bock/Corbis; **61** (BC) The Granger Collection, NY; **62** (BR) ©Delaware Art Museum, Wilmington, USA/Bridgeman Art Library; **63** (B) ©MPI/Getty Images, (CR) The Granger Collection, New York; **64** (C) ©MPI/Getty Images, (CR) ©Topham/The Image Works, Inc., (TL) The Granger Collection, NY;

Unit 4: **67** (Bkgd) ©Scott T. Smith/Corbis; **69** (CL) North Wind Picture Archives; **71** (Bkgd) Hulton Archive /Getty Images; **72** (BL) Jamestown National Historic Park/National Park Service/U.S. Department of the Interior, (TR) The Granger Collection, NY; **73** (BR) Getty Images; **74** (BR) SuperStock; **75** (TC) Stock Montage Inc., The Granger Collection, NY; **77** (C) Andre Jenny/Alamy Stock Photo; **78** (BR) North Wind Picture Archives; **79** (BC) The Granger Collection, NY; **80** (BR) The Granger Collection, NY; **81** (C) ©Private Collection/Bridgeman Art Library; **83** (TR) ©Patti McConville/The Image Finders; **85** (Bkgd) North Wind Picture Archives; **86** (BR) Visivasnc/123RF; **87** (CR) North Wind Picture Archives; **89** (C) The Granger Collection, New York; **90** (B) The Granger Collection, NY; **91** (TR) The Granger Collection, NY; **92** (CR) Getty Images, (CR) The Granger Collection, NY; **93** (Bkgd) North Wind Picture Archives; **94** (B) Getty Images; **95** (TR) APVA Preservation Virginia; **99** Houses of Parliament, Westminster, London, UK/Bridgeman Art Library International Ltd.;

Unit 5: **100** (TR) Bridgeman-Giraudon/Art Resource, NY, (BC) North Wind Picture Archives; **101** (R, CR, BL, BC) Corbis; **102** The Granger Collection, New York; **103** (TC) Corbis, (BR) Stock Montage; **104** (BR) Library of Congress; **107** (R) The Granger Collection, NY; **108** (TR) ©Courtesy of the New York State Museum, Albany, NY, (BC) Library of Congress; **109** (TL) The Granger Collection, NY; **111** (C) Vlad Ghiea/Alamy Stock Photo; **112** (TR) ©Lee Snider/Corbis, (BR) Bettmann/Corbis; **113** (CR) ©Bettmann/Corbis, (T) Corbis; **114** Wwing/E+/Getty Images; **115** (C) The Granger Collection, New York; **116** (BC) The Granger Collection, NY; **117** (TR) Jean Leone Gerome Ferris/SuperStock; **118** (C) GL Archive/Alamy Images, (BC) The Granger Collection, NY;

Credits

Unit 6: 121 (C) Robertstock; **122** (BR) SuperStock; **123** (BR) PhotoEdit; **124** (R) Corbis; **125** (BR) The Granger Collection, NY; **126** (BR) The Granger Collection, NY; **129** (C) The Granger Collection, NY; **130** (BR) North Wind Picture Archives; **131** (TR) SuperStock; **132** (C) Xinhua/Alamy Stock Photo; **133** (CR) ©Bettmann/Corbis; **134** (TL) The Granger Collection, NY; **135** (CL) The Granger Collection, NY; **136** (R) The Granger Collection, NY; **137** (C) SuperStock; **138** (TC) The Granger Collection, NY; **139** (BL) The Granger Collection, NY; **140** (TL) Getty Images; **141** (Bkgd) ©John Adams, Samuel Adams and James Bowdoin Drafting the Massachusetts Constitution of 1780, mural by Albert Herter, 1942, Massachusetts State House Art Collection./ Courtesy Commonwealth of Massachusetts Art Commission; **142** (BR) Bettmann/ Corbis, (BR) Corbis; **143** (BL) Corbis, (BL) The Granger Collection, NY; **144** (C) The Granger Collection, NY; **145** (C) North Wind Picture Archives; **146** (BR) The Granger Collection, NY; **147** (BL) North Wind Picture Archives; **148** (CL) Classic Collection/Alamy Stock Photo; **149** (R) The Granger Collection, NY; **150** (B) North Wind Picture Archives, (CR) The Granger Collection, NY; **151** (BL) The Granger Collection, NY; **152** (TR) ©North Wind Picture/ Alamy Images;

Unit 7: 155 (Bkgd) ©Leif Skoogfors/Corbis; **156** (BR, BL) The Granger Collection, NY; **157** (C) North Wind Picture Archives, (C) The Granger Collection, New York; **158** (TR) ©Massachusetts Historical Society, Boston, MA, USA/Bridgeman Art Library, (TCR) SuperStock; **159** (Bkgd) The Granger Collection, NY; **160** (BR) Ian Dagnall/ Alamy Stock Photo; **161** (BL) The Granger Collection, New York; **162** GL Archive/Alamy Images; **163** (Bkgd) ©Time Life Pictures/ Getty Images; **165** (CR) ©Jeff Cadge/Getty Images, (CR) ©Tom McCarthy/PhotoEdit, Getty Images/Thinkstock; **166** (B) Corbis; **167** (Bkgd) ©Andrea Pistolesi/Getty Images; **168** (BL) ©Ping Amranand/SuperStock, (BR) SCOUS/Alamy Stock Photo, (BC) Mark Reinstein/Alamy Stock Photo; **169** (BL) David R. Frazier Photolibrary, Inc./Alamy Stock Photo; **171** (Bkgd) ©David Butow/Corbis; **172** (BR) ©Alan Klehr/Getty Images, (BR) ©Dave Schlabowske/Time Life Pictures/ Getty Images; **173** (CR) Steve Schapiro/ Corbis/Getty Images, (TL) ©Napoleon Sarony/ Corbis; **174** (BR) The Granger Collection, New York; **175** (Bkgd) ©Chuck Savage/Corbis; **176** (B) ©David McNew/Getty Images; **177** (CR) The Granger Collection, NY; **178** (BC) Macfromlondon/123RF, (BR) Corbis;

Unit 8: 181 (C) North Wind Picture Archives; **182** (BR) Christie's Images/SuperStock; **183** (BL) Corbis; **185** Alamy Images; **187** (C) The Granger Collection, NY; **189** (C) ©David David Gallery/SuperStock; **190** (B) The Granger Collection, NY; **191** (TC) ©Robert Stuart Junior High; **192** (CR) ©National Historical Park, Independence, Missouri, MO, USA/ Bridgeman Art Library, (CR) ©Picture History, (BR) Rhoda Schwartz/PicturesNow.com/Alamy Stock Photo; **193** (T) Charles Phelps Cushing/ ClassicStock/Alamy Stock Photo; **195** (CR) North Wind Picture Archives; **196** Photos/ Thinkstock; **197** (C) Steve Skjold/Alamy Stock Photo; **198** (B) ©The Granger Collection, NY, (T) Amy C. Etra/PhotoEdit; **199** (BL) ©DmitriK/ Fotolia, (CR) AP/Wide World Photos, (CR) Getty Images; **200** Glen Korengold/ZUMA Press/Newscom; **201** (TL) ©J.M. Dunn/ Robertstock, (BR) Hal Lott Photographics; **202** (BR) North Wind Picture Archives;

Unit 9: 207 Call number 1963.002:0313— A/©Courtesy of the Bancroft Library, University of California, Berkeley; **210** (C) ©Bruce Burkhardt/Corbis, (B) ©Wendell Metzen/Getty Images; **211** (B) Jeffrey B. Banke/Shutterstock.